THE LATIN AMERICA READER

Series edited by Robin Kirk and Orin Starn

THE ARGENTINA READER
Edited by Gabriela Nouzeilles and Graciela Montaldo

THE BRAZIL READER
Edited by Robert M. Levine and John J. Crocitti

THE CHILE READER
Edited by Elizabeth Quay Hutchison, Thomas Miller Klubock,
Nara Milanich, and Peter Winn

THE COLOMBIA READER
Edited by Ann Farnsworth-Alvear, Marco Palacios,
and Ana María Gómez López

THE COSTA RICA READER
Edited by Steven Palmer and Iván Molina

THE CUBA READER
Edited by Aviva Chomsky, Barry Carr, and Pamela Maria Smorkaloff

THE DOMINICAN REPUBLIC READER
Edited by Paul Roorda, Lauren Derby, and Raymundo González

THE ECUADOR READER
Edited by Carlos de la Torre and Steve Striffler

THE GUATEMALA READER
Edited by Greg Grandin, Deborah T. Levenson, and Elizabeth Oglesby

THE LIMA READER
Edited by Carlos Aguirre and Charles F. Walker

THE MEXICO READER
Edited by Gilbert M. Joseph and Timothy J. Henderson

THE PARAGUAY READER
Edited by Peter Lambert and Andrew Nickson

THE PERU READER, 2ND EDITION
Edited by Orin Starn, Iván Degregori, and Robin Kirk

THE RIO DE JANEIRO READER
Edited by Daryle Williams, Amy Chazkel, and Paulo Knauss

The Lima Reader

THE LIMA

READER

HISTORY, CULTURE, POLITICS

Carlos Aguirre and Charles F. Walker, editors

DUKE UNIVERSITY PRESS *Durham and London* 2017

Library of Congress Cataloging-in-Publication Data
Names: Aguirre, Carlos, [date] editor. | Walker, Charles F., [date] editor.
Title: The Lima reader : history, culture, politics / Carlos Aguirre and Charles F. Walker, editors.
Other titles: Latin America readers.
Description: Durham : Duke University Press, 2017. | Series: The Latin America readers | Includes bibliographical references and index.
Identifiers:
LCCN 2016054236 (print)
LCCN 2016056568 (ebook)
ISBN 9780822363378 (hardcover : alk. paper)
ISBN 9780822363484 (pbk. : alk. paper)
ISBN 9780822373186 (ebook)
Subjects: LCSH: Lima (Peru)—Civilization. | Lima (Peru)—Social life and customs. | Lima (Peru)—History.
Classification: LCC F3601.2.L563 2017 (print) | LCC F3601.2 (ebook) | DDC 985/.255—dc23
LC record available at https://lccn.loc.gov/2016054236

Cover art: Photo of a *pasacalle* by Agencia Andina / Carlos Lezama.

A todos los limeños y limeñas de ayer y de hoy,
y especialmente a Carlos, Susana, María y Samuel,
nuestros limeños más queridos.

Lima, aire que tiene una leve pátina de moho cortesano,
tiempo que es una cicatriz en la dulce mirada popular,
lámpara antigua que reconozco en las tinieblas, ¿cómo eres?

Lima, air with a slight patina of courtly mold,
time which is a scar in the people's sweet gaze,
ancient lamp that I recognize in the dark, what are you?

—Sebastián Salazar Bondy

Translated by Charles F. Walker

Contents

Acknowledgments

Many people helped us in the long process of putting this book together, sharing their appreciation and passion for the City of Kings. Jorge Bayona, now a PhD student at the University of Washington, proved to be an outstanding translator and thoughtful collaborator. From the beginning, José Ragas and Aldo Panfichi provided suggestions and aided with various *trámites*. We could not have done this without the excellent team at Duke University Press. Many thanks to Gisela Fosado, Miriam Angress, Jesús Hidalgo Campos, Farren Yero, Christi Stanforth, Liz Smith, and the rest of the Duke University Press team.

Dozens of people answered our queries about documents and images. We cannot name them all, but we want to mention (in alphabetical order) Renzo Aroni, Nino Bariola, Andrés Chirinos, Fidel Dolorier, Mary Domínguez, Nicanor Domínguez, Rafael Dumett, Juan Carlos Estenssoro, Iván Hinojosa, Fernando López, Natalia Majluf, Sara Mateos, Ubaldo Mendoza, Lucía Muñoz-Nájar, José de la Puente, Marlene Polo, Carlos Ramos, Ricardo Ramos-Tremolada, Cecilia Rivera, Roberto Rizo, Cecilia Ruiz, Ximena Salazar, Alejandro Susti, Eduardo Toche, Víctor Vich, and Marco Zileri.

Many of the authors helped us gain the rights or answered questions about their texts. We won't list them, but we hope that their presence in the book is sufficient gratitude. We strongly believed in the need to have images accompanying the texts, and we want to thank the following people for helping us assemble a wonderful set of photos and other images: Max Cabello, Fidel Carrillo, Rosario Casquero, Angel Enrique Colunge Rosales, Juan Gargurevich, Enrique Fernando Inga de la Cruz, Hans Kruse, Víctor Liza, the late José Matos Mar, Evelyn Merino-Reyna, Ken Mills, Adrián Portugal, Molly Roy, Herman Schwarz, Vladimir Velásquez, and Carlos Zevallos Trigoso.

Finally, we want to thank our wives, who coined the term *"Lima Reader* widows." Gracias, otra vez, Mirtha y Zoila.

Chronicle of Lima
by *Antonio Cisneros*

> "To allay the doubt
>   that grows tempestuously,
>   remember me, Hermelinda,
>   remember me."
>   ("Hermelinda," popular Peruvian song)

Here are recorded my birth and marriage, the death
of grandfather Cisneros and grandfather Campoy.
Here too is recorded the best of my works, a boy and beautiful.
All the roofs and monuments remember my battles against the
    King of the Dwarfs and the dogs
in their fashion celebrate the memory of my remorse.

                                        I was also
fed up with the base wines and without a trace of shame or
    modesty was master
of the Ceremony of the Frying.

                        Oh city
maintained by the skulls and customs of kings who were
the dullest and ugliest of their time.

                    What was lost or gained between these waters?
I try to remember the names of the heroes, of the great traitors.
Remember me, Hermelinda, remember me.

The mornings are a little colder,
but you'll never be certain of the seasons
—it's almost three centuries since they chopped down the woods
and the fields were destroyed by fire.

                            The sea's close, Hermelinda,
but you can never be sure of its rough waters, its presence
save for the rust on the windows,

the broken masts,
immobile wheels
and the brick-red air.
                              But the sea's very close
and the horizon extended and suave.
                                        Think of the world
as a half-sphere—half-an-orange, for example—on 4 elephants,
on the 4 columns of Vulcan,
                                    and the rest is fog.
A white furry veil protects you from the open sky.
You should see
                    4 19th century houses,
                    9 churches from the 16th, 17th, and 18th centuries,
                    for 2½ *soles,* a catacomb too
where nobles bishops and lords—their wives and children—
shed their hides.
                    The Franciscans
inspired by some chapel in Rome—so the guide'll tell you—
converted the tough ribs into dahlias, daisies and forget-me-nots
—*remember, Hermelinda*—the shinbones and skulls into Florentine
        arches.
(And the jungle of cars, a sexless snake of no known species
        beneath the red traffic-lights)
                                        There's also a river.
Ask about it, and they'll tell you that this year it's dried up. Praise
        its potential waters, have faith in them.
On the sandy hills
barbarians from the south and east have built
a camp that's bigger than the whole city, and they have other gods.
(Arrange some convenient alliance.)
This air—they'll tell you—
turns everything red and ruins most things after the briefest
        contact.
Thus your desires and efforts
                                will become a rusty needle
before their hair or head have emerged.
And this mutation—*remember, Hermelinda*—doesn't depend upon
        anyone's will.

The sea revolves in channels of air,
the sea revolves,
it is the air.
                    You cannot see it.
But I was at the quayside in Barranco
picking out round flat pebbles to skim across the water.
I had a girl with slim legs. And a job.
And this memory, pliant as a pontoon-bridge, anchors me
to the things I've done
and the infinite number of things left undone,
to my good or bad luck, to things I've neglected.
                              To what was lost or gained between
        these waters.
Remember, Hermelinda, remember me.

Introduction

Lima is a vibrant, multiracial city with over 8 million people. Reflecting Peru's centuries-old centralism, it continues to attract migrants from throughout Peru seeking economic and educational opportunities, and it now holds more than a quarter of the country's population. This includes the very rich, who live in well-protected gated communities; the ever-insecure middle class; and the multitudes of working poor, who live in the tenements in the city center, in partitioned-off houses, and in the "new towns" that ring the city in every direction, the Pacific Ocean being the only barrier. The city stretches well over sixty miles north to south and continues to expand. In recent years, coinciding with a period of relative economic and political stability, it has become a hot international tourist destination, famed for its colonial architecture and, more recently, for its creative and diverse culinary offerings.

Limeño/as can be and are of indigenous, African, European, Asian, or, more frequently, mixed descent, but each of these categories has its own complexity. "Indigenous" refers to Quechua, Aymara, dozens of jungle groups, and others. Peruvians use the term *chino* to refer to all Asian Peruvians, including Japanese and Polynesian as well as Chinese. It shouldn't be forgotten that immigrants from Europe and those brought by coercion from Africa also have diverse backgrounds. The mestizo population includes persons of mixed origin, but gradations of skin color and racial status destroy the pretensions of homogeneity that ideologies of mestizaje sometimes suggest.

Race, and its inevitable companion, class, are at the core of the persistent question of who is a limeño or limeña. Many people—including white *criollos* (people seen as eminently coastal rather than Andean),[1] Afro-Peruvians, and coastal mestizos—believe that they have greater rights to the city because their great-grandparents were born and grew up in what in colonial times was called "the City of Kings." This view questions the presence of the millions of Andean migrants and their descendants: they have come to the city since early colonial times, but their numbers have increased dramatically in the last few decades, and many of them maintain their native language and culture as well as strong ties to their towns of origin. Migrants would contend, on the other hand, that they are remaking the capital, adding the Quechua language, Andean food and music, and other customs to the urban sociocultural mix. The perception of Andean limeños as "new" immigrants is clearly false: although the number of Andean immigrants has skyrocketed in recent decades, this migration process began well before the twentieth century.

Lima is a city of contrasts. Class inequalities are immediately visible and frequently appalling, and juxtapositions and disparities stand out in daily life. As in other cities of Latin America, teeming shantytowns can be found on the hills above affluent neighborhoods with mansions. One of the most exclusive neighborhoods, Las Casuarinas, backs up to the much poorer Pamplona Alta (see color insert). While some districts enjoy nice streets, manicured gardens, and security guards, others lack basic services such as water and electricity. In recent decades class segregation has increased as the upper classes flock to the well-maintained districts to the east, having outgrown the traditional upper middle-class districts such as Miraflores and San Isidro. As perceptions about insecurity have grown, many areas—and not just those of the elite—have added gates to what were public streets, while a virtual apartheid reigns in the beaches of Asia to the south of Lima. Nonetheless, the search for any place to call home has led the poor to occupy areas near the affluent. Rich and poor and the light- and dark-skinned continue to mix.

Lima has grown so much that we could argue that there are many Limas today. In their introduction to a set of essays about twentieth-century Lima, Carlos Aguirre and Aldo Panfichi used the image of an archipelago to refer to the multiplicity of social, economic, and cultural spaces that, although sometimes physically segregated, are nonetheless connected in multiple ways.[2] There is the Lima of the *callejones*, where Afro-Peruvians and other members of the city's lower orders created some of the city's great musical traditions and where today large sectors of the urban working poor struggle to survive amid poverty and marginalization. There is of course the Lima of the few remaining majestic colonial mansions and the many churches, monasteries, convents, and chapels that still grace the historic downtown or *centro*. There is the Lima of middle-class chalets and Belle Époque buildings and streets, and the Miami-like suburbs where the wealthy and the superwealthy live. And there is the Andeanized Lima of *polladas* (fund-raising dining and drinking get-togethers), noisy and colorful weekend *chicha* or *huayno* concerts, and impressive economic vitality.

Lima is today a city of cities, a massive human and cultural entity that is at once the continuation of its colonial roots and a completely new (re-)creation by present-day limeño/as. It is diverse and contrasting: it has always been. The debates that mark the city today, especially the question of who is a "true" limeño or limeña, date not from the second half of the twentieth century but from the city's founding by the Spanish conqueror Francisco Pizarro in 1535. And although the city has changed drastically since the sixteenth century—the original city center grid now makes up about 5 percent of its full size—these glaring class inequities, rich racial mixing, and vibrant social life have marked the capital since its creation.

This reader seeks to provide a sample of Lima's complex history— its glories and traditions, its pleasures and charms, as well as its old and new predicaments and tensions. We aim at offering a comprehensive and historically informed view of the city's changing physical contours, its ever-shifting populations, and the competing mythologies and imaginaries created around all of them. We also highlight how different intellectuals (broadly defined) have attempted to address the ever-pressing question of where to locate Lima's identity. Nostalgic traditionalists, critical intellectuals, travelers and scientists, poets and singers: all of them share a fascination with the city and have collectively and conflictually constructed the images of Lima. We hope to transmit to the readers our own fascination with Lima and to help them create their own understanding of the City of Kings.

The Lima Reader is roughly organized into chronological sections; except where specified, all endnotes are our own. We have sought to provide diverse texts but also accessible ones. We reluctantly left out many topics, authors, and episodes, characters, corners, or districts that deserve more attention simply due to the lack of space. Our emphasis has been to provide multiple, sometimes clashing viewpoints. The book's organization reflects Lima's long history and the contentious debates about its "soul" and future, controversies that date from the sixteenth century and continue today. For some, Lima is enjoying its finest moment, with new high-rise apartments, malls, and shopping areas popping up from north to south, not just in the affluent corridor near the ocean and to the east, and with the food boom attracting tourists and prompting culinary nationalism. For critics, the quality of life has actually declined with recent economic growth, due to torturous traffic, fewer and fewer parks and public spaces, growing inequality, distressing crime, the loss of historic monuments and buildings, and minimal or inefficient planning. We underline the historical roots of these tensions, but also incorporate another key aspect of the city: limeños' sense of humor. Perhaps it's safe to say that one thing will never change in

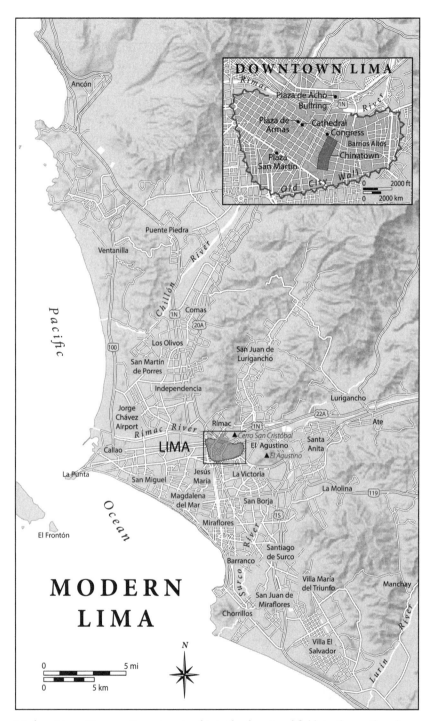

DOWNTOWN LIMA

Plaza de Acho
Bullring
Plaza de Armas
Cathedral
Congress
Plaza San Martín
Barrios Altos
Chinatown
Old City Wall

Rímac River
Rímac River

0   2000 ft
0   2000 km

Ancón

Puente Piedra

Ventanilla

Pacific

Chillón River

Comas

Los Olivos

San Martín de Porres

Independencia

San Juan de Lurigancho

Lurigancho

Jorge Chávez Airport

Rímac River

Rímac

Cerro San Cristóbal

El Agustino

El Agustino

Santa Anita

Ate

Callao

LIMA

La Punta

El Frontón

Jesús María

San Miguel

Magdalena del Mar

La Victoria

San Borja

La Molina

Ocean

Miraflores

Surco River

Santiago de Surco

Barranco

Villa María del Triunfo

Manchay

MODERN LIMA

San Juan de Miraflores

Chorrillos

Villa El Salvador

Lurín River

N

0   5 mi
0   5 km

Modern Lima. Lima continues to extend into the desert and fields to the north and south and up the Andean foothills to the east. The old colonial center, *el centro*, now constitutes about 5 percent of the city. Map drawn by M. Roy Cartography.

Lima: the debates about the city's heart and soul, often conducted over a delicious meal.

The renowned poet Antonio Cisneros (1942–2012) had a clear favorite topic and inspiration: his hometown of Lima. In his aptly titled "Chronicle of Lima" (1968), which opens this book, he brings up his family's deep roots in the city, but also approaches it from many other perspectives. He alludes to its environment, the lack of trees and the corrosive humidity and fog, the often dried-up Rímac River, the Franciscans and the catacombs of their church. But he also underlines the massive presence of Andean immigrants in the shantytowns that surrounded the city, a transformation that, unlike many of the city's older residents, Cisneros embraced. We have included this poem here at the beginning because it provides such a sweeping view of Lima and alludes to themes present throughout the book: the resilience of pre-Columbian and colonial elements; the city's unique setting; and the ongoing Andeanization of the City of Kings.

The reiterated invocation of Hermelinda, in the epigraph and the poem, alludes to a romantic and very popular *vals* written by Alberto Condemarín in the 1920s, one that connects love, loss, and memory: just as Condemarín didn't want Hermelinda to forget him (she apparently did, as she married the famous composer and musician Felipe Pinglo), Cisneros did not want his beloved Lima to forget him. We are confident that the city has not.

Notes

1. The term *criollo* is used for both whites and Afro-Peruvians and also often connotes cunning, the ability to get around bureaucracy, court someone, or confront any challenge with charm and humor.
2. Carlos Aguirre and Aldo Panfichi, introduction to *Lima, siglo XX: Cultura, socialización y cambio* (Lima: Pontificia Universidad Católica del Perú, 2013), 16.

I

Pre-Hispanic, Conquest, and Early Colonial Lima

When Francisco Pizarro and his brothers in arms scouted areas in 1534 and early 1535 to establish a capital of Peru, they had the usual pragmatic concerns, above all securing sufficient water and agricultural land. Jauja in the central Andes had been an original favorite but was rejected, deemed too high and too distant from the Pacific Ocean. Instead, they selected a slightly inland spot along the Rímac River that could protect them from pirates yet lay on the coast, a good distance away from the center of the far-from-subjugated Inca Empire. On January 18, 1535, they laid out a classic Plaza Mayor just south of the river, with the state (what became the viceroy), the church, the municipality, and merchants occupying the four sides of the square and streets running from it at perfect right angles. It received two names, Lima and La Ciudad de los Reyes (The City of Kings). The first derived from a pre-Inca oracle in the valley, called Limaq (which also produced the name of the river and district, Rímac), and the second from the decision to found the city on January 6, the feast of the Epiphany or Three Kings Day. The Spanish believed that they had set in stone (and adobe) an enduring symbol of Spanish rule, one that would house the different components of the conquering Iberians and oversee the domination of the Incas and all of South America.

They succeeded yet created a city very different than the one they imagined. The symbolic power of the plaza and its environs glorified Spanish domination and created a hierarchical society overseen by an omnipresent Catholic Church. Lima and its port, Callao (which now run together as the Lima Metropolitan Area), served as the entrepôt between Europe and South America and continue to be the nation's gateway to the world. Nonetheless, the Spanish built atop an indigenous religious center and decades later added an "Indian quarters" to the eastern part of the city. Colonial Lima counted on a sizable indigenous population—artisans, merchants, servants, and members of the indigenous aristocracy—and today Lima has more Quechua speakers (the Inca language) than any city in the world, approximately half a million. The decision to build the capital far away from Cuzco in no way isolated Europeans from indigenous Peru. Furthermore, the number of mestizos, the offspring of Europeans and indigenous people, increased rapidly.

African slavery bolstered the plantation economy and shaped Lima. By the eighteenth century, some referred to Lima as a predominantly black (African, Afro-Peruvian, and mixed groups) conglomeration. Lima and its nearby port also attracted immigrants and travelers from Asia (the Philippines) and northern Europe (including Protestants and Jews, to the chagrin of the Inquisition). Their presence as well as the surging mixed-race population imploded the official division of Peru into two republics, one of Spaniards and one of indigenous people. It should not be forgotten that Spaniards themselves were far from unified: bloody civil wars among the conquistadors raged for decades after Lima's foundation.

The Catholic Church was a full partner in the establishment of Lima. With the arrival of the Inquisition in 1570 and the building of more than one hundred churches, parishes, monasteries, and prayer houses, particularly of the Mendicant Orders and the Jesuits, the spiritual and social order would seem to have been well guarded. Nonetheless, authorities rapidly complained about widespread disregard for laws that sought to bolster the city's racial and class hierarchies and to control questionable public behavior. They blamed just about everyone, depending on the point of view of the critic, of course: lower classes and elites, men and women. Lima was almost from the start both a highly pious and highly sinful city, part of the nature of baroque cities, as explored in several texts here.

The texts highlight the rich ritual and public life of Lima, particularly its religious processions and festivals. Other writers underline the rich spiritual life behind convent doors. Social relations remained fluid and can be read in different ways. More conservative interpretations stress a harmony among different racial groups built around the shared piety and the devotion to public rituals. Others would stress tensions, noting the uneasiness about possible uprisings among the indigenous in Lima and far beyond as well as concerns about slave resistance. Lima not only feared pirates and European marauders—it also dreaded subversion from within or potential attacks by rebels. The walls that surrounded it from the 1680s to the 1860s aimed to protect the City of Kings from foreign invaders and from invaders within Peru.

Pre-Hispanic Lima

César Pacheco Vélez

Pizarro and his band of conquistadors sought to establish Lima in an area free of indigenous settlements. Not only were they following Castilian policy (disregarded, clearly, by the imposition of "Mexico City" on top of Tenochtitlan), they also feared the Incas and suffered in the high altitude of the Andes. However, finding a suitable place with adequate water and shelter and with no indigenous settlements would prove impossible. Both the Incas and other previous and contemporary cultures had settled in the best valleys and river streams in the highlands and the coast. Lima could never escape its proximity to pre-Columbian settlements, sanctuaries, and peoples. Even today, more than fifty huacas or large monuments and shrines rise up throughout the city, and excavations continue to find buildings and other remains that predate the Spanish. The historian César Pacheco Vélez (1929–89) underlines Lima's foundational ties to the indigenous people who not only surrounded it but also built it.

The Spanish Crown followed a policy—outlined in edicts by Charles V and Philip II—of not founding cities in the midst of preexistent native settlements. This is the case with the new capital of the kingdom of Peru. Chroniclers refer to the site where Pizarro founded the city on that pleasant January morning of 1535. But it so happens that this locale had an elusive, centuries- or millennia-long heritage, as some of the most ancient (over twelve thousand years old) human settlements known have been discovered in its vicinity. These include the ruins of Paraíso in the Chillón Valley, which was probably inhabited up to 4000 BC and constitutes one of the oldest stone monuments of the Western hemisphere; the settlements of Ancón, also ten thousand years old; Cajamarquilla, a pre-Inca village in the Rímac Valley, which was uninhabited when the conquistadors arrived; and the massive and densely populated sanctuary of Pachacamac in the Lurín Valley, which also represented the earliest sign of the region's predestination to host the new capital. The Spanish also discovered numerous *huacas* or shrines between the hamlets of Limatambo, Armatambo, and Maranga. . . .

9

The region boasts abundant evidence of an uninterrupted human presence spanning centuries or millennia: it was the southernmost frontier during the Chavin Period; the northwestern reaches—but not quite the northernmost border—during the Wari Period; a clearly defined local culture during the Late Intermediate Period; and a region recently subjugated by the Incas around the time of the Spanish arrival. The pre-Hispanic ethnic groups of the central coast of modern-day Peru, specifically those concentrated in the valleys of Huaura, Chillón, Rímac, and Lurín, constitute a common entity with those of the highlands of Yauyos, Canta, and Huarochirí, suggesting that the arbitrary borders of the modern Department of Lima—disjointed in both its roads and its economy—respect the cultural identity forged in the first half of the sixteenth century, during which they adjusted to domination by the Inca and subsequently by the Spaniards.

The concrete jungle of the megalopolis now straddles the Chillón, Rímac, and Lurín Valleys of the central coast, the former homogeneous territory of a series of *señoríos* (lordships) and *kurakazgos*. These señoríos carved up the territory in a different pattern than the European one. Due to the importance of irrigation in their desert-based agricultural society—in which hydraulic techniques were the key to well-being—they rebuffed fixed borders and instead favored different types of access. In the lower course of the three rivers that seem to converge into what would later become Lima, irrigation ditches and floodgates bear witness to a pattern of settlement that is both clever and prolific. The Spanish came upon about twenty villages of potters and farmers and four fishermen's coves in the entire region. The central valley of Lima—or Rímac, following the pronunciation by highlanders—features the señorío of Sulco or Surco, with its villages of Armatambo and Guatca or Huatica; the señorío of Lima proper, with its village of Rimactambo or Limatambo; and the señoríos of Malanga or Maranga, Amancaes, and Collique, all of which were associated with or subordinated to the señorío of Ychma or Pachacamac, and in whose ceremonial center priests seemed to wield more power than any *kuraka* could. And it is through the *yunga* valleys that these pre-Inca señoríos—which remained mostly unaffected by Inca conquest—and their neighbors to the north and the highlands (toward Canta and Huaura) articulated the millennia-old bonds between highlands and lowlands. Their alleged antagonism is disproven by this centuries-old relationship.

The *yunga señoríos* that had been recently conquered by Cuzco were peppered with many hamlets or villages, full of millennial human remains, that could not be considered cities in the Western sense. The nucleus of the entire territory was religious in nature: Pachacamac. It was one of these small settlements—Lima—that was chosen by Pizarro to make a reality out of this premonition of a city.

Pizarro followed the tradition of not founding a city next to a preexisting ceremonial center—Pachacamac was located several leagues away. Some believe, however, that the promontory of the atrium of the Cathedral of Lima may betray the presence of a small native *huaca*, or shrine, which was, as was common practice at the time, destroyed prior to the construction of the Christian temple. Nevertheless, pre-Hispanic Lima's main *huaca* lay farther east, by the orchard and mill that would later belong to Jerónimo de Silva. Located behind the convent of La Concepción and the Hospital of Santa Ana, in Barrios Altos, it may have been referred to as the Huaca Grande or Huaca of Santa Ana. It was later destroyed in order to prevent Indian worship of the oracle, the god Rímac, a rather vocal god, as opposed to the silent Pachacamac. It was this oracle that the river and the city of Rimactambo were named after: that is, "the town or village of the god who speaks."

Translated by Jorge Bayona

Note

Suspension points (. . .) in this selection appeared in the original text and do not indicate an ellipsis.

The Foundation of Lima

Garcilaso de la Vega el Inca

Garcilaso de la Vega (b. Cuzco 1539–d. Montilla 1616) embodied two of the conflicts that defined early colonial Peru: raging battles among the first generation of Spanish conquistadors and the debates about what to do with mestizos, the offspring of Spaniards and indigenous people. His mother, Chimpu Ocllo, was related to the Inca Tupac Yupanqui and was the niece of Huayna Capac, the Inca ruler, while his father, Captain Sebastián Garcilaso de la Vega Vargas, was a noble and conquistador. His father became embroiled in the Pizarro-Almagro civil war and was taken prisoner by Pizarro's brother Gonzalo. In 1549, after the defeat of the Pizarro clan, Spanish authorities ordered that all Spaniards who had encomiendas (the right to tax and exploit a group of Indians) marry Europeans. De la Vega Vargas complied, and Chimpu Ocllo also remarried (her new spouse was a less prestigious Spaniard). Their son's position in Cuzco and Peruvian society thus plummeted overnight; a mestizo such as Garcilaso de la Vega would not form part of the colonial aristocracy.

Garcilaso de la Vega grew up bilingual in Spanish and Quechua, well versed in both Spanish and Inca history. He lived in Cuzco at the point when the Incas moved their resistance to the jungle, but left for Spain in 1560. He continued to study, gained military experience, and settled in Montilla, near Córdoba. His landmark work, Royal Commentaries of the Incas, *and its second part, called* The General History of Peru *(published posthumously in 1617), made him the first American-born writer to enter the Spanish literary canon. Baptized Gómez Suárez de Figueroa (in honor of a noble Spanish ancestor), he adopted the name of his father and added El Inca to distinguish himself from a distant relative and great Spanish Renaissance poet of the same name. He is best known for his history of the Incas, glorifying them and casting them in terms that Europeans could appreciate, and of the conquest. While Cuzco was the subject of much of his writing, he also left this precise account of the foundation of Lima, which he incorrectly dates as 1534 rather than 1535.*

As soon as the governor [Francisco Pizarro] had dealt with Alvarado,[1] he sent his companion Almagro to Cusco with most of the gentlemen who had come with Alvarado, so as to confer with Prince Manco Inca and the governor's two brothers Juan and Gonzalo Pizarro. He recommended them to serve the Inca and treat the Indians well, so that the natives should not be provoked or the Inca lose his affection for the Spaniards, to whom he had come of his own free will. The governor remained in the valley of Pacha-camac, desiring to establish a city on the coast and take advantage of the traffic over the sea. Having consulted his friends, he sent people who were experienced in nautical affairs to explore the coast in both directions to find some good port, which was essential for what he had in mind. He learned from them that four leagues north of Pachacamac there was a good port at the bottom of the Rímac Valley. He went there and inspected the advantages of the port and the valley; and decided to transfer thither the town he had begun to build at Jauja, thirty leagues inland from Rímac. The city was founded on the Day of the Kings, Epiphany 1534.

With regard to the years of these events there is some disparity between the various authors, some of whom place events earlier and others later, while others give the decades, such as 1530, but leave the last number blank, so as to avoid errors. We shall leave opinions aside, and count the years by the most notable occurrences. It is certain, and all authors agree on this, that Pizarro, Almagro, and the schoolmaster Hernando de Luque established their triumvirate in 1525. They spent three years on the discovery before reaching Tumbes for the first time, and took two years more to come to Spain and obtain the right to conquer Peru and to return to Panama and prepare the expedition. They reached the island of Puna and Tumbes in 1531. The capture of Atahualpa took place in December of the same year, and his death was in March 1532. In October of this year they entered Cusco, where Pizarro remained until April 1533, when he learned of the coming of Alvarado. In September 1533 he left Cusco to pay Alvarado the sum agreed in their bargain, and he founded Lima on the Day of the Kings at the beginning of 1534. It was for this reason that Lima took as its arms and device the three crowns of the holy kings and the shining star that appeared to them.

The city was beautifully laid out, with a very large square, unless it be a fault that it is too big. The streets are broad and so straight that the country can be seen in four directions from any of the crossroads. It has a river that runs to the north of the city, from which many irrigation channels are drawn. These water the fields and are brought to all the houses in the city. When seen from a distance, the city is ugly, for it has no tiled roofs. As there is no rain in that region or for many leagues around on the coast, the houses are covered with thatch of excellent local straw. This is covered with two or three fingers' thickness of mud mixed with the straw, which suffices for shade against the sun. The houses are well built inside and out, and are daily improved. It stands two shaft leagues from the sea, and I am told that the part that has been built in recent years is approaching the sea. Its climate is hot and damp, a little less than Andalusia in summer: if it is less so, it is because the days are not so long and the nights not so short as they are here in July and August. The degree of heat lost by the later rising and earlier setting of the sun and the greater freshness of the night, which begins earlier and lasts longer, explains its greater coolness as compared with Andalusia. But because in Lima the heat is constant throughout the year, the inhabitants grow accustomed to it and take the necessary measures against it. They have cool rooms, wear summer clothes, and use light bed-covering; and take steps so that the flies and mosquitoes (which are numerous on the coast) shall not molest them by day or night. There are day and night mosquitoes in the hot valleys of Peru. The nocturnal ones are like those of Spain, with long legs and of the same color and shape, though they are much bigger. Spaniards emphasize how fiercely they sting by saying they can penetrate a leather boot. They say this because knitted stockings, even if of kersey or worsted, provide no defense, not even when linen is worn underneath. The mosquitoes are more savage in some regions than in others. The clay mosquitoes are small and exactly resemble those found in wine cellars in Spain, except that they are as yellow as weld. They are so bloodthirsty that I have been assured that not content with sating themselves, they have been seen to burst while sucking. In order to test this, I let some of them prick me and take their fill of blood: when sated, they were unable to rise and could only roll away. The sting of these smaller mosquitoes is somewhat poisonous, especially if the flesh is unhealthy, and produces small wounds, though they are not serious.

Owing to the hot damp climate of Lima, meat soon spoils. It has to be bought daily for consumption. This is very different from what we have said of Cusco, for the two cities are quite opposite from one another, one being cold and the other hot. The other Spanish cities and towns on the Peruvian coast all resemble the city of Lima, for the region is the same. The inland cities from Quito to Chuquisaca, over a distance of seven hundred leagues from north to south, are of a very pleasant climate, neither as cold as Cusco nor as hot as Lima, but sharing temperately in the conditions of both, except in the settlement of Potosí, where the silver mines are: this is a very cool region with extremely cold air. The Indians call the region *puna,* meaning that it is uninhabitable on account of the cold; but the love of silver has drawn so many Spaniards and Indians there that it is today one of the largest, best supplied, and most comfortable towns in Peru.

Note

1. Pedro de Alvarado, a lieutenant of Hernán Cortés in the conquest of Mexico, brought a large force to Peru, arriving after the capture of Atahualpa. In order to avoid conflict, Pizarro bought Alvarado's ships and equipment and allowed the men he brought with him, one of whom was Garcilaso de la Vega, the author's father, to join Pizarro's forces if they chose.

The Form and Greatness of Lima

Bernabé Cobo

Bernabé Cobo captures features of Lima that would obsess residents, visitors, and authorities for centuries. He underlines the city's multiracial composition, providing estimates of the black and Indian population; describes the grandiose and frenetic Plaza Mayor; and even probes environmental issues such as the city's year-round supply of produce, the abundance of bread and wheat, and the scarcity of wood. Cobo argues that the Spanish had created the city with great prudence and precision but had not foreseen the growth of the African and Indigenous population. The Spanish would have to share the City of Kings with the people who did the work. He provides a particularly precise description of the Plaza and the streets that left it at right angles.

Cobo left his native Jaén in Andalusia as a teenager and reached Lima in 1599, at the age of eighteen. He joined the Jesuit order and spent the rest of his life in Lima and Peru's provinces, with a thirteen-year hiatus in Mexico. He planned for his Historia del Nuevo Mundo *to consist of forty-three books in three parts, along the line of Pliny the Elder's* Natural History *(77–79 AD), but only the first part on pre-Columbian society and the first three books of the second on the foundation of Lima exist today, excerpted here. Cobo also mentioned a multivolume history of botany, one of his interests, which was either never written or lost. He died in Lima in 1657. His descriptions of cinchona bark helped lead to the discovery of quinine as a treatment for malaria and thus to the gin and tonic.*

The houses built at the beginning to shelter the settlers were of simple construction that lent itself to the materials available at that time. All the houses fit into the first two blocks surrounding the plaza, the number of residents being so few. The remaining site plan was being established by the regiment for those who came to settle nearby, and there was enough space to allot in this manner for many years. The blocks that were laid out were surrounded by adobe walls and turned into orchards and farmworkers' huts for Indians and blacks, or what we used to call *corrales de negros*, some of which have lasted until our time. In the thirty years since I came to this city, I have seen many houses built, so many that no single block is left in the layout of the city where Spaniards' buildings are not found. Because of the upheavals and civil wars that ensued in this realm three or four years after the founding of Lima and lasted for more than fifteen years, the city experienced very little growth in all that time. But once the noise of arms ceased, the climate improved and the Spaniards began to enjoy peace and quiet. Lima caught its breath and launched into such great growth up to 1629 (the year in which this is being written) that it has achieved a very prosperous course of uninterrupted growth. Nor can one foresee the end or limit to Lima's growth in the future.

It seemed to the settlers that they were greatly extending the city's dimensions and design when they were laying it out, believing that however much the population grew it would take a lot to manage to fill the site they were planning and dividing up. Yet their estimate fell far short of the magnitude that the city has achieved in view of the fact that Lima today occupies twice the space that the settlers allotted in planning it. Four thousand houses have been built here, along with those of the neighborhood and parish of the district, with Indian houses numbering about two hundred. The remainder are for Spaniards, and of these, six hundred stand along the other side of the river in the neighborhood called San Lázaro [what is today Rímac], after the parish church located there. All these dwellings together house five to six thousand Spanish inhabitants, who when combined with those coming and going add up to twenty-five thousand souls. There are thirty thousand black slaves of all ages and sexes, about half of them living most of the time on the small farms and country estates of this valley, and as many as five thousand Indians of every age. All these groups together total sixty thousand persons of every kind living in Lima. Things of this world are so unstable and so subject to change and variation that the industry and foresight of men are not enough to prevent or defend against such changes. We have a good example of this unpredictability in the subject we are discussing. The settlers expended great care and diligence in establishing this city with the order and arrangement noted and in anticipating the accidents that can alter a city without changing its shape and design. Despite all this, in the few years that have passed here, the city of Lima—without having suffered the calamities of fires, sackings, and sieges that have befallen cities in Europe—now has a shape and state so different from the one the settlers provided on founding the city that it is amazing.

The Plazas and Public Buildings

The public buildings of Lima have the advantage over the private residences in grandness and splendor. Most of them are found on the main plaza, the most spacious and best laid out that I have seen, even in Spain. The plaza takes up an entire block, including the width of the four streets that surround it on all sides, and thus on the four sides one can survey more than two thousand feet. The plaza is very level, with a large fountain in the middle, two rows of buildings with porticos featuring stone columns, a brick arcade, and many large balconies and windows. Along one of these two sides are the offices of the *cabildo* [the secular town hall], more imposing and magnificent than the rest of the buildings on that side, with very showy covered corridors in front of the chamber of the *ayuntamiento* [city council], a large and beautiful structure. Beneath these porticos stands the city jail, with a chapel so large, well decorated, and well attended that it could be called a church, along with the offices of the clerks, particularly those of the town hall, where the district magistrates meet and decide legal cases.

The other row of buildings with porticos consists of shops of different kinds, most of them occupied by hatters, silk merchants, and retailers. The block on this side is split in half by a street so narrow that we call it "the Alley." It leads to the street of the silversmiths and is lined on both sides with nothing but shops. On the third side of the plaza are the main church and the archbishop's quarters. The magnificence of these buildings makes this side of the plaza the most ornate and showiest of all. The church fronts onto the plaza via the three main doors (of its seven), with two towers on the sides, one on each corner. The rest of this row of buildings is occupied by the archbishop's offices, which are magnificent and have splendid windows, particularly in the living quarters and the hall of the ecclesiastical council, which were built during the lifetime of the third archbishop. On the fourth and last side of the plaza, which slopes down toward the river along the north bank, are the royal offices, palace, and home of the viceroys. It is the largest and most luxurious structure in this kingdom because of its grand site and the great effort expended by all the viceroys to make it resplendent with new and expensive buildings. Scarcely a single viceroy has not enlarged it with some room or distinguished addition, and hence the structure has acquired the majesty that it represents today. The building is low, only one story tall, with spacious tile and flat roofs. In addition to the rooms and apartments where the viceroy lives with his family are the courtrooms and halls of the *audiencia* [royal tribunal], which deals with civil and criminal matters, all these chambers being expensively appointed.

After the founding of Lima, this plaza stood with few decorations, surrounded by the humble buildings erected at the beginning, with the gallows in the middle, right where the Marqués [Francisco] Pizarro put them, until the administration of Viceroy Count of Niebla undertook to improve the plaza. The first thing he did was to take the gallows out of the plaza and move them to the side toward the river. He also began construction of the porticos and ordered that running water be installed in the city and that fountains be built, beginning with the one in the plaza. All of this was started at that time but was completed only gradually and with the support of Viceroy Don Francisco de Toledo.

The commerce and bustle of those who continually people this plaza is very great. More than a quarter of the plaza, in front of the main church, is taken up by the market, where all kinds of fruits and other foods are sold by so many blacks and Indians that it looks like an anthill. And so that this multitude of common people will not lack for mass on fiesta days, a low mass is said for them from a balcony or corridor of the main church, which dominates the entire plaza. The items found in this market are anything that a well-supplied republic could desire for its sustenance and comfort. Many little stalls are set up by street vendors, Indians selling a thousand trifles. All along the row of buildings of the palace, a string of booths or wooden stalls belonging to vendors with a few things to sell are set up leaning against the walls, as well as many other little portable stalls along the two rows of buildings. In the marketplace, on the side of the town hall offices, public auctions are always being held where old clothes are sold at low prices along with everything needed to furnish a house.

The eight streets that lead into the plaza are the main ones and the most heavily traveled in the city. The street that goes to the Convento de la Merced is the one we call Merchants' Row (part of what is today Jirón de la Unión) because it is lined with expensive shops run by wealthy merchants. It is very beautiful and fresh because the southerly wind fans its length, and, covered by awnings in the summer, it offers much coolness and shade. On Merchants' Row are found all the hustle and bustle of merchandise not only from this city but from all over the realm because every part of the country does business with the merchants along this street. The second-busiest street runs nearby at a right angle to Merchants' Row and is called the Street of the Blankets; it runs westward to Holy Spirit Hospital. This street got its name from the fact that in the early days, most of its shops sold native clothing, Indian garments, blankets, and undershirts. Now the street has expensive shops with Spanish clothing like those on Merchants' Row, although not as many. The rest of the street is occupied by workers plying various trades.

The third-busiest place in Lima is the intersection of the two streets on the corner of the main church: one heads right toward the south and runs into the Convento de la Encarnación, and the other runs east to the Convento de la Concepción, both of which are for nuns. The first road is known as the Street of the Secondhand Clothes Sellers, after the shops along it that sell ready-to-wear clothing, old and new. The second street has only one row of shops because it faces the main church.

The four other main streets also bear much traffic and trade, and although they have no stores, they are lined with the shops of many workers. In addition to these streets that head straight out to the edges of the city are others with lots of businesses, like the ones running into the back of the plaza on all four sides, especially the street of the silversmiths, the one that goes from the Jesuits' headquarters to the parish of San Sebastián, running more than a quarter of a league in length.

Lima's Convents

José de la Riva-Agüero

Lima is a city of churches, monasteries, temples, and other religious sites, although modern sprawl has diluted their predominance and Protestant churches now compete with Catholicism. Well into the nineteenth century, travelers almost invariably noticed the omnipresence of the Catholic Church as well as the high number of priests and above all nuns. In 1700, one-fifth of the city's female population lived in convents: nuns, spiritual women who had not taken vows, and the servants who waited on these two groups. José de la Riva-Agüero captures the physical and spiritual presence that the colonial era, particularly convents, retained in the first half of twentieth-century Lima.

The aristocratic Riva-Agüero (1885–1944) was a historian, essayist, and politician who confronted left-leaning views of Peru, including indigenismo. After serving in the Oscar Benavides government (1933–39), Riva-Agüero's views shifted to the right, and he ultimately became a fascist sympathizer. Yet his views on colonial Lima are nuanced and rich. Although he regarded Spain and Catholicism as Peru's historical backbone, he criticized aspects of colonial architecture and society. Here he brings the reader into the phantasmagoric aura of convents and nuns in modern Peru.

Convents represent and embody the colonial mystique. This holds true in all the Spanish dominions in the Americas, but it is especially so in Peru and particularly in Lima. The soul of our city is convent-like. It lingers, hidden and forgotten, but emerges at times. Driven away from the urban center by the din of modernity and the pretentious vulgarity of newer constructions, it seeks refuge away from the encroachments of factories and those absurd repair jobs we call remodeling. It slumbers serenely in the past of churches, on quiet streets, and within the long fences of the monastery. But there are moments—in the golden sunlight and delicate, deep blue of the summer; or in the cool pallor of a pale sun that scrapes away at the tin-gray sky on certain days of winter—in which, called upon by the ringing of the

La Merced Church and Convent. In Mariano Felipe Paz Soldán, *Atlas Geográfico del Perú* (Paris, 1865).

old bells—sometimes grave, sometimes joyful and silver-like—the soul of Lima awakens and spreads its voluptuous and mystical charm.

The principal churches bequeathed to us by the colonial period are still standing. Despite many earthquake-related repairs, they had kept their unique physiognomy rather well until recently. None of them are master-pieces, however, and should not be afforded such treatment. Most were built in the seventeenth century and thus partake—to differing degrees— in the elaborate *churrigueresque* style that coexists and contrasts oddly with the severe style of the Spanish Renaissance. But that decadent architecture and those affected, florid, and time-weathered decorations are not lacking in interest, as they embody a historical period. Time has idealized the appear-ance of the overly presumptuous baroque by smoothing the shriller colors, dampening the shine of gold, spreading patina on paintings, and imprinting the charm of memory on all those objects. There is no architectural deca-dence that, centuries later, will appear to lack poetic suggestiveness. With their pompous carved altars, profusion of gold, and Solomonic columns, all decorated with unbelievably round and twisted lines, our churches remind us of those old ladies who keep and wear hoop skirts and elaborate bows, following the extravagant fashions of their remote youth. At any rate, they possess historical character and transmit that to the city. But now a wind of ignorance and folly blusters, and it endeavors to make Lima the blandest place on earth. And the religious communities are actively cooperating in this preposterous task. We have enough abominable caricatures of modern gothic (made of adobe and wood!) which are completely out of tune, entirely out of place, and which struggle ridiculously and painfully with tradition and environs.

. . .

Such complete disorder and indescribable abandon were the norm until very recently, when the arrival of foreign friars restored monastic life in the old greater convents, cleansed them of their greater impurities, and raised them from the miserable condition in which they had fallen to their current reasonable and almost decorous mediocrity. Discerning what in the present state of the old convents of Lima is actually artificial or even dangerous—being based exclusively on foreign elements—is a key issue, albeit one whose discussion is beyond the scope of this essay. From an artistic point of view, the damage caused by past carelessness is irreversible. Mosaics are truncated in many parts, and sections of coffers are rotten or broken. Almost all the valuable paintings and furniture have vanished, due to the activities of cunning travelers or avid merchants who hurried to wrest them from the hands of their unwitting owners. But worst yet is that this devastation seems set to continue and will consummate the ruin of everything that is characteristic and traditional within limeño convents. The relative economic comfort that they now enjoy (thanks to the law that allowed them to sell their estates) enables them to rebuild their dilapidated cloisters; one must fear, however, that the good friars may try to modernize them, in all certainty with that same lack of sensibility for local color, with the same pretentious and ill-advised cosmopolitanism that inspires contemporary constructions in Lima and has already transformed churches into unfortunate and laughable parodies. It shall be a great shame if the cloisters follow the terrible fate of those poor churches. Some cloisters, such as the first of San Francisco, for instance, have some actual merit. We definitely find it superior to their corresponding temples, which, despite their agreeable historical memories, are actually in terrible taste, and can be preferred solely to those insipid creatures that contemporary taste foists upon us, making us yearn for the capricious originality and exaggerated luxuriance of the baroque.

Cloisters—along with a few, increasingly rare, old mansions—are the only places where it is still possible to imagine and feel colonial poetry in all its mildness, delicateness, and weakness. The wide, solemn staircases vainly pretend to be magnificent and palatial, while the choir- and meeting-rooms showcase the somber splendor of their carved chairs; the naked El Escorial–esque style[1] reemerges frequently, but to no avail, among the baroque bombast and struggles to impose on our cloisters the dour severity of Spanish monasteries. Any impression of sternness is dispelled by the exaggerated roundness of arches and domes, the prodigious decorations, the golden trifles in *churrigueresque* style, the gay polychrome of the tiles, with their Moorish reminiscences, and the neat gardens, whose fountains laugh and sing in the golden splendor of the sun or in the gentle and warm mist in the tranquil Lima clime.

. . .

History beautifies and purifies it all. In its magic mirror, even the worst times seem beautiful. We must not, however, forget that this is but an illusion. Among the relics of extinct luxury in the old creole convents, let us, with agreeable dilettantism, contentedly taste a feeling of melancholy peace. But deep down, we must congratulate ourselves for not having been born in a time when those convents lorded over society, covering and smothering it with a dark web of fanaticism, ignorance, and silence.

Translated by Jorge Bayona

Note

1. This is a reference to El Escorial monastery, built in the sixteenth century near Madrid.

The Spiritual Diary of an Afro-Peruvian Mystic

Ursula de Jesús

Colonial Lima's rich religious life involved all of the city's multiracial and multicultural population. Ursula de Jesús was born a slave in 1604, the legitimate daughter of a Spaniard and an Afro-Peruvian slave woman. She entered the Convent of Santa Clara in 1617 to work for the niece of her mother's owner. She spent twenty-eight years there, washing, cooking, and cleaning, somehow finding time for her own spiritual development and a diary.

This selection from her diary, taken from the fine biography and compilation by Nancy van Deusen, highlights the mysticism of women such as Ursula and her rich religious life. She describes different appearances and voices and her horrific vision of hell, a hole filled with enemies and insects. She also mentions the scolding of her "companion" and the threats to force her on the streets to beg. Ursula writes, "They tell me to suffer all that happens without complaint or criticism, not letting anyone know how I really feel, as though I were a stone." As shown by her vivid writing, Ursula de Jesús could never be perceived as a stone.

Thursday, on Saint John's Day, as I prepared to take communion before the Latin door, I thought about those nuns who have decided to alter their habits. I commended them to God, so that He would keep them in a state of grace until they reached glory. The voices said, *Pray to God that it will turn out for the best. Saints Francis and Clare were always extremely humble. They saw themselves as the least important people in the world. All the people they saw, whether common or great, seemed better than they.* The voices talked about the nuns' responsibilities and the need for patience and silence. They showed me a skull and said, *We should always keep that skull in mind.* They mentioned the cords they now make with buttons at the waist and explained that whoever wears or makes them would be punished. After this, they came to me with something illusory. Because of God's great mercy, I disregard such things. I thought, "Who tells me these things?" They seemed to say within me, *Jesus Christ, our Lord*. I said, "Jesus Christ?" *No, your angel, look*. "Your grace, I have already asked God to free me from these things. Why would I want them?" I forgot to mention that when they were talking about the nuns' obligations, they said they should always try to imitate our Lord Jesus Christ. He could easily have tied the hands of those who were going to take Him prisoner, but because He was God almighty, He refused to in order to set an example for us.

The following Saturday, I was up to my ears with cooking and other things, desiring only to be in the mountains where there are no people. I turned to God and said that were it not for Him, I would not do this. The voices responded that the Son of God was quite well off in paradise, but still He came and suffered for our sake. The apostles felt very content in Christ's company, but He had to go to heaven so they could work, preach, and call together those around them.

When I began praying to God on Sunday, I felt the presence of a dead soul next to me. This one had died nearly a year ago, and he asked me to commend his spirit, although I could not see him. Later, during the siesta, I saw a horrible hole filled with insects and enemies. I have seen this place before, and the first time I saw it, they explained that it was a cavity in hell. The voices told me that were it not for God's mercy, we would be there because of our sins—and to free us. Then I saw a crucified Christ, and they explained that because of God's mercy, He suffered what He suffered to free us from that place.

A dying nun was very distressed because she could not resign herself to God's will. She felt great anxiety and desperation and asked us to commend her spirit to God. I felt great pity toward her and commended her spirit to God. They told me that because God loves us so much He gives each of us what we need. In time He would give her relief, but for now this ordeal would do her good. Suffering helps to purify the spirit. It all comes in bits and pieces. I cannot explain what happened there. I go to our Lord and ask Him to give me patience, teach me how to suffer for others, and grant me peace of mind so that I do not criticize another in my heart. I am such a bad black woman. Sometimes I feel—I do not know what—toward my companion; with all her scolding I do not know how to get along with her. If I ask her, bad, if I do not ask her, worse. Nothing seems to suit her. Sometimes she says, "Why don't you take your bag and go beg for alms for the infirm?" Other times, "Why don't you heal them?," and other things of this nature that make me laugh. God only knows how. They tell me to suffer all that happens without complaint or criticism, not letting anyone know how I really feel, as though I were a stone. Do I not see it? What happens when they step on the side of a brick that does not move and then on those bricks that are loosely placed?

One day they told me that whoever does not imitate the virtues of our Lord Jesus Christ—humility, meekness, patience, obedience, and poverty— could not be His child or disciple.

One day, while in a state of recollection, I see within myself a Christ figure tied to a column and in a pitiful state. He told me that our sins kept Him bound to that column and crown of thorns and on that cross. What He suffered and what we caused Him to suffer would save us. He tried to inspire us. He awaited us, giving us many opportunities. We needed to commend ourselves to Him and ask His forgiveness. When we were defiant and refused to mend our ways, He also bound us. The Jews acted out of ignorance, but because we know better, we offend Him. It is impossible to explain what happened there, it is all in pieces, only a segment.

Throughout this nine-week period before Christmas, I have been in such a state that even Jesus could not say. I was in the crèche, looking at that child and thinking about that mystery. I complained to the Lord and said, "What is this about, Lord? I spend all my time sleeping and being lazy." They said it was my lot and to see whether I could do something on my own. I started to say, "Virgin and Mother of God," because they told me to say it like that, just as here we say "king." There the greatest honor one can bestow upon our Lady is to call her "Virgin and Mother of God." After that, I saw a representation of what had happened during the Most Holy Sacrament, as real and authentic as in heaven. Because of His love for us, He remained in the host and was transubstantiated. This is all in bits and pieces. For us, He spent nine months in the Virgin's womb, and here a great number of benefits occurred. I said, "Virgin and Mother of God, Virgin before giving birth, during the birth, and after giving birth." The voices explained, *This is the Catholic faith, which the Jews deny.* I cannot recall it all; it is impossible to say what happened there. It all happens in a disorderly manner, upside down. They also mentioned that God's breath formed the Son and Holy Spirit. I said, "Jesus be with me, I do not want breath or faith, only to be taught the Catholic faith. I want to leave here, now." He said, *This is untrue,* and repeated each part of the creed.

On the day of the Innocents, while commending myself to God, the voices told me to thank Him for the love He showed when He came down from heaven to earth, became a man in the Virgin's womb, and suffered such travail for our redemption. One by one, they repeated each. Neither the exile, garden, whippings, nor thorns remained, but the cross did and He remained in the host. They talked about the preparation needed to receive the knowledge of God and the gratitude we should have for such a great gift. After receiving Him, we should throw ourselves at His feet, thank Him, tell Him our needs, and ask for a remedy and mercy.

Auto-da-Fé and Procession

Josephe and Francisco Mugaburu

Published diaries, memoirs, and autobiographies are rare in Peru, past and present, so Josephe and Francisco Mugaburu's detailed account of colonial Lima, which stretches fifty-seven years (1640–96), is particularly welcome. Born in Spain, Josephe lived in Peru from 1640 until 1686, at which point his son, Francisco, continued the account. Josephe wrote little about himself and instead focused on the city's active public life, its countless religious processions and celebrations, political shifts and rumors, and alarming events such as pirates lurking off the coast of Callao.

This 1667 passage describes an auto-da-fé conducted by the Holy Office, the Inquisition. The accused included César de Bandier (Nicolás Legras), a French doctor "and the greatest heretic known in these times"; his nephew Luis Bandier (Luis Legras); and a Carmelite priest, César Pasani Beniboli, who it was said "carnally had known more than three hundred and sixty women, and in a convent of nuns had committed many sacrileges." All three were humiliated and exiled. In fact, they had to be protected from the crowds who sought to stone them. The Inquisition in Peru (1570–1820) had as its mission the defense of Catholicism from Protestants and Jews and the prosecution of heresy, bigamy, sorcery, witchcraft, and other behaviors deemed superstitious or immoral. Indians were not subject to the Inquisition.

Auto-da-Fé

On Saturday morning, the 8th of October of the year 1667, an auto-da-fé was held in the church of the Holy Office wherein four [persons] were sentenced. [One was Doctor] Don Cesar [de Bandier, or Nicolás Legras], the physician brought [to Peru] by the viceroy Count of Santisteban, and the greatest heretic known in these times. [Born in France in 1600,] he was the son of a Christian father and mother, and was a priest. Later he married in Rome and from there went to Constantinople, where he became a great herb doctor and cured the sultan of Turkey. He traveled all over the world, and in this city cured many and killed many more. He was a physician at

29

the royal hospital of Santa Ana of this City of Kings; while he was curing he killed more than two thousand Indians. And he was a doctor of this royal university, a doctor of medicine. This so-and-so denied the immortality of the soul, and his errors were worse than Luther, Arius, Mohammed, or any of the sectarians. He was of such a type that he went up to paintings of the crucified and dying Jesus Christ and one of the Virgin of Solitude, and he said to the holy Virgin, "Why is that [female] liar crying for a son that has deceived the world?" There were so many insults and blasphemies and dishonest words that he said to the holy Virgin, that I do not write them for the great horror and scandal they cause to Christian hearers. They were so bad that in relating his wickedness and evil deeds [at the Inquisition], all those who heard became riled up, and if the gentlemen of the Inquisition had not ordered that no more be read, they would have killed him right in the chapel of the Holy Office. The sentence was to wear a *sanbenito* [a garment of shame], life imprisonment, and exile from these kingdoms of Peru. He went to the Inquisition of Seville to serve out his sentence.

The following day, Sunday, the 9th of October, more than two thousand souls awaited in the event they brought him out to the cathedral to hear Mass, and with determination, young and old [awaited] to stone him to death. But the gentlemen [of the Inquisition] knowing that there was such a tumult, ordered that neither he nor the other two go out to hear Mass. His nephew [Luis Bandier or Luis Legras] was as great a heretic as he. They gave him the same sentence and took him to the Society of Jesus [monastery].

The Carmelite Friar

[The third penitent sentenced by the Inquisition was the Carmelite Friar César Pasani Beniboli, a native of Modena, Italy.] He was a great heretic, and being a priest said Mass, this dishonest and lascivious dog. While relating his evil doings, he said that in a certain city [La Paz, Upper Peru] he had carnally known more than three hundred and sixty women, and in a convent of nuns had committed many sacrileges. They brought him prisoner [from the mines of Puno] en route to Buenos Aires by way of Chile. They gave him the same sentence and took him to the Franciscan monastery of this city.

Procession of the Gentlemen of the Inquisition

Friday, the 14th of October of the year 1667, at four in the afternoon the Holy Sacrament was carried out of the chapel of the Holy Office in the hands of the chief inquisitor, Don Cristóbal de Castilla, whose acolytes were two somber Dominican friars. The first two poles of the canopy were carried by the canons, the others by the prelates of the religious orders, and the insignia by the vicar of Santo Domingo. The same image of the [Virgin of] Solitude and the Holy Christ, towards which the heretic dog [Don César de Bandier] directed so many insults, were brought out in the procession. The image was carried by the clerical priests, and the Holy Christ by four grave religious of the Dominican order.

From the Inquisition to Santo Domingo [Church] all the streets were swept and sprinkled, the ground full of flowers; balconies and windows were hung with great display. All the religious orders and the Society of Jesus attended with lighted candles in their hands. In this procession there were almost eighty students dressed as angels, all very well costumed, [as well as] all the secular priests, *caballeros*, and residents with their lighted torches. The Holy Sacrament was uncovered during the entire procession.

The following Saturday at Santo Domingo [Church] there was rejoicing. Head inquisitor Don Cristóbal de Castilla said Mass. On this day Father Maestro Fray Melendez of the Dominican order gave the sermon in praise of the Virgin. The other two inquisitors, Don Alvaro de Ibarra and Don Juan de la Huerta, participated in the Mass and the procession with their candles in hand. All the [Inquisition] officers attended these two days with their insignias on their chests. The banner of the faith was carried by Señor Don García de Híjar y Mendoza, *caballero* of the order of Santiago and chief constable of the Holy Office.

The inquisitors told Archbishop Don Pedro de Villagómez that His Grace should order and instruct where the two images of Jesus Christ and his Holy Mother of the Solitude should be placed. His Grace chose the convent of Nuestra Señora del Prado.

Margarita's Wedding Dress

Ricardo Palma

Ricardo Palma (1833–1919) was a writer, scholar, and librarian who also held various administrative positions. He rebuilt Peru's National Library after the devastating War of the Pacific (1879–83). Palma wrote in numerous genres but was most renowned for his humorous tradiciones, *which mixed history and fiction, usually building off well-known individuals or events. His* Tradiciones Peruanas *has been released in countless editions.*

In classic Palma fashion, "Margarita's Wedding Dress" both ridicules and lauds the upper classes of colonial Peru. In telling the story of an ambitious but broke Spaniard who comes to Peru to tap into his rich uncle's wealth, he emphasizes the upper classes' penchant for vanity, conflict, and audacious solutions. This brief story explains why the expression "as expensive as Margarita's Wedding Dress" became synonymous with outlandish expenditures that proved to be sage financial decisions.

It is likely that some of my readers have heard old women of Lima remark, when they wanted to think over how much the price of something had gone up:

"Good heavens! Why, that's more expensive than Margarita's wedding chemise."

I would have been left with a lingering curiosity as to who that Margarita was whose wedding dress was the talk of the town, had I not come across, in the Madrid newspaper *La América*, an article signed by don Ildefonso Antonio Bermejo (the author of a noteworthy book on Peru), who, although he touches only lightly on the girl and her wedding dress, put me on the right path to disentangling the skein and getting the story that you are about to read straight.

Margarita Pareja was the most pampered daughter of don Raimundo Pareja, a Knight of the Order of Santiago and collector general of taxes in Cuzco.

The girl was one of those Lima beauties who captivate the devil himself and make him cross himself and throw stones. She had a pair of black eyes that were like two torpedoes loaded with dynamite that caused an explosion in the depths of the soul of Lima's dashing young men.

There arrived from Spain around that time a bold young man, the son of the crowned city of the bear and the madrone tree[1] named don Luis Alcázar. He had an uncle in Lima, a rich bachelor of old highborn Aragonese stock, and prouder than the sons of King Fruela.[2]

It was only natural that as he waited for the time to come when he would inherit his uncle's fortune, our don Luis should be as poor as a church mouse and be going through the pains of hell. When I say that even his love-adventures were on credit, to be paid for when his fortunes took a turn for the better, I need say no more.

Alcázar met the lovely Margarita in the procession of Saint Rose. The girl's eyes sent their darts straight to his heart and inspired his love at first sight. He paid her courtly compliments, and though she answered neither yes nor no, she made it clear with little smiles and other arms of the feminine arsenal that the handsome young man was a dish very much to her liking. The truth is, as if I were in the confessional, that the two of them fell in love to the roots of their hair.

Since lovers forget that arithmetic exists, don Luis believed that his current poverty would not be an obstacle to the prospering of his love, and so he went to Margarita's father, and without further ado asked him for the hand of his daughter.

The petition was not to don Raimundo's liking, and he courteously dismissed the petitioner, telling him that Margarita was too young to marry, for despite her 18 Mays, she still played with dolls.

But this was not the heart of the matter. The negative answer stemmed from the fact that don Raimundo did not wish to be the father-in-law of a poor devil, as he told his friends in confidence, and one of them went with this bit of gossip to don Honorato, which was the name of the uncle from Aragon. The latter, who was prouder than the Cid,[3] fumed with rage and said:

"What's this I hear! Snubbing my nephew! There are many who would give anything to be related by marriage to that young man, than whom there is none more gallant in all of Lima. Who has ever seen such insolence! How far will that petty tax collector go with me?" Margarita, who was ahead of her time, for she was as nervous as one of today's damsels, wept and wailed and tore her hair and had tantrums and if she did not threaten to poison herself it was only because sulfur matches had not yet been invented.

She lost color and weight, her health quite visibly declined, she spoke of becoming a nun, and no one could do a thing with her.

"Either Luis's bride or a nun!"[4] she cried each time her nerves were upset, something that happened from one hour to the next.

The Knight of the Order of Santiago grew alarmed and called in doctors and healers, all of whom declared that the girl was well on her way to becoming consumptive and that the only *melecina*[5] to save her wasn't sold in an apothecary's shop.

Either marry her to the young man of her choice, or soon lay her out in a coffin with a palm frond and crown. Such was the ultimatum from the doctors.

Don Raimundo (finally acting as a father!), forgetting in his concern to take his cape and cane, rushed like a madman to don Honorato's house and said to him:

"I have come to ask you to consent to your nephew's marrying Margarita tomorrow, because if not the girl will go to her last resting place very soon."

"That can't be," the uncle answered rudely. "My nephew is a 'poor wretch' as you put it, and what you ought to seek for your daughter is a man rolling in money."

The altercation was stormy. The more don Raimundo pleaded, the more the Aragonese hit the roof, and don Raimundo was about to depart dejected when don Luis, intervening in the matter, said:

"But uncle, it is not Christian behavior to cause the death of someone who is not to blame."

"Do you declare yourself willing to marry her?"

"With all my heart, my uncle and master."

"Well then, my boy. I agree to do as you wish, but on one condition, which is this: Don Raimundo is to swear to me before the consecrated Host that he will not give an *ochavo* to his daughter, nor will he leave her a *real* as her inheritance."

At this point another even stormier dispute ensued.

"But my dear fellow," don Raimundo argued, "my daughter has a dowry worth 20,000 duros."

"We give up any claim to the dowry. The girl will come to her husband's house with nothing more than what she is wearing."

"Allow me to give her furniture as a wedding gift and her bride's trousseau."

"Not so much as a pin. If that doesn't suit you, leave matters as they are and let the girl die."

"Be reasonable, don Honorato. My daughter needs to have at least a wedding chemise to replace the clothes she is wearing."

"Very well. I agree to her having such a garment so that you won't accuse me of being obstinate. I consent to your giving her a bridal chemise, and that's the end of it."

On the following day don Raimundo and don Honorato went to the church of San Francisco very early in the morning, knelt to hear Mass, and according to their agreement, at the moment that the priest elevated the divine Host, Margarita's father said:

"I swear not to give my daughter anything but her wedding chemise. May God condemn me if I swear falsely."

And don Raimundo fulfilled *ad pedem litterae*[6] what he had sworn to, for neither in life nor in death did he later give to his daughter anything worth so much as a *maravedi*.[7]

The Flanders lace trimming the bride's wedding chemise cost 2,700 duros, according to Bermejo,[8] who appears to have copied this detail from the *Relaciones secretas* of Ulloa and don Jorge Juan.[9]

Furthermore, the drawstring at her neck was a diamond chain worth 30,000 pesos.

The newlyweds made the Aragonese uncle believe that the bridal chemise was worth a doubloon at best, because don Honorato was so stubborn that had he discovered the truth he would have made his nephew divorce Margarita.

Let us agree that the fame that Margarita Pareja's bridal chemise came to have was highly deserved.

Notes

Except as denoted below with "—Eds.," these notes appeared in the original.

1. Madrid.

2. The medieval King of Asturias, known in legend, like his offspring, for his inordinate pride.

3. Ruy Díaz de Vivar (1043–99), a legendary Spanish hero known as "El Cid" (from the Arabic meaning "lord"), was immortalized in the thirteenth-century epic *El cantar de Mío Cid.*—Eds.

4. Umphrey's translation [George W. Umphrey and Carlos García Prada, eds., *Flor de tradiciones* (México: Ed. Cultura, 1943)], 127. The original reads: "¡O de Luis o de Dios!"

5. A corruption of *medicina*, medicine.

6. To the letter (Latin).

7. Any number of medieval Spanish silver coins, used in the thirteenth to fifteenth centuries to value silver and base silver coins, in the fifteenth to eighteenth centuries to value

copper coins; a Spanish copper coin of small value used in the seventeenth to eighteenth centuries, frequently used as a type of worthless or valueless object.

8. Ildefonso Antonio Bermejo (1820–92) was the author of *Repúblicas americanas: Episodios de la vida en la República del Paraguay* (1873).—Eds.

9. Antonio de Ulloa (1716–95) and Jorge Juan (1713–73) coauthored the *Noticias secretas de América sobre el estado naval, militar y político de las Reynos del Perú y provincias de Quito, costa de Nueva Granada y Chile: Gobierno y régimen particular de las pueblos de Indias, etc., etc.* (1826). —Eds.

II

Bourbon Lima

The War of Spanish Succession (1701–14) culminated in the transfer of the control of the Spanish monarchy to the French House of Bourbon. The new rulers (most notably King Carlos III, who reigned from 1759 to 1788) believed that their predecessors, the Habsburgs, had been too lax with their American possessions. The "Bourbon Reforms" heightened social control, implemented "modern" or more direct forms of government, and unleashed fiscal reforms that desperately sought to increase tax revenues from the Americas. These tax increases escalated in the latter half of the eighteenth century as Spain found itself constantly at war with European powers such as Great Britain and France.

For authorities, Lima epitomized Spanish America's problems: its upper classes lived a decadent, vain lifestyle; its lower classes drank, gambled, and showed little respect for social hierarchies; and the city's widespread racial mixing meant that social categories differentiating groups were impossible to uphold. Critics, both authorities and travelers, targeted women and blacks with particular vehemence. Bourbon reformers as well as priests decried women—particularly the *tapadas*, who covered their face and thus their identities—for leading dangerously promiscuous lives and flouting social mores. Administrators and reformers complained that blacks had little respect for authorities and too much presence in public life.

Authors such as Jorge Juan and Antonio de Ulloa, Hipólito Ruiz, and Alexander von Humboldt present critical interpretations of Lima, emphasizing the city's supposed decadence, moral and economic. Other essays highlight unique features of the city, from a massive earthquake and tsunami in 1746 to the threat of an Indian uprising four years later. We also include a description of slave life and religion from 1791 and a comparison of Lima and Cusco from the fictitious travel account *El Lazarillo*. In their own way, each text builds from and contributes to a broad fascination with Lima, along with a debate about whether it was a declining den of inequity or still a majestic capital.

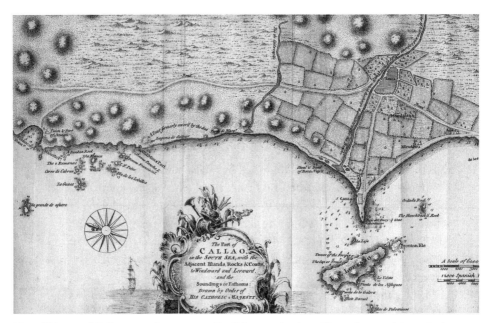

Map of Lima and Callao, 1748. Anonymous English reproduction of Jorge Juan and Antonio de Ulloa's map "El Puerto de el Callao en el Mar Pacífico o del Sur," in *Relación histórica del viaje a la América Meridional* (Madrid, 1748) 2: 146.

Of the Inhabitants of Lima

Jorge Juan and Antonio de Ulloa

Juan and Ulloa were not only explorers, navy officers, scientists, and Spanish officers with positions from Louisiana, to Huancavelica, to Cádiz, but also excellent chroniclers. They formed part of the French Geodesic Mission, which aimed to measure the roundness of the earth, and they remained in the Andean region from 1736 to 1744. Their account of this expedition was translated into English as A Voyage to South America. *In this as well as* Noticias secretas *or* Discourse and Political Reflections on the Kingdoms of Peru, *they stressed the decadence of the Catholic Church (its wealth and the scandalous lives of priests and nuns) and the arrogance of the upper classes. In this passage, they highlight the commercial ambitions and skills of Lima's inhabitants, the city's vanity, and several of its peculiar customs and obsessions. While their publications formed part of a wave of European writings that belittled Lima and, in general, Spanish America, they appreciated certain aspects of the Americas and had a good eye for social tensions. Their critique of the Catholic Church resonated broadly in transatlantic debates about secularization.*

Having, in our accounts of several towns through which we passed to Lima, included also the inhabitants, we shall observe the same rule with regard to Lima; for though amidst such an infinite variety of customs, there is always some resemblance between those of neighboring people, yet the difference is also considerable; and no where more so than on this continent, where it doubtless arises from the great distance between the several towns; and, consequently, I may say, from the different geniuses and dispositions of the people. And though Lima is the capital of the country, it will appear that it is not a model to other places, with regard to dress, customs, and manner of living.

The inhabitants of Lima are composed of whites, or Spaniards, Negroes, Indians, Mestizos, and other casts, proceeding from the mixture of all three.

The Spanish families are very numerous; Lima according to the lowest computation, containing sixteen or eighteen thousand whites. Among these are reckoned a third or fourth part of the most distinguished nobility of

A street in colonial Lima, with characteristic balconies and *tapadas*. In Esteban Terralla y Landa, *Lima por dentro y fuera* (Paris: Librería española de A. Mezín, 1854).

Valladolid Street, c. 1836. In Theodore Auguste, *Voyage autour du monde execute pendant les annees 1836 et 1837 sur la corvette La Bonite*, Album historique, Fisquet (Paris: Arthus Bertrand, [184?]).

Peru; and many of these dignified with the stile [*sic*] of ancient or modern Castilians, among which are no less than 45 counts and marquises. The number of knights belonging to the several military orders is also very considerable. Besides these are many families no less respectable and living in equal splendor; particularly 24 gentlemen of large estates, but without titles, though most of them have ancient seats, a proof of the antiquity of their families. One of these traces, with undeniable certainty, his descent from the Incas. The name of this family is Ampuero, so called from one of the Spanish commanders at the conquest of this country, who married a Coya, or daughter of the Inca. To this family the kings of Spain have been pleased to grant several distinguishing honors and privileges, as marks of its great quality: and many of the most eminent families in the city have desired intermarriages with it. All those families live in a manner becoming their rank, having estates equal to their generous dispositions, keeping a great number of slaves and other domestics, and those who affect making the greatest figure have coaches, while others content themselves with calashes or chaises, which are here so common, that no family of any substance is without one. It must be owned that these carriages are more necessary here than in other cities, on account of the numberless droves of mules which continually pass through Lima, and cover the streets with their dung, which being soon dried by the sun and the wind, turns to a nauseous dust, scarce supportable to those who walk on foot. These chaises, which are drawn by a mule, and guided by a driver, have only two wheels, with two seats opposite to each other, so that on occasion they will hold four persons. They are very slight and airy; but on account of the gildings and other decorations, sometimes cost eight hundred or a thousand crowns. The number of them is said to amount to 5 or 6000; and that of coaches is also very considerable, though not equal to the former. The funds to support these expenses, which in other parts would ruin families, are their large estates and plantations, civil and military employments, or commerce, which is here accounted no derogation to families of the greatest distinction; but by this commerce is not to be understood the buying and selling by retail or in shops, every one trading proportional to his character and substance. Hence families are preserved from those disasters too common in Spain; where titles are frequently found without a fortune capable of supporting their dignity.

Commerce is so far from being considered as a disgrace at Lima, that the greatest fortunes have been raised by it; those on the contrary, being rather despised, who not being blessed with a sufficient estate, through indolence, neglect to have recourse to it for improving their fortunes. This custom, or resource, which was established there without any determinate end, being introduced by a vain desire of the first Spaniards to acquire wealth, is now the real support of that splendor in which those families live; and whatever repugnance these military gentlemen might originally have to commerce, it was immediately removed by a royal proclamation, by which it was declared that commerce in the Indies should not exclude from nobility or the military orders; a very wise measure, and of which Spain would be still more sensible, were it extended to all its dependencies.

At Lima, as at Quito, and all Spanish America, some of the eminent families have been long since settled there, whilst the prosperity of others is of a later date; for being the center of the whole commerce of Peru, a greater number of Europeans resort to it, than to any other city; some for trade, and others from being invested in Spain with considerable employments: among both are persons of the greatest merit; and though many after they have finished their respective affairs, return home, yet the major part, induced by the fertility of the soil, and the goodness of the climate, remain at Lima, and marry young ladies remarkable equally for the gifts of fortune as those of nature; and thus new families are continually settled.

The Negroes, Mulattoes, and their descendants, form the greater number of the inhabitants; and of these are the greatest part of the mechanics; though here the Europeans also follow the same occupations, which are not at Lima reckoned disgraceful to them, as they are at Quito; for gain being here the universal passion, the inhabitants pursue it by means of any trade, without regard to its being followed by Mulattoes, interest here preponderating against any other consideration.

The third, and last class of inhabitants, are the Indians and Mestizos, but these are very small in proportion to the largeness of the city, and the multitudes of the second class. They are employed in agriculture, in making earthenware, and bringing all kinds of provisions to market, domestic services being performed by Negroes and Mulattoes, either slaves or free, though generally by the former.

The usual dress of the men differs very little from that worn in Spain, nor is the distinction between the several classes very great; for the use of all sorts of cloth being allowed, every one wears what he can purchase. So that it is not uncommon to see a mulatto, or any other mechanic, dressed in a tissue equal to any thing that can be worn by a more opulent person. They all greatly affect fine clothes, and it may be said without exaggeration, that the finest stuffs made in countries, where industry is always inventing something new, are more generally seen at Lima than in any other place; vanity and ostentation not being restrained by custom or law. Thus the great quantities brought in the galleons and register ships notwithstanding they sell here prodigiously above their prime cost in Europe, the richest of them are used as clothes, and worn with a carelessness little suitable to their extravagant price; but in this article the men are greatly exceeded by the women, whose passion for dress is such as to deserve a more particular account.

. . .

Besides diamond rings, necklaces, girdles, and bracelets, all seeking to stand out in terms of quality and size, many ladies wear other jewels set in gold, or for singularity's sake, in tombago. Lastly, from their girdle before is suspended a large round jewel enriched with diamonds; much more superb than their bracelets, or other ornaments. A lady covered with the most expensive lace instead of linen, and glittering from head to foot with jewels, is supposed to be dressed at the expense of not less than thirty or forty thousand crowns; a splendor still the more astonishing, as it is so very common.

. . .

With regard to the persons of the women of Lima, they are, in general, of a middling stature, handsome, genteel, and of very fair complexions without the help of art; the beauty of their hair has been already mentioned, but they have usually an enchanting luster and dignity in their eyes.

These personal charms are heightened by those of the mind: clear and comprehensive intellects; an easiness of behavior, so well tempered, that whilst it invites love, it commands respect; the charms of their conversation are beyond expression; their ideas just, their expressions pure, their manner inimitably graceful. These are the allurements by which great numbers of Europeans, forgetting the fair prospects they have at home, are induced to marry and settle here.

One material objection against them is, that being too well acquainted with their own excellences, they are tainted with a haughtiness, which will scarce stoop to the will of their husbands. Yet by their address and insinuating compliance, they so far gain the ascendancy over them as to be left to their own discretion. There may, indeed, a few exceptions be found; but these possibly by rather owing to a want of capacity. Another objection may be made to their being more expensive than other ladies: but this arises from the exorbitant price of stuffs, laces, and other commodities, in this country. And with regard to the independence they affect, it is no more than a custom long established in the country. To which may be added, that being natives, and their husbands generally foreigners, it is very natural, that the latter should not enjoy all that authority, founded on laws superior to custom; and hence this error remains uncorrected. The husbands conform to the manners of the country, as their character is not in the least affected thereby; and this complaisance is rewarded by the discretion and affection of their ladies, which are not to be paralleled in any other part of the world.

. . .

The lower classes of women, even to the very negroes, affect, according to their abilities, to imitate their betters, not only in the fashion of their dress, but also in the richness of it. None here are seen without shoes as at Quito, but they are made of so small a size, in order to diminish the natural bigness of the feet, that they must give infinite uneasiness in the wearing. A desire of being distinguished by an elegant dress is universal. Their linen is always starched to a great degree, in order to display the costly patterns of their laces. After this universal passion, their next care, and indeed a much more commendable one, is cleanliness; of which the uncommon neatness of their houses are sufficient instances.

They are naturally gay, sprightly, and jocose, without levity; remarkably fond of music; so that even among the lowest you are entertained with pleasing and agreeable songs; for the gratification of this passion, they have in general good voices, and some of them are heard with admiration. They are very fond of balls, where they distinguish themselves equally by the gracefulness and agility of their motions. In fine, the reigning passions of the fair at Lima, are shew, mirth, and festivity.

The natural vivacity and penetration of the inhabitants of Lima, both men and women, are greatly improved by conversing with persons of learning resorting thither from Spain. The custom of forming small assemblies has also a great tendency to improve their minds, and give them a ready and happy manner of expression, from an emulation to distinguish themselves in these engaging accomplishments.

The 1746 Earthquake

Anonymous

At 10:30 p.m. on October 28, 1746, a massive earthquake struck Lima. Half an hour later a tsunami decimated Callao, leveling the important port. Property owners fortunate to have been out of Callao that evening could not find where their houses had stood, while a few lucky survivors floated miles south to safety. In the following days, people searched for their loved ones, water, and shelter, dodging tumbling buildings and looters. With hundreds of aftershocks and the scarcity of staples, the agony continued for weeks and months. Five thousand people died in these catastrophes; illnesses and diseases killed many.

The earthquake prompted much international interest. Accounts appeared in Spain, Mexico, Holland, Portugal, and what became the United States (the U.S. account was edited by Benjamin Franklin) as well as this one from London. Voltaire, Kant, and other luminaries would comment on the 1746 earthquake. The catastrophe prompted much debate about the security of Lima and the causes of earthquakes (nature or God). Most people understood it as divine wrath: many pointed their fingers at women's supposedly libertine ways or the Church and its lax codes. This text stresses the destruction of the earthquake and the search for an explanation.

Of all judgments, proceeding from natural causes, which the Deity often inflicts on offenders, in order to satisfy divine justice and manifest his almighty power, the unexpected stroke of sudden earthquake hath ever been the most tremendous, for as much as in one and the same moment they became both the warnings and executioners of its wrath. The total desolation of cities, which have perished through their violence, have been in all ages the terrible witnesses of this truth. These kingdoms have suffered greatly by them. But of all which have happened since their first conquest, so far at least as hath come to our knowledge, we may with truth affirm that none ever broke-out with such astonishing violence, or hath attended with so vast a destruction as that which happened lately in this capital.

. . .

This surprising convulsion of the earth arrived in the night of the 28th of October, 1746: a day dedicated to the two holy apostles, St. Simon and St. Jude, who merited the blessed acquaintance of the most holy Virgin-Mother of our redeemer, whose glorious memorial had been celebrated on that day for some years before with most remarkable and extraordinary devotion; and this perhaps because the Divine Providence had so ordained, that through her powerful intercession the inhabitants of this city should obtain the miraculous preservation of their lives: a thing which would be hardly conceivable to those who should behold the total ruin of the houses and buildings, wherein they dwelt at the time of the earthquake.

. . .

But on this occasion the destruction did not so much as give time for fright; for at one and the same instant almost, the noise, the shock, and the ruin were perceived together: so that in the space only of four minutes, during which the greatest force of the earthquake lasted, some found themselves buried under the ruins of the falling houses; and others crushed to death in the streets by the tumbling of the walls, which, as they ran here and there, fell upon them. However the major part of them happened to be preserved either in the hollow places which the ruins left, or on top of the very ruins themselves, without knowing how they got-up thither; as if Divide Providence had thus conducted them that they might not perish: for no person at such a season had time for deliberation; and even supposing he had, there was no place of retreat in which to trust. For the parts which seem most firm, sometimes proved the weakest: on the contrary, the weakest at intervals made the greatest resistance; and the general consternation was such that no one thought himself secure 'till he had made his escape out of the city.

The earth struck against the edifices with such violent percussions, that every shock beat down the greater part of them; and these tearing along with them vast weights in their fall (especially the churches and high houses) compleated the destruction of every thing they encountered with, even of what the earthquake had spared. The shocks, although instantaneous, were yet successive; and at intervals men were transported from one place to another, which was the means of safety to some, whilst the utter impossibility of moving, preserv'd others.

. . .

To elucidate this it must be observed that there are three thousand houses which make up the hundred and fifty islands of buildings contain'd within the walls of the city. These with the others near adjoining, and the shops where tradesmen and poor people dwell; together with those in the suburbs or borough of St. Lazarus, on the other side of the Rímac (to which there is a passage and communication by the grand bridge) amounted in the whole to a number sufficient to contain sixty thousand persons, for so many there are computed to be constantly resident in this city. Now altho' scarce twenty houses were left standing, yet by the most exact and diligent search that could be made, it does not appear from the lists taken of the dead that the number of them has amounted to much more than eleven hundred and forty one persons.

Lima had arriv'd to as great a degree of perfection as a city situated at such distance from Europe, and discouraged by the continual dread of such calamities was capable of. For altho' the houses were but of moderate height, being confin'd to one story only, yet the streets were laid-out with the exactest regularity, and adorned with all the beauty which a nice symmetry could give: so that they were equally agreeable to the sight as commodious to the inhabitants; and display'd as much elegance as if all the ornaments of the best architecture had been bestowed upon them. To this may be added the delightful appearance of many handsome fountains, for whose supply the water was conveyed through subterranean aqueducts; the towering height of the churches, and structure of the religious convents and monasteries; in which the zeal for divine worship inspired so devout a confidence, as excluded all apprehensions of the danger which such sort of buildings are liable to. It may be affirmed, that the magnificence of these edifices, if it did not exceed, at least might rival that of the grandest fabrics of this king in the whole world: for the beauty of their design, their profiles, their cemeteries, the largeness of their naves, their cloisters and stair-cases, was such as they had no cause to envy any for size and elegance.

. . .

But all this beauteous perspective, which with so much cost had been the care of many years to bring to such perfection, being in an instant reduced to dust, manifested before its time the natural frailty and weakness of its constitution. No relation whatsoever is capable of conveying to the mind an idea of the horror with which the sight of these ruins strikes the beholders. The very sufferers themselves are amazed at what they could not comprehend; and therefore a particular recital of the calamity is not only utterly inexplicable by words; but it is impossible even to form any perfect notion of the horrible destruction which on all sides appeared to view. What force of expression is capable of making the reader comprehend the dreadful astonishment which the mountains of ruins occasion that hinder all entrance to the holy cathedral church, whose elegant structure was destroyed by its own greatness: for the high towers, with which its summit was adorn'd, splitting to pieces and tumbling on its roof, utterly demolished all the arches and other parts of the main body as far as they reached, beside those which fell to themselves; so that not only the Rebuilding of it is rendered impracticable, but it will require an immense expence only to clear away the rubbish. In the same lamentable condition are the other great churches of the five religious orders, where the parts were left standing are yet in such ruinous circumstances, that it would be better to pull them quite down than to think of repairing them.

. . .

To speak the truth, human understanding is utterly at a loss to penetrate the inscrutable judgments of God in thus permitting the destruction of his temples, the affliction of his spouses [i.e., nuns], and so vast an ecclesiastical patrimony to be lost. But it is still more difficult (considering all that havock) to account how so many lives came to be preserved: especially when in the little Monastery of Carmen only, dedicated to Santa Teresa, out of the twenty one nuns thereof that house consisted, twelve perished: Indeed this was the largest number of nuns who suffered on this occasion, for in the other great nunneries they did not amount to so many, although in some of them the number of maid-servants who perished were more. And in the hospital of St. Anne, which was a royal foundation for the relief of Indians of both sexes, seventy of the patients lost their lives; having been buried at the beginning of the earthquake by the roofs of the grand halls of their several apartments, which fell upon them as they lay in their beds, no persons being able to give them any assistance.

A Failed Indian Uprising

Anonymous

Histories of colonial Lima often overlook the city's Indigenous population or present these individuals as apolitical serfs. Nonetheless, they constituted at least 10 percent of the city's total, many moving back and forth through the city's eastern gates to bring goods to and from the Andes. In 1750 authorities learned of a conspiracy by Indians and mestizos, many of them artisans, that entailed seizing houses, flooding the Plaza Mayor, executing Spanish officials, freeing black slaves, and uniting with rebels in the Amazon basin led by the mysterious Juan Santos Atahualpa. The rebels did not call for a rupture with the Catholic Church, and some officials suspected that they counted on the support of dissident priests.

In this account of the uprising held in the Biblioteca Colombina in Seville, Viceroy Manso y Velasco makes clear that he understood that city leaders had been fortunate to prevent a full-scale uprising. Executioners hanged six ringleaders, displaying their body parts—including their "skinned and salted heads"—around the city as a gruesome warning. The viceroy had planned to pardon other participants (or bystanders), but a violent revolt in the Andean area of Huarochirí east of Lima just months later with apparent connections to the Lima rebels put authorities and Spaniards on alert. The repression would be brutal.

On June 26, His Excellency the Viceroy was informed that the Indians of this city of Lima, in connivance with others of this Kingdom and several Provinces, intended to rebel. They had had several meetings to this purpose in the place known as Los Amancaes, the most recent of which was held on the day of San Juan [June 24], which was attended by a freedman, who served and continues to serve a cleric. Said Black told and related all that he saw and heard to the cleric, who in turn told the Captain of the Guard, and then both reported it to His Excellency, who proceeded to act.

Between the evening of said 26th and noon of the following day, the *Alcaldes de Corte* headed for the criminals' homes and apprehended them, isolating them in dungeon cells. Said Ministers began their judicial questioning, going so far as torturing two of them. They have arrested ten conspirators

49

in the days following that night, and despite being summoned by edicts and proclamations for four of the main cases, the rest have not appeared, apparently having fled and disappeared.

Their statements prove that they intended to revolt within the city and throughout the entire realm, with the support of all the Indians of the provinces. The uprising was planned for the day of San Miguel [September 29] this year, which the Indians celebrate by making a procession similar to that of the Virgin Mary's day. With that excuse they planned to take weapons from the armory and requisition all the shotguns, pistols, swords, and even ceremonial swords that they could, so that we should be left disarmed while they were armed, without it appearing strange to see them thus, as it is a common occurrence every year on that date.

At midnight they would have set fire to all the dwellings in the four corners of the city, and unleash upon the city the river that flows through the heights of Santa Catalina, while setting fire to all the Churches. Everyone would flee their homes in panic and surprise, becoming all the more startled upon finding themselves flooded, thus rendering them defenseless and easier to kill. To further this purpose they planned to send 500 men to the Palace to kill His Excellency the Viceroy, his family and his guard, the latter of which would necessarily be reduced, as most of them would have left to deal with the fire. Once they controlled the Palace and the Armory, they would send 500 mounted men to Callao to capture the fortress and its arsenal, and then place 50 men at every four corners—wearing distinctive shirts so to recognize each other—who would kill those who exited their homes. They would also send 50 men to the house of each Minister in order to murder them: they desired to get every Spanish Minister, as the killer would earn the title of his victim.

They also called for the freedom of all slaves in an attempt to forestall their hostility and instead gain their allegiance, having assigned among them some of the main duties so that they should not doubt the enterprise. They said they wanted to put an end to slavery, so all would enjoy freedom, but without renouncing the Catholic faith, for which they planned to spare a small number of regular priests of each order, and some Creole Spaniards. The plan foresaw crowning the Jungle Indian as King, who was in touch with these rebels and had even offered men for the enterprise.[1] However, others did not want him for King, and remaining undecided on this issue, they had planned a General Assembly for the day of San Pedro [June 29] to discuss this point and all related issues.

It was the Lord's will, however, that all this be revealed; and the cases having been substantiated with the supervision of the public prosecutor, the gentlemen of the court sentenced six of the accused to be dragged, hanged, and quartered. The resulting quarters were to be placed in the bastions of the city and the skinned and salted heads in three different places where they had assembled. Another two were exiled for life to the fortress of Ceuta, and two more for life in the fortress of Callao; and lastly, the one whom they say acted as scribe for said Indians—being the most mestizo and almost Spanish—was sentenced to 200 lashes in the streets.

The first six were informed of their sentence on Saturday July 18, and were placed in the chapel. One of them argued that, having had accomplices, there was no reason that they should go unpunished, for which he wanted to turn on them. It was, however, merely a ploy to lengthen his life somewhat, which he did accomplish, as the notification was delayed for a day. But despite spending the day locked up with a scribe and a judge, nothing of worth was extracted, proving that it was, in fact, nothing but a ruse. So, on the 20th they were notified of their sentence and were placed in the chapel, whence they were taken one by one on the 22nd. The first one was executed at 8 o'clock in the morning, and upon his death another one was taken, and the last was executed at 11 o'clock in the morning, and they were left hanging from three gallows.

And thus, justice was served on the wretches who came up with this egregious folly, which would never succeed, but which did perturb the Kingdom. In fact, they say that in the highlands all the Indians are acting uppity, and they will not be quelled until they know of the justice that was meted out here.

This discovery must remind us Spaniards that we ought to live with some caution and that we must no longer lend our weapons to anyone. Instead, we must try to keep them ready to fulfill our duty to defend the Crown—and ourselves—as these Indians and Blacks bear us ill-will. May God's will be carried out in everything, for his greater honor and glory.

Translated by Jorge Bayona

Note

1. This is a reference to Juan Santos Atahualpa, who was leading a rebellion in the Amazon region at that time.

Lima and Cuzco

Concolorcorvo

El Lazarillo, a Guide for Inexperienced Travelers between Buenos Aires and Lima (1773) is a wry account of late colonial Peru, written in the form of a dialogue between an Inca scribe and a postal inspector. Although he published it under a pseudonym, Concolorcorvo (with dark skin), the Spaniard Alonso Carrió de la Vandera (1715–83) was the author. A resident of Peru for nearly half a century, Carrió de la Vandera had conducted an official review of the postal system of the Peruvian viceroyalty in the early 1770s, the basis of this account.

The text points out some of the city's idiosyncrasies, such as the lack of rain and the impact this had on architecture; the high number of carriages; and the profusion of servants in elite households, which made young children indolent "and unable to dress themselves at the age of 12." The author ultimately defends limeños' wit and ability to learn, while declaring that the bilingualism of Cuzco, where residents spoke both Spanish and Quechua, prompted bad syntax and the delayed mastery of Spanish in the highlands.

I attempted to write a description of Lima, but the inspector told me it was an undertaking which many intellectual giants had been unable to accomplish and that it would be ludicrous for a pygmy to undertake it. "But, Señor inspector, is it possible that I should end such a detailed itinerary without saying anything about Lima?" "Yes, Señor Inca, because this is not a matter for you, but rather for me, since my commission ends here. Señor Don Jorge Juan," he added, "Don Antonio de Ulloa, and the greatest cosmographer in the kingdom, Doctor Don Cosme Bueno, described the singular aspects of this city with the quill from a swan, and you cannot add anything of importance with your goose quill." "Nevertheless," I replied, "please tell me what difference there is between this city and that in which I was born." "I suppose, Señor Inca," he answered, "that you are devoted to Cuzco, your homeland, and you want me to say that it surpasses Lima in all aspects, you are mistaken because, leaving aside its location and its common lands, you must have observed that the King maintains a viceroy in splendor in this great capital with an assignation from the King which is equivalent to all the income from family estates in Cuzco. It has, as well, three military financed by the Crown: a well-equipped and well-paid cavalry, an infantry, and halberdiers—who serve not only for ostentation and splendor, but also for the personal security and peace among the large population—to which is added a complete *Audiencia*, courts of higher accounting and of the Royal Inquisition, a university, a theater for plays, and public parks near the city, which are not found in Cuzco or in any other city in the kingdom.

"Lima supports 250 carriages and more than a thousand calashes, which are different from the former only in that they have two wheels, are pulled by a mule, and are more subject to being upset. There is nothing of this in your great city. In the matter of clothing, one is as foolish as the other, the only difference being in the matter of tastes, size of families and commerce, in which Lima greatly surpasses Cuzco. In this city there are many titles of marquis and count, and an even greater number of gentlemen belonging to the orders of Santiago and Calatrava, who, with the exception of one or two, have sufficient income to maintain themselves with splendor, to which are added many first-sons and gentlemen who support themselves with their farms and other respectable businesses, giving luster to the city. I have no doubt that in the city of your birth, as in the others of this vast Viceroyalty, there are illustrious families, but the total of all of them does not match that of this city, where little notice is given to the conquistadors, for although there was no lack of noble families among them, such families increased as the conquest became firmly established.

"With the selection of men for the tribunals and other honorable positions, there came to this capital from Spain many second-sons of illustrious families, some already married and others who acquired the state here, and even many of those who were destined for the interior provinces came to establish themselves here in the capital, as has happened in the courts all over the world. Many subjects who came from Spain for the sole purpose of seeking a fortune kept their nobility concealed until they acquired their fortune and could maintain their luster in such an expensive place where luxury is too well established. In Cuzco and the other cities in the sierra and part of the valleys, the only costly items are dress and the household furnishing which maintain their splendor for centuries. The most important lady in Cuzco has five or six maid servants, serving her well, on whose clothing she scarcely spends as much as is spent here on one Negro servant of average account. In this city, without considering the farms, there are 1½ million pesos squandered, because generally speaking, there is not a slave who saves his master as much money as is spent on him. Their infirmities, genuine or feigned, are not only expensive to the masters because of the medicine, physician, or surgeon, but also due to their absence and lack of service. Every Negro child born in one of these houses costs the master over 700 pesos before he reaches an age when he may be put into service. This evil situation has no remedy as long as they are products of legitimate marriages, but it could be remedied in part by reducing the male servants to a smaller number, as is happening every-where in the world.

"The multitude of servants adds to the confusion of the household, invites anxiety, obstructs service, and causes the children of the family to become lazy so that they can scarcely dress themselves at the age of 12, besides other difficulties which I shall pass over. This present situation, along with the expensive clothing which is provided from the cradle onward, due to the overindulgence of some mothers, are two bleeding sores which are noticeably draining the wealth.

"I have no doubt, Señor Concolorcorvo, that you, since you have seen only the exteriors and roofs, or I should say flat roofs, of the houses, probably think that the one in which I live is the best in the city, since it has the coat of arms above the main door and three or four rooms of considerable size. This house, in its present state, should be considered as one of the fourth-class houses, that is, there are many others which are three times better. The residents of Lima do not fancy the adorning of the doorways with embossments and large coats of arms which add beauty in the large cities. The tile roofs here are useless, due to the lack of rain, which may be considered a serious lack for clearing their skies and cleaning their streets, for although a number of ditches cross the streets, pure water does not flow in them; since they are of little depth and the water is scarce, they hold only excrement and urine, which are prejudicial to health and ruinous to the buildings as is publicly known to all. The great palace of the viceroy, viewed from the façade, appears to be a town hall such as those in the two Castilles, but its interior shows the grandeur of the person inhabiting it. The same is true of other houses belonging to distinguished people, as you will see in time.

"The nobility of Lima is not debatable, unless it can be in the rest of the world as well, because every year we are seeing Creoles inherit some of the oldest seigniories and primogenitures of Spain. I do not give examples so as not to offend those families on which I have no definite information and because it is not my intention to offer a defense for them. The present viceroy, His Excellence Señor Don Manuel de Amat y Junient, greatly enhanced the city with parks and other public works of advantage to the State. I cannot make mention of them all, for it would be necessary to write a large, bulky volume and to have another pen, but no one can deny that his genius and ingenuity are, and have been, superior to that of all viceroys in matters of culture and good taste.

"The people of talent of Lima seem to be outstanding in all the kingdom. This stems from their having an earlier and more permanent cultivation of the mind. A child from this city expresses himself well at the age of four, while highlanders can scarcely express themselves in Castilian at eight, making many solecisms, which comes from the fact that they are studying two languages at once: Castilian and their native tongue, which is the most common at home among the nurses, maids, and mothers; and thus, when they go to the Spanish school, which is usually taught by an ignorant man, instead of 'Give me a glass of cold water,' they say, 'A glass of cold water give me' (which corresponds to *Uno chiri apamuy*), considered gross and stupid by ignorant persons. The Biscayans (I speak of the common ones) use the same word order and, for this reason, understand Quechua much better.

"I protest to you, Señor Inca, that for 40 years I have been observing the peculiarities of the talented Creoles in both Americas, and comparing them in general, I find them no different from the peninsulars. The comparison which has been made up to the present between the Creoles from Lima and those from Spain who take up residence here is unjust. Here the white youth is rare who does not devote himself to learning from an early age, while rare is the one who comes from Spain with even the slightest superficial knowledge, except for those publicly employed for letters. It is notorious that the outstanding are not always selected, because in addition to the fact that they, trusting in their merits, can always find positions in Spain, they do not wish to risk their lives in a long sea voyage and change of climate, or in having no patrons with whom to locate satisfactorily here. If the stage were changed, that is, if all vocations were made available in Lima, one would clearly see that proportionately there were as many learned men as on the peninsula and that any city in Spain comparable to this one would be matched in creative talent, good judgment and literary production, without considering the several giants in this area, so rare that one scarcely finds two in one century—like the great Peralta,[1] the Lima son so well-known in all of Europe, who was praised so highly by the most beautiful and critical pen Galicia has produced in this century."

Note

1. This is a reference to Pedro Peralta y Barnuevo (1663–1743), a prominent creole intellectual and president of the San Marcos University in Lima.

Slave Religion and Culture

Hesperióphylo

Slavery was a central feature of Lima's cultural, social, and economic landscape from the time of its Spanish foundation. African slaves constituted a significant proportion of Lima's population, most of whom performed domestic duties or were hired out to work in Lima's artisan shops or as street vendors. For many visitors and witnesses, Lima resembled a "black city." One of the most important manifestations of black culture in colonial Lima was religion. Slaves and free blacks joined brotherhoods, participated in processions, developed syncretic cults, and infused Catholicism with their African cultural heritage.

This text, published in the seminal Mercurio Peruano *(1790–95), an outlet for the dissemination of enlightened thought and creole nationalism, describes slaves' religious practices. Even if shaped by prejudice and loathing toward blacks, it gives us a glimpse of the importance of those practices for both people of African descent and, more generally, for life in Lima toward the end of the eighteenth century.*

  . . .

These wretched souls find comfort in religion. Overburdened, they turn to it, seeking to attain the relief they cannot find in pleasures, wealth, and mundane honor.

  . . .

The gospel beatifies the plights of man, whereas human wisdom knows only to exaggerate or elude them. Even the most barbaric nations resorted to this principle during their hours of peril, and found no consolation other than assuming that the Supreme Divinity had a prior interest in the realization of their misfortunes. Attacked by the Spaniards, and terrified by the novelty of their weapons and excessive bravery, Mexicans believed that sacred omens had predestined them for conquest many years before. Peruvians looked on their conquerors as heaven-sent demigods; believing this, they remained loyal, served them obsequiously and abided by their rule. The Blacks of Guinea believe that God expressly commanded them to acquiesce to slavery. In view of such ideas, that are part and parcel of their

Black pallbearers at a funeral, c. 1790. In Esteban Terralla y Landa, *Lima por dentro y fuera* (Paris: Librería española de A. Mezín, 1854).

rhetoric, it is not strange that all the entertainments of our *Bozal* slaves are directly related to Religion. The first thing they do is assemble *Cofradías or brotherhoods*: these congregate for worship and holy sacraments, preserve the social links of their respective communities, and allow them to partake in their entertainments.

We are served by ten main Black castes: *Terranovos, Lucumés, Mandingas, Camburidas, Carabalíes, Cangaes, Chalas, Huarochiríes, Congos,* and *Mirangas*. Their names are not derived precisely from each caste's country of origin; some are arbitrary, such as the *Huarochiríes*, and others stem from where they were disembarked originally, such as the *Terranovos*.

All these castes jointly choose two senior chiefs-for-life to lord over them. The election is carried out in the Chapel of Our Lady of the Rosary, founded and funded by the Nations in the Great Convent of Saint Domingo. Vote-wielding electors are comprised of the Black Foremen and the *Twenty Fours* (whom we would call *Senators* should we not fear profaning that word) of each Nation; they carry out the election in the presence of the Chapel Father of their *Cofradía*, and tend to always nominate the oldest members descending from their founders. The name of the anointed one is written in the book they have for this purpose, without Royal Justice being present or influencing this act in any way.

The same formalities are observed when a junior chief is appointed for each Nation, or one of the *Twenty Four Brothers*; but in order to be confirmed, the chief contributes ten pesos, and the brother, twelve. Half is spent on the worship of Our Lady and on refreshments for the electors, whose decisions are recorded in the aforementioned book.

Amongst those of his Tribe, these dignities bring much consideration to him who bears them; they do not purvey him with any relief, however, in other matters pertaining to his slavery and services. It is amusing, or poignant, to see the Sovereign of an African Nation cutting weeds with his subjects at two or three in the morning, and perhaps being whipped by one of them, the Majordomo. A few days ago, one of us asked about the identity of a Black man who was upside down in the stocks of ——'s plantation. He could not hold back the tears when he was told: *He is the King of the Congos.* Such an August title, which we have learned to venerate from birth, deserves respect and is a near sacred gift, even when it has been granted in irony, or abusively.

All the aforementioned Nations promote the worship of Our Lady of the Rosary through the annual collection of half a *real* [eight reales made a peso] per member, which is carried out on the Sunday after *Corpus* at a table set up in Santo Domingo Square, without there being a tradition of an excessive amount being contributed. The money collected is used to bankroll the annual party in honor of the Image, as well as other costs associated with her worship.

The funerary service has similar endowments. Each *Cofradía* supplies six *reales*, and these cover the costs for the Masses and the prayers for the dead. The senior Chiefs receive the remainder whenever there should be any, and spread it among the rest of the junior Chiefs and Brothers, who are absolutely subordinated to the decisions of the aforementioned Senior Chiefs.

In previous times, the *Terranovos* and *Lucumés* worshipped the Image of Christ the Savior in the great Convent of Our Lady of Mercy. Black *Congos*—whose *Cofradía* is located in the banana fields of San Francisco de Paula—practice this devotion in the daytime, solely with the alms that they collect voluntarily among themselves. The *Mandingas* also had a brotherhood devoted to the Holy Virgin in the Church of the great Convent of Saint Francis, under the appellation of *Nuestra Señora de los Reyes*; it currently lies in ruins, much as the remaining *Cofradías* that were based in the Churches of Saint Sebastian, Monserrat, *Capilla del Baratillo,* and another small one from across the bridge. Black and Mulatto teamsters have a brotherhood in San

Agustín for the worship of Saint Nicholas. Most of these are Creoles: despite having no other funding than the voluntary contributions of their members, their Majordomo is chosen under Royal Justice supervision.

Their most important Feast is on the Sunday after *Corpus Christi*. On that day, all the Tribes gather for the procession that departs from the great Convent of Santo Domingo. Each one takes its flag and a parasol that protects the King or Queen, who bears a scepter in his or her right hand and a cane or other instrument in his or her left. The rest of the Nation escorts them with loud instruments, most of which produce a most hideous sound. The subjects who form the retinue that precedes the Kings make an effort to wear appalling costumes. Some dress like Devils or feathered men; others don skins to imitate bears; others appear as monsters with horns, feathers, beaks, lion claws, and snake tails. They all carry bows, arrows, clubs, and shields; they paint their faces red or blue, according to their customs, and accompany the procession with atrocious shouts and gestures that make it seem as though they were attacking an enemy. The severity and fierceness with which they represent these scenes give us a notion of the barbarity with which they would wage war. These decorations, which would be agreeable in a carnavalesque masquerade, appear indecent in a religious ceremony, all the more so in a procession in which the smallest impertinent object profanes the dignity of the sacred act and dissipates the devotion of those in attendance. Our offspring may see to the reform of these and other similar abuses, whose extirpation we desire today. The authorities have sensibly restrained the Negroes from bearing and firing arms during the procession, as they used to do.

All these aforementioned gatherings, which sprouted from the palliative of religion, lead to others that are purely for entertainment. Along different streets in the city, Blacks have rooms that resemble lodgings (which they refer to as *Cofradías*, and amount to sixteen in all) that constitute their centers of operations during festive days. Each Tribe uses one of these places for their congresses; and the larger ones have two or three. They purchase the land to build these rooms, for which they pay but a small rent, with the voluntary oblation of those in attendance.

. . .

We have already stated that the music of the *Bozales* is exceedingly unpleasant. The drum is its main instrument: most are made with clay jugs, or with cylinders of hollowed out wood. They are beat by hand, not by sticks. They play little flutes and make some kind of musical noise by beating the fleshless and dry horse or donkey jawbone whose teeth have been loosened. Something similar is accomplished by rubbing a smooth stick on a grooved one. The *marimba* bears some semblance of melody. It is made up of a set of thin, long, and straight pieces of wood placed a third of an inch from the mouths of a group of dry and hollow pumpkins; both sets are fastened on a wooden arch. It is played with sticks, as though it were a Bohemian psaltery. The shrinking diameter of the aforementioned pumpkins makes them subject to modification according to the alternatives of tuning, and produces a sound that even refined listeners find tolerable. As to the rest, we must confess that as far as music, dancing, and many other areas that depend on talent and taste are concerned, Blacks are even further behind the Indians than the Indians are from the Spaniards.

Translated by Jorge Bayona

Note

Hesperiófphylo was the pseudonym of José Rossi Rubí.

Faces of All Colors

Hipólito Ruiz

The Spanish botanist Hipólito Ruiz (1754–1816) led a scientific expedition sponsored by King Carlos III that explored Peru and Chile for more than a decade, from 1777 to 1788. Although Ruiz was a leading figure in natural history and ethnobotany, he showed little sensitivity to Peru's population. His writings are among the most acidic of eighteenth-century European travelers' accounts: they use terms such as "perversity" and "monstrosity" to describe Lima's racial mixing. In fact, he claims that Spaniards born in Peru were indelibly harmed by the fact that they were raised by mestizos, mulattoes, and other mixed-race women. Ruiz also blamed humors and heat in the blood in order to explain why Creoles were purportedly inferior to their European brethren. Ruiz has little good to say about the women of Lima, although he deems them more honorable than the city's men.

It would seem that the makeup of the inhabitants is self-evident. They are as unlike in social and economic rank and complexion as they are alike in their behavior. Hardly a middle-class home can be found without faces of all colors; in them we can recognize the races that make up the population. There is the Indian; the *cholo* (Indian-Spanish); the chino, resulting from the cohabitation of a *cholo* and a negro woman; the mulatilla, the result of intercourse between a Spaniard and a negro woman; and the *zambo*, the result of intercourse between a negro and an Indian. There is likewise the offspring that each of these has begotten with each of the different women of this mixture, which are called *tercerones, quarterones, quinterones, salta atrás*, etc.

Some of these mixtures are slaves and others are free, according to the position of the mother, even though all might be born in the same household. Few are legitimate offspring and, like as not, all are brought up together. Those children of Spanish blood among them are fed from the breasts of any of the mothers, for the white or Spanish woman does not look upon the nursing of her own children as at all important.

The Indian is sensual and, like his native land, warm of temperament; he easily falls prey to deception, is prone to cowardice, and is drawn more to superstition than to religion. The negro is inclined to be a thief almost from birth and to be arrogant, mercenary, and inclined to all the vices that servitude and recent conversion open up to him. The mulatto is intrepid and bold, vainglorious, pompous, and fond of keeping up false appearances—even with what does not belong to him—and boastful of even his licentious behavior. The germs of all these defects and qualities are as mixed, in as many different ways, as are the results. The sum total of much of this, making up a physical monstrosity, naturally produces a moral monstrosity: this multiplied perversity of tendencies and passions is picked up by the unfortunate Spaniard who is born, reared, and nurtured by them, unless—as rarely happens—some good fortune separates him from it.

Wickedness early lays claim to all the children, so much so that a tendency to thievery is evident even before they attain the age of four. Lewdness usually associated only with adult years and, very frequently, envy and vanity not manifest in any other country are also common in these children, even at the age of 12 or 15. They are possessed by a vivacity, restlessness, and impishness characteristic of persons incapable of exercising common sense and behaving calmly. They are, naturally, troublesome to their families in a proportionate degree. Their intelligence and motivation are usually astonishing. Everything points to the presence of acrid humors and great heat in the blood and in the imagination, which in time engenders very vehement passions, all the stronger when one adds to them the causes of association and the example of so many of similar nature.

All this means merely that the Spaniard born in this country is to be pitied, for he tends to be superficial, haughty, cowardly, false and untrustworthy, light-fingered, and very skillful in the exercise of these traits. We can see, then, that all this is part of the recklessness, lack of honor, faultfinding, pride, and haughtiness that lead them to consider themselves better than their European-born parents, to believe themselves worthy of all honors and employment even though their unfitness is evident, and to give themselves over to such vain and extravagant ideas that any well-balanced man might think them mentally deficient.

This, generally, is really the character of the Spaniard born in Peru—those known as creoles. The same is true of many other Europeans who grow up or settle in Peru. They try to mimic the others in a kind of self-defense calculated to soften the implacable ill will that the natives usually show towards them.

This generality, nevertheless, does not include many honorable and illustrious families. Experience, religious obligations, and social station have led these families to be extremely cautious, and a praiseworthy and overcareful training enables them to correct or alter the natural course of affairs. One finds among them true models of the strictest civility, honor, and virtue, which are passed down to their noble descendants.

Impressions of Lima

Alexander von Humboldt

The Prussian geographer, naturalist, mining engineer, and explorer Alexander von Humboldt (1767–1835) not only wrote about volcanoes, glaciers, and electric eels in his 1799–1804 exploration from Mexico to Peru; he also commented on towns, cities, and local residents. In this frank letter, based on his visit in 1802, he expressed his disappointment with Lima, stressing its decline in the face of competition from other cities, its filthy streets, its shabby cultural life, and the widespread gambling habit. He took advantage of his stay in Peru to examine guano, the bird droppings that would prove to be an important fertilizer and global commodity later in the nineteenth century.

Humboldt joined many other foreigners in criticizing the City of Kings on these fronts, allegations that Creoles and others contested. Countless scholars have cited the passage of this letter that begins "I have not learnt anything about Peru in Lima" to highlight the deep breach between Lima and the Andes and the city's determination to look toward Europe rather than to its interior provinces.

Our stay in Lima lasted a little over two months, which sufficed to get acquainted with a place that is in no way different from Trujillo, although it does have more population and activity. Back in Europe, Lima had been described to us as a city of luxury, elegance, and beautiful women. I did not witness anything to that effect, even when it is known that this capital has decayed significantly with the development of Buenos Aires, Santiago de Chile, and Arequipa. As to its customs and social culture, it cannot be compared to Havana and much less with Caracas. In the latter city, dominated by agriculture due to the abandonment and absence of mines, there are families with an income ranging from 35000 to 40000 pesos. In Lima nobody reaches 30000 and very few make it to 12000. I did not see magnificent homes nor splendidly dressed women, and I know that most families are completely bankrupt. The hidden reason for this situation lies in social animosities and a passion for gambling. Apart from a mediocre and poorly attended theater and a very showy bullfighting arena, there is a dearth of

Portada de Maravillas

The Maravillas city gate, one of the original entrances to the walled city in the colonial period. The wall was demolished in the 1860s. In Manuel Atanasio Fuentes, *Lima: Apuntes históricos, descriptivos, estadísticos y de costumbres* (Paris: Firmin Didot, 1867).

entertainment. Barely three carriages amble through the streets. At night, the filth in the thoroughfares—which are littered with dog and donkey carcasses—and the irregular cobbling, hinder the movement of carriages. Gambling and family feuds (those unfortunate dissensions promoted by the government and which slowly render inhabitable one of the most beautiful regions of the earth) quash all social life. In Lima, conversation circles never surpass eight participants and when they gather to gamble, such as today at the house of Gainza or of the Marquis of Medina, their ephemeral society does not last more than the time required for one of them to lose his entire patrimony. All this, in addition to the completely barren landscape, makes one feel like he has been transported to the heart of the desert that spreads between Chancay and Pisco; a very sad thought for a man like me, who is so sensitive to the beauties of nature and who prefers the plateaus of Saraguro and Tomependa to the castle of cards that is the capital of Peru. Despite Lima being the last place in the Americas where one would want to reside, I nevertheless did spend a pleasant season here. With the invitations received and returned in the entire city, time flies by. The Viceroy and the Regent—to whom we had been recommended by señor Mendinueta—as well as Inspector Villar, Aguirre, Gaenza and, one may say, all of Lima, greeted us with the greatest consideration, respect, and cordiality. Urquizo is the most learned and affable man in this city and, apart from Mutis, we have not found a similar talent in the Americas, but his fellow-citizens do not hold a nongambler in high esteem.

The following realization proves a very sad fact, which also sheds light on the government's priorities. I have not learnt anything about Peru in Lima. Nothing pertaining to the public happiness of the kingdom is ever dealt with there. Lima is farther away from Peru than London is, and though no other part of Spanish America is guilty of excessive patriotism, I know not any city in which this feeling is more muted. A cold selfishness permeates everyone and that which does not concern one, concerns no one.

Translated by Jorge Bayona

III

From Independence to the War of the Pacific (1821–1883)

Peru's independence from Spain, proclaimed in 1821 and completed in 1824, jeopardized Lima's preferred role as the capital of Spanish South America. Peru itself emerged smaller than it had been as a viceroyalty, as Bolivia and Ecuador became nation-states. Buenos Aires, Santiago, Caracas, and other cities sought to replace it as both a political and economic center, while Callao faced challenges to its near monopoly as a port. Nonetheless, Lima remained the center of Peru and an important cog in the transpacific economy, which expanded rapidly in the latter half of the nineteenth century with the development of long-distance steamships.

Socially, Lima increased its diversity with the arrival of new immigrant populations (most notably the Chinese). For many commentators, changes taking place in the post-Independence era (the abolition of slavery or of the death penalty, for instance) threatened social order in the city. Popular culture was seen as a symptom of the loosening of social boundaries. New mechanisms of social control (legal codes, the erection of the penitentiary, the creation of police forces) were imposed. Political and economic turmoil led to episodes (riots, caudillo battles, foreign wars) that increased the sense of decay that many commentators felt.

The writers selected here discuss different aspects of Lima: the war of independence against Spain; the slave and Chinese populations; festivities such as carnival, bullfights, and the Amancaes Parade; and the destruction caused by the Chilean occupation during the War of the Pacific (1879–83).

From different perspectives, these authors recognize that Lima was changing, transformations that would only accelerate with the advent of the twentieth century. Nostalgia for Lima's supposedly "glorious" colonial period, the apogee of the city for many, marks some of these accounts.

Lima in 1821

Basil Hall

*The British naval commander Basil Hall (1788–1844) led military and scientific ex-
peditions around the world. A Scot, Hall met Napoleon, explored South Africa, and
ventured into Mexico and South America in the midst of the Wars of Independence.
His detailed journals allowed him to publish numerous memoirs of his adventures.
In this section of* Extracts from a Journal, Written on the Coasts of Chili,
Peru, and Mexico *(1823), Hall lands in Lima just as General San Martín and the
Royalist Army jostle to take control of the capital. He underlines limeños' political
flexibility (or "versatility") as the population, according to Hall, supported whoever
held power or at least control of the city. Both the Argentine San Martín and the
Venezuelan Simón Bolívar, however, contended that the city, or at least its patri-
cians, favored the Spanish. A firm proponent of free trade, Hall sustained that Independence would open Peru to international commerce, bringing political stability
and economic growth.*

Our stay at Lima, upon this occasion, was short, but very interesting. We
arrived on the 9th, and sailed on the 17th of December 1821. In the interval
of four months, which had elapsed since we left Peru, the most remarkable
change had taken place in the aspect of affairs. The flag of Spain had been
struck on the Castle of Callao; and in its place was displayed the standard
of Independence. The harbor, which we had left blockaded by an enemy,
was now open and free to all the world; and, instead of containing merely a
few dismantled ships of war, and half a dozen empty merchant vessels, was
crowded with ships unloading rich cargoes; while the bay, to the distance
of a mile from the harbor, was covered with others waiting for room to
land their merchandise. On shore all was bustle and activity. The people
had no longer leisure for jealousy; and, so far from viewing us with hatred and distrust, hailed us as friends; and, for the first time, we landed at
Callao without apprehension of insult. The officers of the Chilean expedition, whose appearance, formerly, would have created a sanguinary tumult,
were now the most important and popular persons in the place, living on

perfectly friendly terms with the very people whom we well remembered to have known their bitterest, and as they swore, their irreconcilable foes. It is true there is nothing new in this degree of political versatility; but it is still curious to witness the facility, and total unconcern with which the sentiments of a whole town are at once reversed, when it suits their interest. As the population of Callao depend for subsistence entirely upon the port being open, their anger had formerly been strongly excited against the Chileans who had shut it up, and thereby brought want of employment and consequent distress, upon the people. But now the Independent party had not only restored the business of the port, but augmented it much beyond its former extent. The inhabitants of Callao, therefore, whose interest alone, quite independent of any speculative opinions, regulated their political feelings, were in raptures with the new order of things.

In the capital, also, a great change was visible. The times, indeed, were still far too unsettled to admit of ease, or of confidence in the society. The ancient masters of the city were gone; its old government overturned; its institutions, and many of its customs, were changed; but, as yet, nothing lasting had been substituted; and, as circumstances were varying every hour, no new habits had as yet been confirmed. In appearance, also, everything was different: instead of the formal dilatory style of doing business that prevailed in former days, all was decision and activity; even the stir in the streets looked to our eyes quite out of Peruvian character: the shops were filled with British manufactured goods; the pavement was thronged with busy merchants of all nations, to the exclusion of those groups of indolent Spaniards, who, with their cigars in their mouths, and wrapped in their cloaks, were wont, in bygone days, to let the world move on at its own pleasure, careless what turned up, so that it cost them no trouble. The population appeared to be increased in a wonderful degree; and the loaded carts and mules actually blocked up the thoroughfares.

While viewing all this, the probable result becomes a curious but intricate subject for speculation. That eventual good will spring out of the increased knowledge and power of free action which the recent changes have introduced, there can be no sort of doubt: but in what manner it may be modified, and when or how brought about; into what state, in short, the government may settle at last, cannot, as I conceive, be predicted. In the midst, however, of the great confusion and uncertainty which prevail in these countries, it is satisfactory to think, that, in every variety of aspect under which they can be viewed, there is none in which the advantages of free trade are not likely to be insisted on by the people; who have acquired, with wonderful quickness, a clear and comprehensive view of the subject, as contradistinguished from the ancient system of restriction. There needs no time, indeed, nor education, to teach people of every class the direct benefits of having a large and constant supply of useful merchandise at low prices: and although the means of purchase, and the disposition to spend capital in that way, must be greatly increased by the establishment of a steady government; yet, even in the most ill-regulated and unsettled state of public affairs, there will always be found, in those countries, extensive means to make adequate commercial returns. It is not, as I conceive, any want of power to pay for imported goods that is to be apprehended; but rather the absence of these wants, tastes, and habits, the hope of gratifying which is in every country the surest stimulus to industry. The mining and agricultural resources of South America are very great; as we already know, by what they produced even when under the unfavorable circumstances of the ancient system: and, from all we have seen of late years, it is highly improbable, that, with the worst form of government likely to be established, these resources will be less productive than heretofore. The desire to enjoy the luxuries and comforts, now, for the first time, placed within reach of the inhabitants, is probably the feeling most generally diffused amongst them, and would be the least easily controlled, or taken away. Perhaps the wish for independence is, at this moment, a stronger emotion, but it is not yet so extensively felt as the other: to the great mass of the people, these abstract political ideas, standing alone, are quite unintelligible; but, when associated with the practical advantages we have been speaking of, they acquire a distinctness unattainable by other means. Had the Spaniards, some years ago, been judicious enough to concede a free commerce to the colonies, there can be little doubt, that, although they would, by that means, have involuntarily sown the seeds of future political freedom, by giving the inhabitants a foretaste of its enjoyments, they might have put off what they considered the evil day, to a much later period: and the cry for Independence, now so loud and irresistible, might, perhaps, not have yet been heard in South America.

It may be remembered, that, when we left Peru on the 10th of August, General San Martín had entered Lima and declared himself Protector; but that Callao still held out, and, as long as this was the case, the Independent cause remained in imminent hazard. San Martín, therefore, employed every means of intrigue to reduce the castle, as he had no military force competent to its regular investment. It was supposed, that, in process of time, he would have succeeded in starving the garrison into terms; but, on the 10th of September, to the surprise of every one, a large Spanish force from the interior marched past Lima and entered Callao. San Martín drew up his army in front of the capital as the enemy passed, but did not choose to risk an engagement. The Spaniards remained but a few days in Callao, and then retired to the interior for want of provisions, carrying off the treasure which had been deposited in the castle. As they repassed Lima another opportunity was afforded for attacking them, but San Martin still declined to take advantage of what many of the officers of the army, and some other persons, conceived as a most favourable moment for gaining an important advantage over the Royalists. A great outcry was in consequence raised by all parties against him, on account of this apparent apathy; and his loss of popularity may be said to take its date from that hour.

The fortress of Callao, nevertheless, surrendered to San Martín a few days afterwards, and with this he declared himself satisfied. Being all along, as he declared, certain of gaining this most important object, by which the independence of the country was to be sealed, he did not conceive it advisable to bring the enemy to action. It is asserted, indeed, by many who were present, that San Martín's army was much superior in numbers to that of Canterac, the Spanish general: but his friends, while they admit this, assert, that it was at the same time necessarily defective in discipline and experience; since more than two-thirds of the original expedition had sunk under the effects of the climate at Huaura, and the new levies consisted of raw troops recently collected from the hills, and the surrounding countries. Canterac's army, on the other hand, consisted entirely of veterans, long exercised in the wars of Upper Peru. San Martín, therefore, thought it better to make sure of the castle, than to risk the whole cause upon the doubtful and irremediable issue of one engagement. With Callao in their possession, and the sea open, the Patriots could never be driven out of Peru. But the slightest military reverse at that moment must at once have turned the tide; the Spaniards would have retaken Lima; and the independence of the country might have been indefinitely retarded.

The Passion for Bullfighting

William S. W. Ruschenberger

A surgeon for the U.S. Navy and eventually a distinguished author and president of the American Academy of Natural Sciences from 1869 to 1881, Ruschenberger (1807–95) visited Lima in the mid-1820s, as a very young man, and then again in 1831. In this section he depicts a bullfight in Lima's famous Acho Bullring. Begun in 1765 in San Lázaro (known today as Rímac) on the north side of the river, Acho is the oldest bullring in the Americas and continues to hold corridas de toros. It is celebrated by many as a mecca for the city's traditions and protested by those who decry bullfighting as an anachronistic cruelty. Ruschenberger captures Lima's lively street scene, with vendors, water carriers, musicians, as well as the bloody ritual of the bullfight itself.

About half past two o'clock on a Monday afternoon, in December, people of all classes were to be seen pouring from the plaza into the street that leads over the bridge to the suburb of San Lázaro. The tailor left his thimble, the cobbler deserted his awl, the donkey of the water carrier enjoyed rest for a time, the collegian threw aside his book, the workshops were closed, the merchant left his store, the lady gave up the siesta, and the president of the republic joined in to fill up the living stream, that moved towards the Alameda del Acho. Towards that point rolled gay *calesas* [small carriage], accompanied by gaily dressed equestrians; the street was thronged with mulattoes and negroes, *tapadas* and priests—all going to see "los toros"—the bulls!

Along the street leading to the Alameda, armed lancers from the president's guard, were stationed about a hundred yards apart, gazing quietly on the passing crowd, with hands folded over the pommel of the saddle, and lance resting on the foot and reposing against the shoulder. Great earthen jars of chicha were leaning against the trees, here and there, from which negresses and mulattoes, bedizened with jasmine, were pumping through great canes, "the nectar of Peru," and dispensing it to groups of the lower orders, standing around them. The sounds of harp and guitar, and fandango-

Street vendors, 1830s. In Léonce Angrand, *Imagen del Perú en el siglo XIX* (Lima: Editor Carlos Milla Batres, 1972), 45–46, fig. III.

footing, streamed from houses in the vicinity. It was a heartfelt holy-day, for all classes delight in the spectacle of bull-baiting.

The Plaza de Acho, which is enclosed in a square, is a large amphitheater, capable of containing in the boxes, and on the benches which surround it, rising one above the other, not less than twelve thousand persons. The boxes and benches are supported on brick pillars, and are accessible by narrow stairs from the outside. The arena is about four hundred feet in diameter, surrounded by a barrier seven feet high, through which are horizontal slits a foot broad, opening into the pit beneath the benches. In the middle of the arena, just far enough apart to allow a man to pass between them, are several posts planted in the form of three rays diverging from a center. At one point are a large and a small door, side by side, opening into the pen where the bulls are kept, and over them is the box of the Prefect of Lima, who presides over the exhibition, and bestows the rewards on those who distinguish themselves in the fight. Opposite, but a little to the right, is a large box, occupied by the president and his suite, and to the left is a large door through which the slaughtered bull disappears from the arena.

About a quarter before three, the place seemed full, yet people were still pouring in. The ladies appeared in their usual extravagant style of dress, and the *tapadas* or cyclop beauties were numerous in every direction. The motley assemblage, which we had seen in the street, now occupied the benches. A busy hum of conversation arose continually from the multitude; and above it bawled the *dulcero*, with his tray of sweets, the *almendrero*, with his comfits, the *caramelero*, with his bons-bons. Then the *aguador*, with pitcher and glass, cried ever and anon, "un vaso de agua"—a glass of water. The *segarrero* [*cigarrero*, cigar maker], proclaimed "segarros de mi amo, que los hace bien"—my master's cigars, he makes them well. Occasionally this fellow paused in his walk, and holding the fingers of his right hand to his mouth for a moment, smacked his lips as if tasting something delicious, and, bowing as he swept away his hand, ejaculated in a tone horribly nasal, "que cosa tan rica!"—how exquisite! Other negroes, with trays of square packages of boiled corn, resembling homony [*sic*], done up in plantain leaf, were crying, "maíz blanco, bien caliente!"—white corn, very hot!

In spite of the discordant hum, and out-of-time cries of those fellows who sell trifling sweets and sugar plums to the crowd, to amuse its excitement, (which must be spending itself on something,) those in the arena appear perfectly calm and unconcerned. The *matadores*, and *capeadores* on foot, with their red cloaks flung carelessly over one shoulder, so as to discover the pink or green silk jacket, and bright yellow breeches, trimmed with jaunty bows of gay ribbon, and with the hat set knowingly on one side of the head, sauntered about the ring smoking cigars. The *rejoneadores* and *capeadores* on horseback, armed with short spears,

"In costly sheen and gaudy cloak array'd," slowly walked their animals over the ground, or awaited patiently the commencement of the sport. The mayors of the plaza, better mounted than the rest, occasionally dashed after a half dozen ragged urchins, who were playing, and chasing each other about the arena.

At last the *despejo* or clearing of the field commenced. Part of a well dressed regiment entered the arena, headed by a fine band in a Turkish uniform, playing a quick step. They marched and countermarched, and performed several military evolutions, which ended in a sham fight with a second party, that attacked them from several points at the same time. The orders were given by blast of trumpet and tap of drum. This part of the exhibition was highly interesting, and very creditable to the troops.

Precisely at three, the president and staff entered his box, and were received by the troops with presented arms. The Turkish band took its place in front of the president's box, and the troops separated, and springing over the barrier, mingled with the crowd on the benches.

The *rejoneadores* and *capeadores* on horseback, preceded by the mayors of the plaza, and followed by the *matadores* and *capeadores* on foot, marched slowly round the whole circle, bending low before the boxes of the president and prefect, and saluting the spectators generally as they passed along. This ceremony ended, the *matadores* and *capeadores* on foot distributed themselves in various parts of the arena; the mayors took a position of safety, and the *rejoneadores* and *capeadores* on horseback, holding their spears by the end in the right hand, the points down, trotted gallantly up to the prefect's box and halted. In the mean time, a caricature figure of a belle, constructed of paper and reeds, was placed not far from the center of the ring. The din and buzz of the multitude were for a moment hushed. A trumpet sounded a charge, and a rocket whizzed high and exploded in the air. Expectation was mute. The den flew open, and a noble bull, having a cloth ornamented with tinsel and ribbons stitched to his back, sprang forth. He stood for a moment gazing fiercely right and left, lashing his tail in the air, and pawing the earth; he wavered for an instant, then lowering his head, dashed at a *rejoneador*, who, with admirable skill, flirted a short red mantle in his eyes, and saved himself and horse from the bull's horns. Foiled in this attack, the enraged animal opened his eyes for a second, (bulls always close them to attack,) and rushed at a *capeador* who received him on the point of his spear; thrusting him three times in the neck, he turned the bull, and received the applause of the assembled multitude; then galloping to the prefect's box, held out his cap and obtained a rouleau of four dollars, which was tossed into it as his reward. Blood trickled over the bull's broad chest and down his legs, as he stood wavering in which direction to make his next attack. Now the *capeadores* on foot approached, shaking their red cloaks and stamping and shouting in defiance. He rushed at one of them, and bore off the cloak in triumph on his long, sharp horn, amidst shouts of "qué buen lance, qué buen lance!"—a good feat, a good feat! Next, his furious attentions were bestowed upon the paper belle, and he met a warm reception, for she was a "fire ship" of rockets and squibs, which burst about his ears in a hundred irregular explosions, enhancing his violence and rage. Shouts, laughter, and clapping resounded from all sides. He turned impetuously upon a *rejoneador*, who poised his spear and drew up his horse to receive the charge. His aim was true; he struck just behind the skull, and the bull rolled lifeless on the ground, amidst the deafening shouts and plaudits of the spectators!

Besides the public approbation, the *rejoneador* received a reward of three rouleaus, of four dollars each, from the hands of the prefect.

So soon as the bull fell, the band of hautboys and squeaking clarionets, stationed near the prefect's box, ceased, and that in the Turkish costume struck up the national air called La Sama cueca [*zamacueca*]. Four horses that "spurned the rein," bedecked with waving plumes, pranced into the arena under the guidance of two postillions. A mulatto held the traces, and leaned backwards with all his strength, as he was dragged forward. An axle with two low wheels or trucks, was secured under the bull's head, and the horses were attached. Under rapid applications of whip and spur, they sprang forward, and with a great sweep disappeared with the load from the ring.

The pools of blood were carefully swept over with sand, and another paper figure, representing a jackass playing a guitar, was placed on the spot where the belle had been so unceremoniously treated. Again the trumpet sounded, and again a rocket was fired. Another fierce animal bounded forth. The *capeadores* and *matadores* shook their red cloaks to invite him to attack; but they danced backwards as he trotted towards them. At last he rushed upon one, and received a slight wound in the shoulder from the sword of a matador, which served to inflame his fury. He gored the musical jackass, and struck such notes as neither jackass nor guitar ever before produced. Wild with rage, he darted upon a *rejoneador*, and received a spear wound in the neck, from which the blood flowed freely. He evidently suffered pain, but did not complain, though he stood at bay. The *capeadores* on foot, and the *matadores* approached, shook their cloaks, stamped, and shouted, but he heeded not. Small darts loaded with lead were showered upon him, and hung quivering in his hide; this roused him, and with a well directed aim he rushed upon "a light limbed matador," who received the attack dexterously upon his cloak; the attack was renewed, but the cloak quit the hand, and quick as thought the long blade was sheathed in his broad chest. His career was arrested; he staggered once, but recovered; instinctively he separated his feet to gain a broader and firmer base; his limbs trembled; he hung his head, and making an effort to cough, belched forth a torrent of gore; the next instant he reeled, and his feet kicked in the air! From the moment the wound was given, the multitude was silent; nothing was heard except the discordant and tearing notes of the hautboys, but when he fell, the welkin rang with applauding shouts, "buen lance, buen lance," and the band struck up El Chocolate, another of the Peruvian airs. The matador received his reward, the car was brought, and the carcass whirled swiftly away.

Pancho Fierro

Natalia Majluf

No artist is more closely identified with the image of Lima than Francisco "Pancho" Fierro, a nineteenth-century mulatto painter who captured the vibrancy of life in the capital. His now classic watercolors have left us playful and at times satirical images portraying street celebrations, public authorities, priests, lawyers, urban peddlers, diverse ethnic groups, and a myriad of other characters.

Fierro's rendition of Lima's daily life in hundreds of unforgettable images has deeply shaped collective memories of the city's past and has decisively contributed to our understanding of material culture and social relations in the post-Independence era. In the following essay, art historian Natalia Majluf offers a biographical sketch of this extraordinary artist, some of whose works are reproduced in these pages.

Francisco Fierro (1807–79), better known as Pancho Fierro, one of the most influential artists of nineteenth-century Peru, was born in Lima on October 5, 1807. He was the illegitimate son of a slave, María del Carmen Fierro, and creole priest Nicolás Mariano Rodríguez del Fierro y Robina, scion of a wealthy Lima family, who served as priest in the Indian parish of San Damián and taught at the University of San Marcos. Nothing is known of his training as an artist, but by 1833 he already appears as an established painter in the Lima tax registers. It is likely that he took classes in the drawing academy run by the painter Francisco Javier Cortés (b. Quito, 1775, d. Lima, 1839), a pioneering figure in the development of *costumbrismo*, the visual tradition devoted to the representation of local imagery that Fierro would popularize in the 1830s. This early period saw the production of many of his most complex compositions, such as *Holy Week Procession in Lima* (Hispanic Society of America, New York), a paper scroll almost five meters long that shows dozens of priests, soldiers, and vendors on the city streets. Such elaborate scenes, however, are rare in Fierro's career, as most of his known works follow regular commercial formats of loose single-leaf images, usually showing one or two figures against a blank background.

Even if Fierro's repertoire of city scenes and street peddlers owes much to the preceding tradition of images of Lima, his early watercolors depart from the exacting style of his predecessors. By the 1830s he had developed the characteristic loose manner of broad washes, which gave the impression that his figures were quickly drawn from the bustle of the city streets. Yet as the frequent repetition of images in his work indicates, most were not drawn from life; rather, they were serially produced.

French consul Léonce Angrand claimed that Fierro made substantial earnings by selling his work to foreigners. This indeed seems to have been Fierro's main market in the first half of the century, and explains why a substantial part of his watercolors are found in collections outside Peru. Foreigners passing through the city bought his watercolors either individually or in sets, bound in albums with titles like *Souvenirs du Pérou* or *Recuerdos de Lima*. Throughout the 1850s, most of his images were sold in the music and lithograph store of Inocente Ricordi, who also produced a series of prints broadly inspired by the artist's works. The regular reproduction of his images through different means in fact ensured the enormous influence of his work. Through the repetition of the same typical figures, such as the *zamacueca* dancers or the *tapadas* (the veiled ladies of Lima), a particular image of the creole culture of the city entered the popular imagination.

A new local market for his work emerged toward the 1860s based on a major shift in the understanding of his watercolors, which were no longer regarded as representations of the present; they were now considered historical objects that recorded the past. Indeed, by the 1870s, as modernization seemed to seal the final disappearance of traditional Lima life, his images, which continued to repeat the repertoire fixed in the 1830s, suddenly became documents of a bygone era. Historian and educator Agustín de la Rosa Toro, the author of school textbooks, commissioned one of the best-known series of works by Fierro in the 1870s (now housed at the Pinacoteca Municipal Ignacio Merino, Municipality of Lima), with the express purpose of "bringing to life the costumes, traditions, and institutions of the colonial period in our country."[1] No doubt through the historian's influence, Fierro's watercolors suddenly became more complex, returning to the broad narrative compositions he had explored in his early works. Significantly, La Rosa Toro's watercolors were passed on to Ricardo Palma, founder of the nostalgic literary genre known as the *tradición*. By the early twentieth century, his works indeed served writers and historians of old Lima like Teófilo Castillo and Pablo Patrón as illustrations of their nostalgic accounts of lost customs and traditions.

By the time of his death Fierro had already acquired a mythical status, and his fame as a central figure in the national imagination only grew over

the following decades. Wittingly or not, the image of Lima that Fierro contributed to construct was that of a white creole city that looked back to
Spanish traditions and incorporated Indians and Afro-Peruvians only as
marginal plebeian counterparts to aristocratic society. His watercolors of
types and customs, which can be counted as the most broadly reproduced
images in Peruvian history, have become the paradigmatic emblems of the
capital and a central element in the constitution of Latin American visual
costumbrismo.

Note

1. Cited in José Flores Araoz, "Pancho fierro, pintor mulato limeño," *Cultura Peruana* 5, no.
20–21 (May 1945).

A Slave Plantation

Flora Tristán

Feminist, social activist, writer, grandmother of the artist Paul Gauguin, and much else, Flora Tristán (1803–44) visited Peru from 1833 to 1834. It was the land of her father, Mariano Tristán y Moscoso, whose death had submerged the family into poverty. She traveled to Peru to gain the aid of her prominent uncle, Pio Tristán y Moscoso, and to seek her inheritance. This economic mission did nothing to silence her sharp tongue and pen. She wrote a brilliant account of this journey, Peregrinations of a Pariah, *that was highly critical of Peru's conservative social structures, political instability, and limited opportunities for women.*

In her visit to a sugar estate just south of Lima, the technology and vegetation impressed her, while the conditions of the plantation's slaves distressed her. Although her host claimed that the slave population declined due (somehow) to their laziness and weak will, Tristan understood that the low life expectancy reflected the desperation of the overworked and seemingly hopeless slaves. She taunted the owner that perhaps his slaves would reproduce and work more if they were treated better. Tristan was herself not free of the period's prejudices: she deems the slaves "repulsive." Nonetheless, here and in other sections Tristan presents a rich, critical portrait of Lima and Peru.

Señor Lavalle's sugar mill, the Villa Lavalle, two leagues from Chorrillos, was a magnificent establishment of four hundred negroes, three hundred negresses and two hundred children. The owner was kind and courteous enough to show us round the entire place and took pleasure in explaining everything to us. I was most interested in seeing the four mills for crushing the canes, run by water power. The aqueduct which brought the water to the factory was fine and had been very costly to construct owing to the difficulties of the terrain. I was shown round the great building containing a number of cauldrons, in which the juice from the cane was boiled. We then went into the refinery attached to it, where the sugar dripped out its molasses. Señor Lavalle explained to me his plan for improvements. "But, mademoiselle," he added, "it is desperately difficult to find negroes. The shortage of slaves will ruin all the sugar mills. We lose them in large numbers, and three-quarters of the children die before they are twelve. I used to have fifteen hundred negroes, and now I've only got nine hundred, including the puny children you have seen."

"But such a mortality is alarming," I said, "and indeed casts serious doubts on the future of your undertaking. Why is it that the balance between births and deaths is not maintained? This is a healthy climate, and I would have thought that the negroes would thrive as well here as in Africa."

"You do not know negroes, mademoiselle. They let their children die from laziness, and one can get nothing out of them without the whip."

"Do you not think that, if they were free, their needs would be sufficient to make them work?"

"Their needs are so few in this climate," said Señor Lavalle, "that they would have to work very little to supply them. Moreover, I do not believe that man, whatever his needs, can be induced to work regularly without being forced."

. . .

Señor Lavalle's sugar plantation was one of the finest in Peru; it was vast in extent and its situation was admirable. It ran along beside the sea, where the waves broke on the rocky shore. The tropics are rich in fruit, and Señor Lavalle's orchard had them all. The soil was suitable, and they flourished. The sapodilla trees were so tall that they seemed to be trying to keep out of reach their large green "apples" whose juicy pulp combined the most delicious flavors. The mango-tree, as high as an oak, bore its oval fruits, fibrous to the taste and smelling of turpentine. How I admired the beautiful dark green foliage of those great orange-trees, bending under the weight of their thousands of round fruits whose color delighted the eye and whose smell scented the air! It was like a new Garden of Eden. Bunches of pomegranates and Barbadoes cherries held out the cool refreshment of their fruits for the taking, and here and there the banana-plants, bowing under the weight of their fruit, displayed their long, tattered leaves. And this tropical orchard was made even more beautiful by a very varied show of European flowers, reminding one of home. In a delightful spot, full of coolness and fragrance, stood an observation tower, from which the view was magnificent. On one side lay the sea, whose great breakers rolled on to the beach or broke violently against the rocks; on the other were the vast plantations of sugar cane, so beautiful when in flower. Here and there groups of trees provided relief and variety for the eye.

It was late when we returned. As we passed by a kind of barn in which negroes were working, the angelus sounded. They all stopped working and fell to their knees, bending down until their heads touched the ground. The faces of all these slaves were repulsive to look at, full of baseness and treachery; they all, including the children, had a dark, cruel and unhappy expression. I tried to chat with several of them, but all I could get was "yes" and "no," spoken with coldness and indifference. I went into a cell into which two negresses had been shut; they had allowed their babies to die by depriving them of milk. They were both stark naked, and were huddled together in a corner. One of them was eating raw maize. The other, young and very beautiful, turned her large eyes on me; they seemed to say: "I let my child die, because I knew he would not be free like you. I preferred death for him, rather than slavery." The sight of this woman was most painful to me. Under that black skin there are some proud, great-souled human beings. Negroes have to go suddenly into slavery direct from a natural state of independence; some are untamable souls who suffer torments and die without ever bowing to the yoke.

The Saddest City

Herman Melville

As a shipmate for the USS United States, *Herman Melville reached the shores of Callao on New Year's Day 1844 and made the long trek to Lima (fearing bandits on the way). He returned to the ship forty-eight hours later. One biographer contends that no city, not Boston, Manhattan, or Quebec, "ever caught and haunted his imagination the way Lima did."[1] In* Moby-Dick, *Herman Melville included the following evocative description of Lima, underlining its foggy grayness (and "tearless" skies where rain never fell), long history, earthquake-scarred cityscape, and intriguing decadence. In this chapter he reflects on the association of white and evil. Lima reappears in* Moby-Dick *in chapter 54, "The Town-Ho's Story," and in other works, such as* Benito Cereno.

Nor is it, altogether, the remembrance of her cathedral-toppling earthquakes; nor the stampedoes of her frantic seas; nor the tearlessness of arid skies that never rain; nor the sight of her wide field of leaning spires, wrenched cope-stones, and crosses all adroop (like canted yards of anchored fleets); and her suburban avenues of house-walls lying over upon each other, as a tossed pack of cards; —it is not these things alone which make tearless Lima, the strangest, saddest city thou can'st see. For Lima has taken the white veil; and there is a higher horror in this whiteness of her woe. Old as Pizarro, this whiteness keeps her ruins for ever new; admits not the cheerful greenness of complete decay; spreads over her broken ramparts the rigid pallor of an apoplexy that fixes its own distortions.

Note

1. Hershel Parker, *Herman Melville: A Biography*, vol. 1: *1819–1851* (Baltimore: Johns Hopkins University Press, 1996), 281.

Water carrier (*aguador*). In Manuel Atanasio Fuentes, *Lima: Apuntes históricos, descriptivos, estadísticos y de costumbres* (Paris: Firmin Didot, 1867).

Plaza Mayor, 1865. In Mariano Felipe Paz Soldán, *Atlas Geográfico del Perú* (Paris, 1865).

Inquisition Plaza, 1853. *L'Illustration* 22 (July–December 1853).

Lima's Carnival and Its Glories

Manuel Atanasio Fuentes

Manuel Atanasio Fuentes (1820–89), nicknamed "the Bat," was a lawyer, urbanist, and satirist who wrote extensively on legal history, Lima, and contemporary Peru. A major figure in Peruvian letters in the nineteenth century, he designed parks, compiled statistical collections, satirized his political foes and allies, and chronicled Lima in its slow path toward modernization.

In this text, he reviews Lima's Carnival tradition of soaking passersby, often with stinky water and even eggs. Fuentes derides Carnival's turmoil and its dark-skinned participants. He also ridicules public balls and masquerade parties, belittling all who participate.

Who will waste his breath speaking out against the horrid Carnival of Lima? Who, I insist, in a town where the fair sex (there are, of course, exceptions) enjoys soaking the unwitting pedestrian with water that may be clean or foul? Who would dare call barbaric the custom of men in ragged clothes walking the streets with baskets full of eggshells that they inelegantly throw at balconies and windows? Who would dare fume about the odious spectacle of mobs of dark people of both sexes gallivanting through the streets, soaked in water and full of alcohol, who, in order to foster an atmosphere of fun, sometimes speak dirty and obscene words, and boldly splash with water from the sewage ditch all those sorry souls who cannot spend three days in complete isolation?

Who would dare, finally, to demand that authorities suppress this barbaric amusement?

Nobody: for one would appear as the enemy of the people, wishing to deprive the innocent folk of an innocent pastime. But that does not prevent us from being guileless enough to call them civilized and cultivated, nor the modesty of considering ourselves South America's best.

Oh, if we were the best

How would the worst be!

This year, Carnival has been tempestuous, in other words, fun; for it is

El son de los diablos.

Son de los Diablos (Devil's Dance), one of the most popular dances among the
Afro-Peruvian population. Watercolor by Pancho Fierro. Colección Ricardo Palma,
Municipalidad de Lima.

doubtlessly fun to see a drenched person, clothes clinging to his or her body
and dripping all over the place; for it is fun to smash a balcony's windows;
for it is fun to poke out an eye, or lose a tooth; for it is fun to turn the streets
into puddles; and for it is fun to hear our cultured plebes speak appallingly
foul words.

"What a wonderful time!" exclaims the woman of dubious virtue, seeing her house invaded by a gang of good-humored citizens who have left it as horrible as Furies out of Avernus. "What a wonderful time!" says the follower of Bacchus after having degraded his dignity as a man, prancing around the streets in a grotesque costume, and staggering due to the effects of free liquor. And when it becomes impossible for the authorities, important or petty, to not be persuaded that during those days we cease to present ourselves as moderately civilized beings, Carnival becomes more vigorous with each passing year, with a larger train of obscenities and disgraces, that is, more fun! God keep us from such honest and recreational fun!

My readers know that there have been masquerades in four places over the three nights of Carnival, which I have attended—despite my age and disenchantment—in order to be able to say something about them.

In the house of Tiravanti, I witnessed many lights, few musicians, fewer masks, and yet fewer dancers.

In the garden of La Aurora I found no more than eight musicians playing polkas that no one danced to; the businessman of this establishment *has made a profit.*

In the garden of Los Descalzos things were pretty much the same as in La Aurora.

The Teatro Principal had a large turnout; especially in the final evening.

The largest amount of masks was worn, as far as men are concerned, by Frenchmen and Italians; very few by the badly dressed Creoles; and as to women, it seems unnecessary to state what genre the majority of the masked "ladies" belonged to.

As to outfits, the majority of them were trivial and in bad taste; a few were rather amusing in a grotesque fashion, such as those of a dandy and his page. Certain young gentlemen were remarkable insofar as they—probably quite impressed by their natural beauty and the embroidered capes they rented from the theater—flaunted their faces sans costume or mask, putting in evidence that if they were not born in a land where flashy outfits were worn, they would happily play the role of coachmen and clowns. It must be noted that these youths did not even indulge in the pleasure of dancing, and surely had been motivated to attend solely by the desire to show off.

Though it may be true that in the theater the expected turmoil, due to the nature of the spectacle and the high turnout, did not occur, there was no lack of individuals who, having refreshed their esophagus with several drinks, spoke in a language offensive to morality and indulged in certain indecent choreographed steps that insulted the audience.

One or two subjects of Napoleon III, *Cancan* enthusiasts, forgot that in their country, a flippant gesture or movement would inevitably get them in trouble with the police; but we are more tolerant in this sense and there was thus no lack of *expressive Cancan steps.*

During the second evening, the sovereign people demanded *zanguaraña* or *zamacueca.* The band played something that the devil himself would have a hard time recognizing, but the couples readied themselves and danced the *mozas malas* and the *mozos no buenos* with such charm, grace, and poise that they seemed to be in a tavern in Malambo. The director of the band was warned not to repeat the *zamacueca,* but the sovereign people, captained by a Señor Lieutenant Colonel whose career is a *zanguaraña* in itself, asked for an encore . . . and the *zanguaraña* was played and danced . . . and the orders of the authorities were superseded by the yells of the *jefe.* Witness the value of a couple of epaulets!

This jefe argued that anything goes in a *popular* dance, as long as *order is not disrupted.* Offending decency matters not to this jefe; attacks on public morals matter not to this jefe; obscene dances matter not to this jefe. What kind of jefe is this?

Those of us who have had the fortune of attending masquerades in other lands, have witnessed how the police and gendarmerie closely watch the dancers and above all the public; a dishonest word, gesture, unseemly step, and the individual who disrespected the public is immediately ejected from the locale, even if he were the most presumptuous jefe; it is also true that jefes in other worlds are not made from the same muck as ours are.

Translated by Jorge Bayona

Note

Suspension points (. . .) in this selection appeared in the original text and do not indicate an ellipsis.

The Amancaes Parade

Ismael Portal

Ismael Portal (1863–1934) fought as a young man in the War of the Pacific and re-portedly bought books stolen from the National Library from Chilean soldiers. He worked in public administration but published broadly on the history and folklore of Lima. Whereas Ricardo Palma glorified but also ridiculed Lima's colonial past, Portal cast it in more positive tones, exalting religious and other traditions. His Lima religiosa *(1924), published at a point when immigrants from Japan, Europe, and above all the Andes as well as incipient industrialization were transforming the city, honored Lima's fervent Catholicism under the Spanish. Nostalgia permeated Portal's evocations.*

This essay praises the parades to and picnics in the Amancaes meadow, to the north of Lima. For centuries, limeños crossed the Rímac River to celebrate San Juan Day (June 24) and, after July 28, 1821, Peruvian Independence Day, in the lovely Amancaes fields. The Amancay flower blossomed just around this time. Vendors sold food, musical groups performed, and the more fortunate showed off their means of transportation, whether the coaches described by Portal or subsequently auto-mobiles. In the 1960s urban sprawl converted Amancaes into the Urbanización El Bosque, leaving no trace of the open fields and festive traditions.

As limeños are a vivacious and loquacious people who actively pursue hon-est entertainment, the meadow of Amancaes was destined to become—from the very moment the Spanish arrived—a congenial gathering site that would later become the melting pot from which the new nation would emerge. Its proximity to the capital city, the vastness of the mountain-flanked land, the vigorous atmosphere, the abundance of flowers . . . this symphony of beautiful elements of nature attracted the locals to this garden of delights. This custom began in the early days of the conquest when the settlers, just like the eager hawks in the nearby hills, cheerfully hunted for birds and deer in the meadow, and ended up being organized and followed very enthusiastically—with June 24 as its official date—hence becoming a magnificent parade that, due to various and fortunate circumstances, has always aroused interest throughout the entire country.

The parade to the meadow of Amancaes thus took on a new form, and as a result the aristocracy gained more space for their revelries and glittery displays. Coaches and litters—transporting beautiful ladies in their finest dresses, driven by handsome horsemen on splendid beasts—gracefully crossed the central streets of the city on the assigned day and headed toward their destination. At the historic bridge of Montesclaro—a monument of underrated Viceregal architecture—thousands of limeños anxiously awaited the enthusiastic parade.

Many, many years went by, and the parade to the meadow of Amancaes became even grander after the nation attained political independence. It is from this period that the most fervent memories of the wise and overflowing joy that gives limeño tradition its special flavor belong.

Parade season lasted until July 28—National Independence Day—and many people spent a few hours in that field, especially on Sundays, never lacking well-prepared vending ladies to prepare exquisite *picantes* on the spot.

Old-time topographers who have known this place and visited it again after many years have noticed that its topographic configuration has changed, which they ascribed to the earthquakes that have stricken the Peruvian capital over the course of the colonial and Independent periods. In any case, the view of the city from any point of the meadow of Amancaes—one does not even need to climb the hills—is breathtaking, and its beauty captures one's imagination and prompts one to think, for a few instants, about the infiniteness of Creation.

Our inspired ruler, Grand Marshall don Ramón Castilla [president 1844–51, 1855–63], was particularly keen on this parade. As the army carried out a grandiose exercise in the immense meadow every year, he planned to erect a small building—which later got built—from where the president and his large retinue could view the maneuvers from a vantage point, while safe from bothersome drizzles and savoring succulent local dishes.

This modest construction was known as "The Palace," and it has been abandoned since we were attacked and ruined during the iniquitous war of 1879. It crumbled slowly over time and collapsed a few years ago; only a few adobe bricks from its foundations remain, as though to remind us of the customary negligence Tadeo Haenke has accused us of.[1]

Translated by Jorge Bayona

Note

1. Tadeo Haenke was a German explorer who visited Peru in the early 1790s. See his *Descripción del Perú* (Lima: Imprenta de "El Lucero," 1901).

Chinese Are Not Welcome

Mariano Castro Zaldívar

Peru received approximately one hundred thousand Chinese contract laborers from 1849 to 1874, the vast majority of them Cantonese men. They worked on estates up and down the Peruvian coast as well as in the malodorous guano trade, shoveling bird excrement into ships that would take the nitrogen-rich fertilizer to Europe. After the abolition of slavery in Peru in 1854, they in many cases replaced slaves. Not surprisingly, labor conditions were wretched. Revolts broke out from time to time, and many took advantage of the chaos of the War of the Pacific (1879–83) to desert. Some even fought for the Chileans, prompting broad anti-Chinese sentiment.

After their labor terms ended (often extended illegally by unscrupulous bosses), many Chinese settled in Lima, opening small shops and restaurants. Even today, el chino is synonymous with the corner bodega. Lima's Chinatown emerged in the late nineteenth century, centered around Capón Street just east of downtown. In the early twentieth century, bohemians such as José Carlos Mariátegui and the visiting Mexican intellectual José Vasconcelos described nights turning into days in the barrio chino's opium dens. Authorities targeted the neighborhood for crackdowns, often alleging health risks, as this nineteenth-century document does. In recent decades, a new wave of immigrants has arrived from China. Chinese food, or chifa, is a mainstay of Lima's vibrant culinary scene.

Lima, December 21, 1883

Having reviewed the report submitted by the commission in charge of inspecting the tenements of Capon Street wherein a large part of the Chinese community resides, and considering:

1.— That said report states that the tenements known as Otaiza and Salaverry constitute a permanent source of diseases that afflict the populace and are the focal point of unhygienic and immoral practices;

2.— That we must not expose the city center to a continuous threat against the health of its residents, which is all the more important insofar as it may contribute to the outbreak of epidemics;

It is resolved:

1.— That the Asian population residing in the tenements known as Otaiza and Salaverry be notified that they are to vacate the premises and relocate to various parts of the city without concentrating in large numbers.

2.— That the owners of the aforementioned tenements must repair them and bring them up to hygienic standards; Lima City Hall shall supervise the execution of these orders;

3.— That the Prefect of the Department be informed so that he may enforce this resolution and order that the police watch over the Asians and prevent their concentration in the city center.

Have this communicated and recorded.

Signed,

His Excellency Castro Zaldívar

Translated by Jorge Bayona

The National Library and
the Chilean Occupation

E. W. Middendorf

Ernst W. Middendorf (1830–1908) was a German doctor who lived in Peru for many years in the late nineteenth century. His intellectual interests included archeology, geography, and linguistics, important themes in his publications. Today the museum in Lima's much visited zoo, the Parque de las Leyendas, carries his name.

In the War of the Pacific (1879–83), Chile occupied Lima from 1881 to 1883. They plundered the National Library, sending cases of books and manuscripts back to Santiago. One estimate claimed they looted over 5,500 pounds of books. In 2007 the Chilean government returned 3,778 books to Peru's National Library. Middendorf provides a history of the National Library before and after the War of the Pacific. The National Library is now housed in a modern building on Avenida Javier Prado. The old one on Avenida Abancay serves as a reading library.

One of the first institutions founded after Peruvian Independence was the National Library. On July 9, 1821, General San Martín entered Lima with the Chilean army; on the 28th, Independence was proclaimed, and a month after that, the Protector of the newly founded state issued a decree ordering the creation of a National Library. A reading room and space for the books were set aside in the former School of Caciques, which had been founded by Viceroy Prince of Esquilache and was dedicated to educating the sons of Indian nobles. The consecration and opening took place on December 17 the following year, shortly before San Martín's departure, and all authorities attended.

There were 11,256 volumes available to the public, 600 of which had been donated by General San Martín and his Minister of War García del Río, while the rest came from the university's or convents' libraries. Shortly thereafter, Dr. [Miguel] Fuentes Pacheco donated 7,000 more volumes. By 1830, almost 30,000 books were on hand. Early interest in the library notwithstanding, collections grew slowly afterward. Despite the assignment of an adequate staff—comprised of two librarians, two subordinate employees, two preservers, and two assistants, to be paid for with a yearly budget of five thousand soles—the amount earmarked for the acquisition of new books was negligible. A full catalog of the existent books was never made even though the library, for a very long time, never had more than 30,000 volumes, which makes one wonder how these employees whiled away their time.

From 1835 onward, the library was put under the direction and care of Dr. Francisco de Paula González Vigil, who spent the last forty years of his life there. A liberal priest and patriot, Dr. González Vigil had led the Liberal Party in his youth and became its patriarch; he was well known in South America for his defense of the state and church from papal meddling; his Christian virtues and severe and selfless behavior earned him fame and respect. The library's relocation to its current site was due to Dr. González Vigil's efforts. As the three halls of the School of Caciques proved insufficient, the library was expanded, incorporating the adjoining rooms from the old Jesuit convent.[1] In order to house the collections, the great hall of the refectory was carefully remodeled. Brighter days shone upon the institution; there was a noticeable increase in the number of books, which were stored in tasteful bookcases and shelves within a skylight-lit and spacious reading hall.

The war with Chile brought progress to a standstill. It appears that the library aroused the victors' voracity, perhaps because they overestimated its worth. Shortly after the fall of Lima, the quartermasters of plunder were ordered to ship all the books of value to Chile. Although as a general rule Chileans were shameless in their looting, the library was pillaged in secret. I had frequently consulted its books up to the time when Lima was occupied, and had subsequently—thanks to the German minister—obtained permission from the Chilean authorities to continue my studies. However, and despite this explicit authorization, I was prevented from entering the library. The reason was revealed to me on my third attempt. The main entrance was flanked by several hundred wooden boxes destined for transporting books. A few weeks later, as I casually passed by, I noticed that the door was open, so I went in, without the guards preventing me from doing so. It was a sorry sight. The reading halls, previously so well kept, looked as though they had harbored creatures from a Greek tragedy. The bookcases and shelves were empty, and half-ruined books were scattered all over the place. Soldiers sold them to storekeepers, who, over the course of the following weeks, wrapped their parcels in pages torn from the writings of the Church Fathers.

For all the grief caused by the loss of the library and the astronomy equipment and other scientific collections, nobody in Lima was surprised about their fate. It was not the first time that Chileans had entered the city as victors, and though they had previously done so as allies of at least a faction of the Peruvians, this time they came as enemies and did not need to show any restraint. Peruvians had always believed that their southern neighbors were distinctive among American nations in their insatiable appetite for other people's property. Although the Chileans showed the Peruvians that they also had some redeeming qualities, acts such as these proved sufficient to reinforce their old reputation.

Underneath it all, this war was just an outburst of long-simmering envy, precipitated by Peruvian diplomatic carelessness. When the frivolous and indulgent neighbor finally showed his weakness, Chile eagerly made the best out of the opportunity: whatever the government got its hands on belonged to the state, and the rest was scooped up by individual Chileans. Their greed was insatiable and their voraciousness amazing, ranging from the appropriation of entire provinces and the imposition of heavy war reparations, to the pillaging of the most insignificant and incredible items, such as the public urinals of the Plaza Mayor, which must have also been shipped to Chile. Overall, discipline still held sway, at least among the troops stationed in Lima. Looting was organized by the high command, and carried out with the order and meticulousness that are the hallmarks of Chilean administration. Among the measures with which the Chileans tainted their well-earned military fame, the most loathsome was the looting of all scientific collections, as it made manifest the wicked intention to deprive the defeated nation of these means of instruction, humiliating it in the spiritual aspect, much as its power had been militarily annihilated.

In the short period that has transpired since the war ended, the National Library has managed to recover surprisingly quickly from the calamities visited upon it. The old library had sixty thousand volumes acquired over the course of sixty years; the new one is only two years old and already houses thirty thousand. Formerly, the bookcases contained many thousands of old theological folios, bound in parchment, which nobody cared about and had never been consulted, while relatively small quantities of newer books were acquired with the meager resources available. The current library, conversely, is mostly made up of modern books. This institution's satisfactory progress is mainly due to the efforts of its new director, Don Ricardo Palma, a writer well appreciated in all of Spanish America and whose fame reaches even Europe, who appealed for aid from all American libraries and garnered the support of the most renowned writers of South America.

The library is accessed through the former School of Caciques. It contains a yard that resembles the cloister of a convent; the second story above has fluted Ionic columns in each of its four sides. Beyond it lies an antechamber, whose left wall is almost entirely covered by a great oil painting by Peruvian painter [Luis] Montero, depicting Atahualpa's funerals. Farther ahead is the reading hall, which is visited by a daily influx of between forty and fifty people. The books are kept in well-made cedar bookcases and shelves, in two rooms. The first room, the more important one, used to be the Jesuit refectory. It is 150 feet long, 60 feet tall, and 30 feet wide. It still preserves its old roof with dark, artistically carved wooden beams that blend well with the color of the bookcases. The second room, the smaller one, is reserved for books dealing with America and America-related matters. The National Archive is kept in the third room; in the fourth we find paintings, old and modern, which have not been hung yet, and among these are life-size portraits of all the viceroys and presidents.

The library's staff comprises a director, a deputy director, and two preservers, who are paid four thousand soles. Very few books are published in Lima, and those that are especially voluminous are printed and published in Paris. There is a lot of writing in Lima, but literary production is limited to pamphlets and periodicals.

Translated by Jorge Bayona

Note

1. The Colegio de Caciques was a school for the children of Indigenous elites that functioned during the colonial period.

IV

Modernizing Lima (1895–1940)

The reconstruction efforts after the War of the Pacific began to bear fruit around 1895: that year, caudillo Nicolás de Piérola began his second term, one that set the foundation for a period of relative economic prosperity and political stability dubbed the "Aristocratic Republic" by Peruvian historian Jorge Basadre. Lima went through a period of rapid, albeit quite uneven, transformation. The old Lima wall had been demolished; foreign investment began to pour into Peru, especially its capital, where banks and factories began to multiply; modern artifacts and customs—imported from Europe and the United States—were eagerly adopted; and new avenues, boulevards, and residential areas for affluent people extended the city's reach. The "old" Lima, in the eyes of many commentators, was disappearing before their eyes, rapidly and inevitably. Some welcomed these transformations; others lamented them. By 1919, an energetic leader, Augusto B. Leguía, came to power with a modernization agenda that included the beautification of Lima. By the 1930s, Lima had definitively acquired a new physiognomy.

But the transformation of Lima was not only driven from above: subaltern groups—Chinese and black communities, working-class groups and their labor unions, residents of popular neighborhoods, and others—played a central role in the way Lima was leaving behind its "traditional" appearance. They occupied new social and physical spaces, repeatedly made their political presence felt, developed or appropriated new cultural manifestations, and infused life in the capital with their vibrant economic presence.

The modernization of Lima during this period was certainly uneven: to some extent, it reinforced traditional social and racial hierarchies. As in other cities in Latin America that pursued urban reforms and Belle Époque embellishment, ample sectors of the population did not benefit from the (in many cases quite superficial) modernization impulse. Poverty, crime, and marginalization continued to be central dimensions of the urban experience; policing, repression, and cultural derision not only did not decrease,

La Colmena Avenue and Bolívar Hotel, 1929. In Fabio Camacho, *Aspectos de Lima*, 3rd ed. (Lima: Editorial Incazteca, 1929). Photograph by Fabio Camacho.

but in some cases were loudly invoked as the necessary response to what was still considered the scum of society.

The texts included in this section range from panoramic views about the transformations Lima was undergoing to accounts of specific aspects of both the changes and the continuities. We learn about efforts to beautify the city; life in middle-class neighborhoods; the increasing popularity of sports, especially soccer; and life for domestic servants and other working-class people. We also include accounts of how intellectuals and artists experienced these transformations: changes in sensibilities were among the many transformations the capital city confronted at the turn of the twentieth century.

The Transformation of Lima after 1895

José Gálvez

By the end of the nineteenth century, economic prosperity and political stability led to a modernizing impulse in various realms of society, such as state institutions, urbanism, legal codes, military and police forces, and education. The transformation of Lima triggered a sense of nostalgia among limeños and limeñas: the traditional and romantic city, they felt, was giving way to a new metropolis filled with crime and danger. Many perceived the new rhythm of daily life and demographic growth as detrimental to the quality of life they associated with the old city.

José Gálvez (1885–1957), a poet, journalist, and politician, chronicled the changes that Lima went through during that period in a seminal book titled Una Lima que se va (A Lima That Slips Away; 1921). *Although those pages are filled with a sense of nostalgia, Gálvez did not offer an indictment of modernization; in fact, he praised it, with an excess of optimism, for putting Lima on the path to civilization, palpable in such varied manifestations of public life as the practice of sports, the incorporation of the working classes into the political process, and the emergence of a vibrant intellectual life.*

Under [President Nicolás de] Piérola, the country underwent a radical transformation. I am unable to describe all the positive changes that took place in every aspect of this country—all thanks to his messianic arrival. Quickly, one witnessed how everything was transformed and how our enfeebled nation started to show initiative and true hopes of reemergence. It is unnecessary to delve into the merely political aspect that marked the victory of *civilismo* in order to evoke the essential differences that were noticeable almost immediately. Lima became a city in all the senses of the term. Even customs changed quickly, which can only be explained by the prior evolutionary standstill caused by war and government blunders. A sense of purpose and confidence was instilled in all spheres, especially the economy, which was echoed in all aspects of life. When Piérola handed over power in 1899, a different Peru had risen from the ruins and misery he had started with.

Tapadas inside the Torre Tagle palace, c. 1900. Archivo Courret, Biblioteca Nacional del Perú.

. . .

The year 1895 marks the beginning of our total transformation, so much so that it seems amazing that we should have changed so much in so little time.

. . .

The Palace of Exhibitions at Paseo Colón, currently the Lima Art Museum (MALI), c. 1900. In *Album de Lima y sus alrededores* (Lima: Librería e Imprenta Gil, n.d.). Photographer unknown.

Everything started to change. The whip and the dungeons, as well as the perpetual hatred between students and teachers, disappeared, albeit slowly, from schools. Students caught a glimpse of healthier and nobler entertainments than the old group brawls, brutal sling fights, and insatiable duels over kites. Harmonious foot races, soccer, and cricket replaced the deforming and acrobatic systems of bars, trapezes, and rings. The illustrious youth gathered in the open air, under wide skies, to play British sports. The Club Unión Cricket was founded and two youthful and enthusiastic spirits— Don Pedro de Osma and Don Ricardo Ortiz de Zevallos y Vidaurre—gave this healthy activity a huge and pleasant boost. Those notorious scuffles between schools were replaced by classical-flavored athletic challenges. The upper class organized sporting events, first in Santa Sofía and later in Santa Beatriz, which led to noble emulations and lasting comradery.

Intellectual activity seemed to come back to life. Figures such as [poet José Santos] Chocano took center stage. A slew of enthusiasts took on new fields, and a febrile inquisitiveness shook up the postwar mental slumber. Newspapers started paying their writers and focusing on certain services. Specialized information started to appear, while the vile communiqués di-

minished and the old and variegated chronicle started to lose its manifold
character. A select circle of bohemians and lovers of art formed a brotherhood of sorts that surrounded the very noble and fine Master Valle Riestra
with a kindness that was excessive at the time. There was a renaissance in
entertainment too. The tradition of those great troupes that visited us before
the war was reestablished by Adalguisa Gabbi, who came with Perelló de
Segurola and Castellani. Fondness for tearoom rhythmic waltzes, bouncy
polkas, and sappy romances heard during conversations over limeño tea was
largely abandoned in Lima homes. Even the interior design of homes underwent modification and refinement, although that led to many carved consoles and wonderful antiques ending up in the hands of foreigners or antique
dealers. The young became more serious in thinking about their future. It
was no longer shameful to become a paid employee. A young Dr. Villarán
actually spoke some hard truths about our decorative and venerated liberal
professions.

. . .

There has been striking improvement in political order. The revolution of 1895 has been, without a doubt, the last of the mass revolutions that
used to rock the country, sometimes halting it to gain more impulse, other
times making it regress. Many grotesque and harmful habits disappeared.
Out went the vehement and often rude debates that took place between
candidates vying for the same seat in Congress, and although we have not
progressed much in civics—perhaps there is disparity between social and
merely political progress—the atrocious clashes over polling stations vanished and political life doubtlessly took on a more serious and even peaceful
character.

. . .

The police earned more respect: the grotesque *cachaco* [cop] with the huge
cloak and gargantuan rifle became the Señor Inspector with low-cut shoes
and soft baton, thus somehow curbing our peoples' proverbial irreverence.
Graffiti on freshly painted walls was reduced. Lower-class people started to
orientate themselves; many humanitarian or artisans' agencies were created
or reorganized; institutional spirit evolved somewhat decoratively, but with
good intentions; grocery stores stopped being taverns where our workers
whiled away the hours drinking pisco and gambling with marked cards. For
the first time, a working-class deputy, Don Rosendo Vidaurre, was elected
to Congress; brawlers slowly lost their air of boastfulness; even courtship
started to change with foreign immigration; the increase in vehicles and
the improvement of the trolley service boosted the intermingling of people
from all corners of the city; neighborhoods stopped having an autonomous

character and being hostile toward outsiders; and finally, religious practices changed notably as well, as Archbishop Monsignor Don Manuel Tovar suppressed many extravagances and impressed a grander aura upon rites.

Piérola, an exceptional man in our land, was immensely fortunate to know how to channel the country's development with his genius. Lima's village spirit disappeared, certainly; many overzealous modernistic spirits strongly contributed—and still do—to making a characterless city out of Lima, and much of the old and sweet limeño personality has been lost in the pursuit of progress. Even lovemaking has changed. It is truly admirable how, despite the old habits' tenacity for survival and conservation, all spheres of social life have been changed so thoroughly. And although this profound mutation has a melancholy aftertaste, we cannot deny that we have turned out for the better, and it appears that we have doubtlessly joined the mainstream of civilization.

Translated by Jorge Bayona

A Middle-Class House in 1900

Luis Alberto Sánchez

By the turn of the twentieth century, Lima was still a very traditional city in at least one sense: its streets and neighborhoods, particularly those of the downtown area, had not yet gone through the process of social and economic segregation that would be typical of later decades. One single block could contain the residence of an aristocratic family, the house of middle-class professionals, one or more callejones *where poor working-class families lived in overcrowded spaces, a grocery store, and even a clandestine brothel. The same goes for its racial makeup: limeños of European descent coexisted (not always in harmony) with people of Indigenous or African background. This proximity favored the forging of relations of patronage and clientelism, but at times also produced tensions and friction.*

This excerpt from Luis Alberto Sánchez's memoirs (1900–1994) offers a detailed description of his middle-class house and of the entire neighborhood in those early years of the twentieth century. Sánchez was a prolific literary critic, historian, writer, and biographer; a prominent educator (he was elected president of the University of San Marcos three times); and a well-known politician of the APRA Party and public figure, elected to Congress several times and serving as vice president of the Constitutional Assembly of 1978–79. His memoirs contain colorful and entertaining depictions of life in twentieth-century Lima.

I was born in Monopinta Street, which began at the corner of Ocoña (known as "Pilitricas" back then) and ended in Quilca. It was respectably long, measuring about 130 meters from end to end. Like the rest of Lima, except for a few colonial palaces, it was bereft of any two-story houses. The Buenaños, across the street from me, added a second floor later on, and so did the Prietos, a few doors down. There were three kinds of residences: *casonas* with two or three patios; remodeled houses whose style led to them being referred to as "American"; and the *callejones.* I remember four of the latter: Rosario, Don Lázaro's, González's, and the Brombergs'. As their name indicates, each *callejón* was an alley flanked by two rows of rooms made of adobe and wattle-and-daub. A faucet with a drain was located in the middle

Gil Bookstore and Print Shop, a symbol of Lima's vibrant cultural scene in the early twentieth century, c. 1900. In *Album de Lima y sus alrededores* (Lima: Librería e Imprenta Gil, n.d.). Photographer unknown.

Maury Hotel, c. 1920, where many believe the pisco sour, the famous Peruvian cocktail, was invented. The bar continues to feature it. Photographer unknown.

Military parade at Plaza San Martín, 1924. Photographer unknown.

of the entryway; it was used as laundry, water supply, and toilet by the entire black community that gathered there at the rate of five soles a month per pigsty. There usually was a sacred image at the back, decorated with brass "miracles" and tallow candles. The doorwoman lived in the first room to the right. The street door was never closed.

The main *casonas* were, on one side, Gutiérrez Quintanilla's, later owned by Juan Boix, which is still standing and almost intact until now; ours or Señora Cisneros'; Señora Portalanza's; the Prietos'; and, across the street, the Zamoras', Señora González's (one of whose daughters married the Liberal Deputy Wenceslao Valera), and the Maldonados' and the Prentices'. I do not recall the section of the street that was knocked down by the city council in order to open up La Colmena Avenue.

Grocery stores and wine shops rounded out the neighborhood; one of the former, located in the corner of Pilitricas (Ocoña), still stands today. Across the street, Pinasco's wine shop featured enormous casks and bottles in which various spirits were fermented. The wine merchant was a burly Italian, who always wore a dark sweater and aviator cap. He specialized in macerating cherries, which he later sold at two cents apiece, rolled in paper; he called them "drunken cherries." It was truly delightful to suck on them until one was saturated with their tasty and sweet alcohol. One of the first times I got drunk—unintentionally—was due to those magical cherries.

My family's house had a gate that divided the vestibule from the first patio featuring a date: 1860. We knew that was not the year it was built, but the year it was rebuilt. Anyhow, by the time I was born that gate had already been in use for forty years.

The façade was classic: a huge door with an ample wicket gate and, to the sides, two wide and barred windows, guarded by brass gratings that acted like Moorish shutters. The door was wide enough for a coach. The entryway was paved with river stones, while flat stones adorned the passageway. There were screen doors on each side of the vestibule that led to the apartments corresponding to the grated windows.

Beyond the gate, from which we playfully dangled to commit all sorts of mischief, one could see the patio, which had a corridor at the far end, shadowed by a leafy fig tree. Next to the handrails, three-storied racks held pots with geraniums, basil, white lilies, carnations, and daisies. A creeper with yellow and white flowers wrapped around the fig tree. Jasmines permeated the place with their warm aroma. For several years, one of these handrails was ruled by Martín (a.k.a. The Monkey), my childhood friend. On another, Lolita the parrot pranced around, insolent and talkative as La Celestina.

Off to the right side of the patio was the alley, which led to the pen, whose troughs were empty at the time. At the center of the patio, a door with colorful glass gave access to the living room.

The half-light that shrouded the living room gave it the appearance of a monastery. A dozen and a half pieces of Louis XV furniture with ochre lining and black drawings populated the room. An enormous marble table was placed in the center. Hat racks and counters lined the walls. An exquisite wounded Napoleonic soldier in porcelain decorated one of those counters. On another, a marquise dressed in lace. There was also a pendulum clock on the table. The curtains were dark and dusty, the carpet the same color as the furniture. A twelve-light chandelier lit up the room on festive days. Gas lighting was still used. The gas meter was behind the door in the vestibule. Inquiring about its location was unnecessary: it was given away by the rancid smell of constantly venting monoxide.

The living room was followed by a room known as the *cuadra*, a spacious sitting room whose sparse furnishings comprised a Louis XV table with a marble countertop, two somewhat rickety couches, an armchair, and four chairs in the aforementioned style. A window full of pots faced the second patio, in whose center was a *poza*, a kind of garden shaped like the Peruvian coat-of-arms, where plants in the national colors flourished. In the middle of the *poza* was another fig tree, more pensive than the one in the previous patio. To the sides, there were whitewashed porticos with wooden columns. We hung the rings and trapeze from one of these porticos. Then came the dining room. To the left of the gated window, there were seven rooms with skylights. The first two were occupied by my Aunt Celinda and her children; the next two, by my grandparents; the fifth and sixth, by my father, my mother, and me; the last, by my Aunt Zoila and two of my cousins.

The dining room was vast, with a gated window facing the second patio and also direct access to the antekitchen. The table seated fourteen. On holidays, extra boards were added, thus seating up to twenty. There was an auxiliary table—as always, Louis XV—; an English cabinet that had been my grandfather Leopold's; and an "auxiliary carving table" from the same country.

Next to the antekitchen was the only bathroom in the entire house; all the rest were merely "sinks." The tub was made out of zinc and was cold as stone. The showerhead was so moldy that it spewed as much mildew as water. We all preferred baths: we could not stand the shower for more than ten seconds. The toilet was raised on a dais as if it were a throne. Thus, my father referred to the act of using it as "going to the throne." After all, one can rule anywhere.

The kitchen looked like a ship's, made out of bricks, with iron sheets, blackened by smoke and soot. The pots resembled military cauldrons: black, heavy, and enormous. Furthermore, a staircase led to the attic, our headquarters for mischief.

. . .

Monopinta held a good reputation back then. Among its close to six hundred residents, there were only three or four *chuscas*, or prostitutes. One was retired and was the mother of a poor whitish kid, whom we nicknamed "dull turkey" due to his shyness. My grandmother spoke derisively of the *chuscas* or the "little-wigged ones," referring to the two tenants of don Lázaro's corral who shone a red light over their doors, which were open after 7 p.m. So that we should not lack anything, we also had a wise neighbor, Dr. Rodolfo Zavala. A creole Quixote of sorts, he was a professor of the Facultad de Letras and a teacher in the Colegio de Guadalupe; a lonely, bearded, and frail man, who was an enthusiast of flowers and the silence of dogs. He was dead one morning without anyone knowing why. I still do not know whether I feared or respected him.

Translated by Jorge Bayona

The Growing Popular Taste for Soccer

El Comercio

As in other cities and ports in South America, soccer was brought to Lima and Callao by English sailors, merchants, and other travelers and immigrants. Initially an activity exclusive of English immigrants and the Lima elite, it rapidly became the favorite pastime for young people and the growing working classes of Lima and Callao. The ease of practicing the sport helps explain its popularity. Schools, factories, and neighborhoods became the spaces where soccer was played with growing enthusiasm.

For authorities and elites, soccer presented a welcome opportunity to instill in its practitioners notions of discipline, temperance, and bodily hygiene that would hopefully keep young and poor urban men away from crime, vice, and even political activism. Ideas about masculinity and race also informed the enthusiastic endorsement that different commentators (journalists, businessmen, state administrators) gave to the sport: it would help develop virile men and improve the bio-racial configuration of the Peruvian population. As early as 1908, the newspaper El Comercio *published this brief note praising soccer as "healthy entertainment" and asking authorities to promote its practice.*

For a few months now, an evolution in the entertainment and pastimes of our lower classes has become noticeable: they are gradually leaning toward sports, and soccer in particular. This is a most convenient turn of events that must be encouraged by all available means, as this evolution constitutes a step forward in the culture of our lower classes.

The growing fondness for this kind of healthy entertainment is most manifest in the population centers closest to Lima. In an open field in Barranco, next to the national tramway line, two groups of young people gather every day and play soccer with great enthusiasm. In Chorrillos there are two other groups who practice their daily physical exercises in the lots next to the chalet of the Mothers of the Sacred Heart.

Municipalities could encourage these positive trends by sending officials to the sport fields to hand out free soccer balls to the underprivileged youths and also by setting apart convenient closed fields for their use.

The upcoming national anniversary could be celebrated by promoting this sport among the lower classes of Lima and neighboring towns, by aiding them in the aforementioned fashion, and rewarding those who excel in these endeavors.

Pertaining to the spread of these sports, there is a large expanse of land in the outskirts of Callao, in the fields of Mar Bravo, that are suitable for cricket and soccer as they encompass many flat, grass-covered areas.

This place has been frequented for many years by the Callao cricket and soccer clubs, whose virile games have become increasingly important. In their leisure time, once they finish their work, young chalacos and limeños head for the outdoors, for that splendid air that can only be enjoyed close to the sea. The beautiful fields of Mar Bravo exhibit an attractive and joyful vista on Saturdays and Sundays.

Unfortunately, Callao authorities have been using the area as a shooting range, and therefore soldiers are almost always present in the best parts. All games are thus precluded, and residents are prevented from taking their customary walks. The soldiers also happen to appear mostly on Saturdays and Sundays, which are precisely most people's days off.

Because the fields are one of the best places for this entertainment, and there being many other appropriate and nearby sites for a shooting range, it would be very convenient for the authorities to order its relocation, thus preventing terrible accidents and encouraging the development of games that are of such benefit to our young citizens.

Translated by Jorge Bayona

The Lord of the Miracles Procession

José Carlos Mariátegui

In 1655, a powerful earthquake destroyed large areas of Lima, but a wall inside a Catholic convent withstood the tremor. An image of Jesus Christ had been painted on that wall by an African slave, which gave birth to a religious cult that has survived for more than three centuries. The devotion to the "Lord of the Miracles," as he came to be known, began to spread first among the black population of Lima and later to the rest of society. Every year, in the month of October, hundreds of thousands of devotees fill the streets of Lima, one of the largest religious processions in the Catholic world.

José Carlos Mariátegui (1894–1930), who became the most important Marxist intellectual in twentieth-century Peru, wrote a brilliant account of the procession in 1917. Mariátegui offers not only a description of the procession and the variety of people that followed it, but also an interpretation of the place of faith, mysticism, and piety in the mentality of the Lima population. And he does so with admirable perception and empathy.

A mystical and tumultuous parade that sings, prays, and thrills

Springtime in Lima—an anodyne, foggy, gray, vague, and cowardly spring —features two days that suddenly revivify tradition and faith in the city. During these two days, the procession of the Lord of the Miracles testifies to the renewal and flourishing of a metropolitan religiousness that sends a strong, melancholic, and picturesque wave of emotion through its hybrid, colonial, or modern streets.

A history of terrible tremors that shook and battered the city bolsters the fervor that is felt during these spiritual days, during which Catholicism— usually just sung in bell towers and murmured in chapels—is experienced in a very pure and profound fashion.

The metropolis that progress has transformed, curtailed, and jaded is driven back, inhibited, and concealed for a moment so that the believing, regal, and colonial metropolis may emerge, vibrate, and pulsate.

Holy Week procession, 1885. Archivo Courret, Biblioteca Nacional del Perú.

During these days Lima's mysticism—usually asphyxiated and subjugated by the unpredictability and amnesia of the modern city—undergoes an intense resurrection. And this rebirth is similar to those pious awakenings that suddenly seize the souls of men turned skeptical, cold, and cerebral by analysis, life, and doubt.

Lima is a Catholic city, but not a fervent one. It is not a sentimental city. It is merely fearful. Faith exists in it perhaps due to the survival of tradition and fear of a mysterious, unknown, and dreaded powerlessness. Those who weep in the churches are part of a sinful and unsentimental population that is afraid of the end of the world and of damnation. They love weakly but repent easily.

And during these two days of vacillating and spiritless springtime Catholicism and piety are suddenly exalted, and the city kneels humbly and submissively before the litter of the crucified Lord, who defends it from tremors and blesses it from the old adobe wall on which he was depicted by the rustic hand of a colonial black man.

The procession of the Lord of the Miracles fills the streets of the city with melancholy

The outward manifestations of the crowd's faith are striking. They will dominate, impress, seduce, oppress, woo, and move. Contemplating a throng that calls on God always moves one with irresistible force and deep tenderness. The march of the procession of the Lord of the Miracles through the streets of Lima produces a very deep emotion in a city that is taken by surprise by a naive, soothing, and religious feeling.

From the clear, serene, and luminous moment in which the doors of the Church of Las Nazarenas are opened for the Lord of the Miracles to exit into the streets, to the twilight, melancholic, and gloomy moment in which the litter is lost within the somber and murky emptiness of the same church, Lima feels the palpitations of a very refined, very sincere, very great solemnity and sadness.

Experiencing this soft and innocent emotion will come as much from awaiting the procession in a doorway or a street corner as from seeing the image enter either a sumptuous or humble church, or from joining the throng that follows the Lord of the Miracles in his peregrination through the streets of the city.

However, it is a singularly pleasant and intense experience when the rumble of the procession, the ringing of bells, and the Christian fragrance of incense surprise us at home, unexpectedly, suddenly, at an ordinary hour during which the spirit is far away from devotion and piety.

I have felt and seen the procession in said fashion. That is how I understood what it means and represents in the life of the city. That is how I loved the instant in which the magnificent spectacle of a tumultuous and sonorous gathering suddenly inhibited and touched my heart.

The voices of the hasty advance guard of the parade were the first to be heard under my balconies. Their voices sounded different from those in the multitude. They were livelier, louder, almost joyful. They announced the arrival of the procession with glee and merriment.

And then came the voices of chanting and prayer, female voices, languid and parsimonious, that seemed to never weaken and never become fatigued.

Slowly, the procession finally arrived. Its pace was sluggish and slow. Its solemnity was always majestic and sonorous. Picturing it brisk and restless is unfeasible. It has the same gravity as the gesture with which the priest blesses the faithful during mass and uses the aspergillum in the morning of Ash Wednesday.

The procession marched to the rhythm of a military band. The march was martial and grand. However, due to the influence of the décor, it became religious and liturgical. And it became especially poignant. Each chord matched a heartbeat full of melancholy.

That was when I knew why the spectacle of this mystic and tumultuous procession so impresses souls, touches hearts, silences everything, and makes eyes water, knees hit the ground, and hands clasp together, for the sign of the Holy Cross, etc.

The litter of the Lord of the Miracles

The Lord of the Miracles' litter is heavy, strong, and lavish. Upon it, an oscillating and shimmering silver arch acts as a glorious halo for the image of the Lord, who is painted on a canvas that the light of the candles makes appear oily and which—on the reverse side—bears an image of our Lady of Sorrows, the despondent Virgin whose heart is pierced by seven swords.

The litter cannot be moved in haste. It is too heavy and weighs down on the backs of the brothers who bear it. They must carry it slowly. Furthermore, gasping and trembling under its weight, they have to pause every so often.

The litter is carried by burly men—*zambos*, blacks, or mestizos. They relieve each other every now and then. Carrying the litter leaves them sweaty, abated, and exhausted. They all are the Lord of the Miracles' brothers. Brethren of a humble and pious working-class congregation, they are charged with bearing the litter and taking care of the wax of the Lord.

And the men who bear this burden never complain. More than resignation, they find pleasure and joy in their task. They know that their obscure lives and profound devotion are the stuff of legends. The legend is that the Lord of the Miracles takes one of them to heaven every year. They believe that this is an uplifting and Christian death and that it is tantamount to a blissful reward.

The litter is ancient. It is repaired year after year, but it is never rebuilt altogether. It carries the overwhelming and momentous weight of the cross. And it seems to become ever heftier because of the flowers that it carries during the procession days. As it advances, more flowers appear on the litter. Some of them are placed with the ceremony of a religious offering. Others fall from balconies like a mystical rain. They become so profuse and abundant that they seem to make carrying the litter even more fatiguing.

As the litter moves, it sometimes creaks; other times it only shakes, and yet other times, it vibrates sharply. For an instant it seems to waver. And when it is set on the floor and the procession halts, so that the "brothers" may rest or a prayer may be sung from the patio of a house or the atrium of a temple, the litter makes a gruff and loud sound.

The route of the procession

The procession always follows the same route. It has for many years. The sole difference may amount to not entering a given church. The procession's route encompasses most of the old city. It does not go *abajo del puente*.[1] But neither does it approach the aristocratic suburbs of La Exposición. When the route was set, these suburbs—which are not where the city grows old, but where it is renewed—did not exist.

The procession winds its way from one side of the city to another. Its first destination is the church of Santo Domingo, after which it heads to the cathedral and then to La Concepción. It pauses at the same places every year. At noon, October 18, in La Concepción. That evening in Las Descalzas. At noon, October 19, in Santa Catalina. The people simply say that the Lord "sleeps" at Las Descalzas, and "has lunch" one day in La Concepción and in Santa Catalina the next.

The reliability and unchanging nature of this route testifies to the strength of tradition. Nothing can modify it. Nothing can transform it. The litter goes from one church to the next with unwavering precision. And the devout are always aware, more or less, of where it may be found at any given time.

The Lord's entry into a church is always carried out with grave solemnity. When it is a humble conventual church, oh how simple, ineffable, and naive do the ringing of the bells seem! Adoring nuns or gruff friars sing in the choir. There is a devoted and passionate homage that vibrates and resonates in the bell tower and the pipe organ. When the church is large and ostentatious, oh how majestic and magnificent do the ringing of the formidable bells seem! There are groups of friars who welcome the Lord with a high cross and incensory while singing a monotone and sonorous chant. And sometimes, a prelate or bishop of proud tonsure and arrogant or mean demeanor is among them.

There is a little bit of everything along this route. Metropolitan pavement and suburban pavement. Paving stones, debris, river stones, or granite. Comfortable paths and hostile paths. Rough and neglected floors and soft and clean floors. Here, a smooth stretch that the penitent's bare feet will welcome; over there, a harsh and cruel stretch that ought to be welcomed too due to the love of God and the memory of how much Our Lord suffered in his passion and death, etc., etc., etc.

Incense women, penitents, ex-votos, prayers, chants, rosaries, and other diverse people, items, and happenings of the procession

The followers of the Lord of the Miracles are variegated, heterogeneous, immense, loving, devoted, and believing. It spans the aristocracy and the riffraff. It brings together the elegant dandy and the ungainly butcher. It encompasses the well-dressed lady of noble birth, the lass from the boondocks, the self-important mistress, the circumstantially repentant plebeian prostitute, the humble maid, and the washing woman. In addition, the neat and fair male, the badly dressed and unwashed worker, the mournful beggar, the contrite criminal, the fervent hobo, and the coarse and rustic peasant, all rubbing elbows without displeasure, annoyance, or discomfort.

The *zambos* and their tunics are a key part of this tradition. They constitute its banner, heraldry, and parchment. They give the festivity and its customs an intense color. Without them, both would be stifled. The purple tunic is both suggestive and beautiful. It is always a liturgical color, and it is full of wisdom and emotion. During the days of mourning preceding Easter, Christian images are always covered with purple linens. Purple is associated with sacred items. This applies to both the prelate's suit and the priest's chasuble, as well as a sacristy and in a funeral. Purple is harmonious and gentle. It is soothing and melancholic. Science surely knows that purple, in being pious and good, never harms human eyesight.

The incense women of the Lord of the Miracles are Christians who use neither the liturgical incensory nor the oriental perfume burner. The incense that burns in their hands and is blown in their breath is kept in a turkey-shaped container made out of silver or nickel; this is somewhat puzzling, as the turkey is not known to be a Christian symbol.

Some penitents wear dresses made out of coarse cloth, others don purple; they follow the procession barefooted while burning incense or carrying candles. They sing rogations or pray the rosary. They are imbued with a priest-like gravity that inspires passersby. They start to chant or pray, and everyone follows graciously and obsequiously; the penitent may be a *mulata* and the follower in prayer or chant a noblewoman. Along with the incense women and penitents, there are also peddlers selling candles, cords, and prints. Furthermore, within the ambience of the festivity, *turrón* hawkers and vending ladies sell candy and delicacies suited to the limeño taste.

Everything is emotional, picturesque, soft, melancholic, and pleasant in the procession of the Lord of the Miracles. Ex-votos always tell a story, whether they are made of gold or silver, big or small, polished or unrefined, with numbers or words, or lacking them altogether. And the chants are like the ex-votos. And the prayers are like the chants. And the holy rosary with its fifteen mysteries and fifteen evocations also has much grace and virtue.

Two all-powerful days revive the city's tradition and faith; an image painted on an adobe wall by a black slave impresses upon us devotion and solemnity. Lima once again becomes the colonial city of tremors and rogations; Roman Catholic prayer saunters undaunted and generous through the streets; martial music sets the rhythm for a sweet and mystical parade; the legend of balconies decorated with garlands comes back to life; friars and children sing praises in the threshold or atrium of a church while the throng falls silent; loud street vendors are supplied with local sweets; electric trolleys and mundane traffic come to a stop at the street through which the litter and its followers pass; metal collection boxes chime and hand out prints or other blessed items that will free us of all evil; the naive words of catechism are heard once again; hearts are truly moved and sincere tears are shed; for an instant, the sinful city repents for all its wrongdoings in thought, word, and action; and Our Lord Jesus Christ, who died on the cross to redeem us from original sin, triumphs above all things. Amen.

Translated by Jorge Bayona

Note

1. It refers to the current area of the Rímac district.

Dance in the Cemetery

El Tiempo

On November 5, 1917, a Swiss dancer known by the artistic name of Norka Rouskaya staged a performance at the Lima cemetery and danced to the music of Chopin's "Funeral March." This truly unusual act drew plenty of criticism from conservative media and official circles, who considered it an act of desecration and a sign of moral degeneration, and led to the arrest of the dancer and her companions. Young intellectuals, however, praised Rouskaya's performance, understanding it as a manifestation of artistic beauty. The episode had been promoted by, among others, José Carlos Mariátegui, then a young bohemian journalist and soon to become a socialist and Marxist writer and thinker, who was present at the cemetery that night.

The scandal and polemic generated by Rouskaya's dance at the cemetery must be seen as symptoms of the clash of sensibilities that was taking place in Lima in the early years of the twentieth century: a powerful and quite conservative mind-set, fed by traditional Catholicism, that condemned irreverence and dissent contrasted and clashed with a new, purportedly modern sensibility among important but still reduced sectors of the population eager to experiment with new emotions, sensations, and forms of expression. Lima's Belle Époque, like that in other Latin American cities, saw contradictory reactions to modernizing trends. This excerpt reproduces an account of the cemetery dance by an unnamed eyewitness.

One of the persons who accompanied Norka Rouskaya to the Cemetery relates events in this way, establishing their true sequence, which lamentably has been distorted by a local daily newspaper in its edition of yesterday morning:

A group of writers and artists, friends of Norka Rouskaya, gathered in her quarters Friday afternoon. They conversed animatedly about various matters, childish and transcendental. Someone spoke about a nocturnal visit to a cemetery. The graceful interpreter of Chopin's "Funeral March" became enthusiastic about the idea of going in the middle of the night to the Lima Cemetery which had been praised highly to her, and she recalled that among other cemeteries which had impressed her was the Milan Cem-

University Park, with the San Marcos University building on the right, 1920. In Fabio Camacho, *Aspectos de Lima*, 3rd ed. (Lima: Editorial Incazteca, 1929). Photograph by Fabio Camacho.

etery. At that point some of those present promised Norka Rouskaya to solicit permission so that she could visit our Cemetery on Sunday night, and a journalist promised to write an account of his impressions of the event, provided there were no obstacles to carrying out the excursion.

The requirements necessary for permission having been ascertained, it was understood that it was indispensable to forward the petition to Señor Don Pedro García Irigoyen. The date of the visit could not be postponed and the proposal awoke a lively interest in the artistic temperament of Rouskaya and in her friends. One of the latter gentlemen came to see Señor García Irigoyen at 8 p.m. on Sunday, accompanied by Señor Don Juan Vargas Quintanilla, an undersecretary in the Charity Society, who gallantly accepted the duty of introducing him.

That gentlemen expressed to Señor García Irigoyen the artist's desire, supported by himself and other writers, and their hope that it could be considered since it was in no way disrespectful or unusual. Señor García Irigoyen pointed out that the Cemetery regulations ordered it to close at 6 in the afternoon. The answer was that, indeed, what was requested was an exception. So Señor García Irigoyen called the Administrator of the Cemetery, Señor Valega, on the telephone and authorized him to allow the visit that had been requested. Finally, he stated to the petitioner that, indeed, there existed on his part no difficulty in granting the request and that Señor Valega and Señor Vargas Quintanilla would accompany him.

Later the time and place was arranged with Señor Valega for meeting with Norka Rouskaya and her companions.

In the Cemetery

A few minutes before 1 in the morning Norka Rouskaya the dancer, her mother, the guests, and Señor Luis Cáceres, the first violinist in the Colón Theater's orchestra, went off to the Cemetery in automobile number 68.

The dancer and her companions entered the Cemetery through the main entrance. They went through the New Cemetery and the Old Cemetery filled with a sense of seclusion.

Chopin's March

After going around the different parts of the Old Cemetery attentively, Norka Rouskaya and her companions paused at the *gradin* of the central passage. At that moment Cáceres the violinist began to play Chopin's "Funeral March" on his violin.

Norka Rouskaya appeared at the top of the *gradin*, dressed in white, with her hair loose, and in a majestic invocative posture. Two watchmen helped by lighting the way with candles, illuminating the dancer's face.

Cáceres continued playing Chopin's marvelous religious music, to the funereal harmony of which Norka interpreted several moments of supreme pain.

The moment was of deep and fervent devotion. All those present remained silent, filled with emotion, their gaze fixed on the dancer's emotional posture. Several of the watchmen drew close to Norka, trying respectfully to assist her, doubtlessly believing that she was a penitent.

Norka descended the *gradin* and kneeled in a posture of profound sorrow. Her body doubled over her knees and her hair covered her face completely. Norka seemed like one of the doleful statues from the tombs.

Then, this being observed by Señor Valega, an end was put to this essentially artistic act, for the purpose of avoiding distortions. Norka remained prostrate on the ground for a few seconds and those present did not move, all in silent and solemn devotion.

After an instant the dancer, deeply impressed, raised herself from the ground and wept. The others present came up to her and surrounded her in silence. Señora Franciscus covered her again with a cloak of black silk and covered her hair.

At that moment the departure from the Cemetery began. With great devotion and respect, and still thrilled by Chopin's music and by the dancer's interpretation, those present passed along the paths that lead from the Old Cemetery to the exit to the street.

This is the true report of the event, as we said, by one of those present before the intervention of the police.

On the Streetcar

Martín Adán

The social and urban transformations that Lima underwent in the early decades of the twentieth century were accompanied by a change in sensibilities and modes of expressing the experience of living in a "modern" city. These changes were not unique to Lima: avant-garde art and literature spread across much of the globe. In Peru, César Vallejo and Martín Adán, each in his own way, resorted to new forms of expression, linguistic inventiveness, and oneiric images to reflect the new subjectivities emerging at that time.

In 1928 Adán (née Rafael de la Fuente Benavides, 1908–85) published a short literary gem: La casa de cartón *(literally,* The Cardboard House*). More than a novel, it was a series of vignettes in which the author offered his own account of life in Lima (more precisely, of Barranco, a southern, oceanfront district of Lima that would eventually become a sort of bohemian shelter). Filled with irony, each portrait (of characters, spaces, or episodes) reflected the unique form in which the artist experienced and projected urban life, denouncing its false morale, its hypocrisy, and its asphyxiating modernity.*

On the streetcar. Seven-thirty in the morning. A glimpse of the sun below the lowered shades. Tobacco smoke. An upright old lady. Two poorly shaven priests. Two clerks. Four typists, their laps full of notebooks. One schoolboy—me—. Another schoolboy—Ramón—. It smells like beds and disinfectant. The color of the sun poses on the windowpane from outside like a cloud of pale, translucent butterflies. A sudden excess of passengers. A sinister old lady with skin like crepe, like the crepe of her shawl, in the seat where Ramón had been. Ramón, hanging from a door—the driver's door—turns his head and his eyes in opposite directions. Ramón's glasses reflect a meek philosophical brilliance. Ramón carries the last afternoon—yesterday's—in his satchel. He is going to school, because he is late, and he is late, because he is going to school. I go with him, near him, darkly disgusted that my feet may not reach the ground. Yet, on the contrary, I can hold in my oversized hand the spines of all my textbooks. And this is a pleasure,

Trujillo Street in the Rímac district, c. 1930. The trolleys eventually ceased to exist. Photographer unknown.

almost a consolation, at my pedantic fourteen years of age. My life hangs from the grade on my first test as a crumb of bread hangs from a spider's web. Ramón suddenly reaches over a bald head to hand me an engraving that shows an angel with a constipated look on its face and a wicked twilight at the forefront. A gift from Catita: *rra, rre rri rro rru,* boarding school nonsense, pranks of nuns, and a long jump rope that creates afternoon ellipses. Catita, date of a desert palm tree . . . But the gentleman only enjoys dates from the palm trees pruned by "Mamere": the only dates the unlikely Mr. Chaplain graciously accepts come in a small basket with a perfect white silk bow on the handle: a lying butterfly. Innocent dates, Palestinian dates . . . The outskirts of Lima. An oil factory swells its greasy belly and belches like an old drunk lady: Lima.

The police, on a deep-blue sky morning, toss back and forth from uniform to uniform an infant whistle that screeches and covers its eyes with its fists. Suddenly, the shadow of the school building gets in my eyes like the night.

Note

Suspension points (. . .) in this selection appeared in the original text and do not indicate an ellipsis.

Leguía's Lima

Guillermo Rodríguez Mariátegui

Between 1919 and 1930 Peru was ruled by Augusto B. Leguía, a businessman who came to power through a coup d'état and whose administration (also known as El Oncenio), although initially promising to foster social reforms, became increasingly authoritarian and repressive. Leguía put forward an aggressive modernizing agenda that did not, however, alter the traditional socio-racial structures that kept Indigenous and other groups marginalized.

During the Oncenio, Lima went through significant urban changes, described (somewhat hyperbolically) in this excerpt from one of the many books published during and after the Oncenio to celebrate Leguía's accomplishments. He was at times called the Napoleon of America and was the subject of a widespread cult of personality. The author, an engineer and collaborator in the Leguía administration, adhered to that cult, so the text reflects both his admiration for the former president and his outrage about what he considered ingratitude toward his legacy.

Back in 1919, Lima was but a small town surrounded by miserable and insignificant hamlets. Lima's borders were, to the south, the Colón Promenade, and to the west the now-splendid Alfonso Ugarte Avenue. Back then, the latter was a pathetic, hideous boulevard flanked by dried-out willows, bereft of any kind of pavement, where wind whipped up deathly, disease-spreading clouds of dust. Miraflores, Barranco, and Chorrillos, deprived of pavement, vegetated, making do without the amenities of modern life, and hence, in incipient decadence. The picturesque hamlet of El Olivar did not exist. Infant mortality rates spelled doom for the future of the race. Hygiene was unknown among the plebeian classes. Walking through the dusty, ill-paved streets was a huge risk due to the thousands of germs that surrounded the city, quietly recruiting tenants for the cemetery. Buses, lacking appropriate roads, were impractical, despite their widespread usage among people of equal culture; an automobile excursion back then involved enduring jolts and shakes while trudging through the potholes.

It was only natural that in such a Lima—sans Plaza San Martín, sans

Carnival in Lima's Plaza Mayor, c. 1930. In *La ciudad virreinal* (Lima: Casa Baselli, c. 1930). Photographer unknown.

Veracruz House with colonial-era balconies, 1929. In Fabio Camacho, *Aspectos de Lima*, 3rd ed. (Lima: Editorial Incazteca, 1929). Photograph by Fabio Camacho.

Lima from the air, 1930. In Lieutenant George R. Johnson, *Peru from the Air*
(New York: American Geographical Society, 1930), 95, fig. 88. Courtesy of the
American Geographical Society.

Palacio de Gobierno and the Archbishop's Palace, sans the Ministry of
Public Works, sans the Pasaje Carmen, sans Leguía Avenue, devoid of new
neighborhoods, pavement, efficient transportation, hygiene, with only a
limited supply of awful drinking water, and with the local cops loitering in
intersections—banking and mercantile institutions did not consider beauti-
fying it with the luxurious and artistic buildings they later built. The concern
was that in Lima everything—even commercial transactions—languished;
a statesman of genius was required in order to stimulate the dormant energies that the shortsightedness and selfishness of other rulers did not detect,
desire, or know how to rouse. But the time came, the Statesman emerged
and the miracle happened.

Commercial workers and employees were at the boss's mercy: arbitrary
terminations, zero compensation, no insurance, wretched salaries and wages.
Officials and public employees, officers of the court, sailors, soldiers, policemen, and municipal employees all earned meager wages, barely enough to
subsist. Overseas, the country lacked the prestige it would later earn from
the sumptuous Centennial celebrations and the "Peace" (Tokyo 1922) and Se-

ville (1929) World Fairs, in which the hitherto unknown industrial, artistic, and historical qualities of Peru were disseminated. Foreign loans were but myths; no country would lend a cent to the indolent sibling of the Americas.

This depiction is no impressionist etching—it reflects the situation in as recent a year as 1919; thus, many will confirm that it is no exaggeration.

How about Callao? No chalaco[1] has forgotten the cartwheel ruts on Colón Street, which made it resemble a recently ploughed pasture, or the façades full of the dust whipped up by the ambling of exhausted, wagon-pulling beasts . . . the pickup soccer games of the stevedores . . . the road from the bleak plateau of the May 2 Monument . . . the pestilent sewer cart . . . poverty, hunger, filth, and so on . . .

Suddenly, a bright light shone through the shadows of pessimism that enshrouded the energies of the nation: the morrow of July 4 announced itself as the hope of Peru. Leguía! And like the Napoleonic eagle that flew from bell tower to bell tower, from Cannes to Paris, Leguía's tenacious spirit, inherited from his Basque forefathers, irradiated torrents of progress from the capital to the hamlet that thrust Peru forward, and whose momentum we still leisurely enjoy. We must always bear this in mind. The initial push came from this short, albeit great, man who during eleven years put all his energy to the service of the fatherland, deviating not an inch from the guiding ideal of national aggrandizement. Who cares if "National Reconstruction" was talked about afterward in pompous speeches and ridiculous billboards, when everyone is aware that those so-called rebuilders had to destroy things first in order to fancy themselves the pathetic simulacrums of a great man? Who cares if the rustics are told that our current standstill is progress? Who cares if Leguía Avenue has been rechristened as Arequipa, that the Parque de la Reserva, the Plaza San Martín, and many other public works of the Oncenio have all been reinaugurated? Who cares, in the end, about this sinister conspiracy of cowardly silence, when the Leguía Terminal was built by Leguía and no one else? Believing that silence kills is asinine; on the contrary, it elevates and exalts, while cliques and coteries attempt to conceal tangible truths in order to sully the great figures of history. General Bonaparte, surrounded by the silence of the allies, died alone in Saint Helena; France recovered his remains, and today Emperor Napoleon lies venerated at the shores of his beloved Seine and lives gloriously in the heroic soul of Frenchmen.

January 1935. Lima glitters. Sunlight boosts the joy of the citizenry. There are parties at the Hotel Bolívar, at the Country Club, at the Club Nacional, at the racetrack, in all the social centers that Leguía promoted with his administration's support and even with his own money. Cars drive speedily on asphalt. Foreign Affairs officials swagger among distinguished guests, proudly showing off the modern Lima of the "Arequipa" Avenue; the terminal . . . , the sumptuous furniture of the Palace; the official buildings; the martial, disciplined, and sharp-looking Guardia Civil and police . . . music . . . flowers . . . beautiful women. Champagne flows abundantly; popular joy manifests in gay laughter. Official ceremonies . . . Foundations are laid and abandoned . . . Commemorative inscriptions honoring all the benefactors of Lima, even those who actually weren't . . . Plaques and more plaques, plaques even on flies . . . Leguía is absent, not even a timid memory remains . . . , he never existed, Leguía was but a myth, a legend; pavement is not pavement; the new Lima is not Lima. Everything came from nothingness and was built by nobody or, what is worse, by those who today unsuccessfully try to mystify public opinion. In the afterlife, Leguía's fine-tuned sense of irony would be amused by contemplating so much misery and triviality, incomprehensible to his lofty and magnanimous soul. There is, however, a note of chivalry, of civic bravery that warms the spirit and which therefore shall never be recognized; it is the hearty attitude of the town councilmen who, in the name of the people, requested a plaque for this old fighter and principal benefactor of the city.

There it is! Among the peeling walls, sooty door- and window-frames, smashed window panes, rickety manorial door, all of which exude melancholy and abandonment, lifeless between the stylish paint jobs of the neighboring houses. There it is! It is the plaque of ingratitude with which today's administration memorializes the creator of modern Lima. The board that covers a hole in the wicket gate of the house of Pando is the tribute of the appreciation of a people . . .

Translated by Jorge Bayona

Notes

Suspension points (. . .) in this selection appeared in the original text and do not indicate an ellipsis.
1. *Chalaco* is a colloquial term used to refer to people born in Callao.

The Paperboy

Felipe Pinglo Alva

Felipe Pinglo Alva (1899–1936) was one of the most prominent and prolific composers of so-called creole music (música criolla) in Peru. Born in the traditional Barrios Altos neighborhood, where working-class people of various ethnic backgrounds lived in mostly modest and overcrowded callejones, *Pinglo Alva was nurtured by both the vibrant and festive culture of that environment and an early concern for social issues such as poverty and discrimination. He authored hundreds of songs, mostly valses or Peruvian waltzes, in which, besides addressing the themes of love and disillusion typical of the genre, he represented the tribulations, hopes, and sacrifices of the poor population of Lima: migrants, journeymen, beggars, and working women and children. His most popular composition, "El plebeyo" ("The Plebeian"), is considered a cry for social equality and an indictment of the hypocrisy of traditional values and hierarchies sanctioned by religion and education. In "The Paperboy" Pinglo Alva pays tribute to a character who reflected both the development of a print and information culture and the economic penuries that poor families and children had to face.*

Announcing the newspapers
that he sells
the paperboy strides
sweaty and quickly
running purposefully
to be one among the first
to sell the newspapers
and earn his pay.

Perhaps my eyes
have caught sight of
a boy who toils
to buy bread for his home
or it may well be

El Comercio newspaper, c. 1930. The headquarters remain in this downtown building. In E. Centurión Herrera, *El Perú en el mundo o El Perú y sus relaciones exteriores* (Bergamo, Italy: Instituto Italiano d'arti grafiche). Photographer unknown.

that I was inspired
by the humble orphan
out in the streets
without parents to love.

"El Comercio" calls
urgently the little one,
"The interesting Crónica,"
he'll say right away.
"La Nación" and *"La Prensa"*
we'll hear him cry.

Should many of us
come to discover
the cruel and sad truth
of this daily labor
in an instant
of fatal revelation,
we'd buy the newspapers
just to provide the bread.

Rascally paperboy
playful and loud
with a soul that was pure yesterday
and shall remain so forevermore;
if very early you cross
the streets of your town
you resemble a worker
heading for his job,
later when you run
announcing the newspapers
you prove to be a grown man
toiling for bread . . .
and taking your earnings
to your parents and siblings
your childlike minuteness
faces down cruelty.

Translated by Jorge Bayona

Daily Life of a Domestic Servant

Laura Miller

Domestic servitude has been, and continues to be, a central element of family, domestic, and social life in Lima. Since colonial times girls and women of African and Indigenous background have performed the typically harsh labor required from them by middle- and upper-class employers. Long workdays and physical abuse were made worse by the overwhelming presence of racism and impunity.

Social, urban, and economic transformations in Lima did not significantly alter the widespread abusive practices against domestic workers. In the following account of domestic servants in the first decades of the twentieth century in Lima, historian Laura Miller uses personal interviews conducted in 1981 and 1982 to shed light on the miseries inflicted on poor women of color by one of the most egregious forms of exploitation in the history of Peru. The history of domestic work, however, is much more complex than just a tale of suffering and oppression, and Miller highlights the ambiguities that intimacy and familiarity generate in the relationship between servants and masters.

Girl Wanted: Domestic Servants

Work as a domestic servant was often the first employment that a woman or girl found outside her home, and for highland women, it amounted to their first contact with the capital city, Lima. In 1931, 18.12 percent of the female economically active population was employed in the domestic service sector. This was perhaps the kind of employment that was most abusive and closest to slavery for women, involving endless hours and living-in.

Employment could be obtained in many ways by limeño women or girls who spoke Spanish and were probably literate. The use of acquaintances was perhaps the most frequently used.

An interviewee used this method to find work in the parties of the wealthy. One would spend the entire night moving and washing, picking up the dishes of the people who ate. They would say that they needed someone (to help out in the party) or they'd tell me "Do you

Child and black maid, 1880. Archivo Courret, Biblioteca Nacional del Perú.

know anybody?" and I'd say "I can go," "The pay is so and so," then I'd say: "OK" and they'd pay me.

A limeña could also find work through newspapers or an agency:

> You'd buy *El Comercio* or *La Prensa* and in the want ads, you'd look for the women's section. "Live-in maid," "cleaning lady," cooks, nannies, housemaids . . . Through the newspapers too, but I went to the agency, so you'd go look for work at the agency, and the agency would have a notebook that recorded: Family so and so. The agency sent me, the agency paid for my fare. They got a cut from my first paycheck, but it was only once, no more.

Highland women—39.2 percent of all maids—arrived in an unknown capital city and in many cases spoke only Quechua. They experienced greater difficulties finding work due to their obvious linguistic and cultural limitations. In most cases, they were at the mercy of a relative or godmother. According to a woman from Ancash, in her first months in Lima at age eighteen:

> I had taught myself a little Spanish, then, a woman, who was my guardian, who treated me like a daughter. So she cooked in a house. So she took me in and looked out for me. So she tells me, "Felipa" she says, "Where I am cooking the maid is leaving, so I want you to go

see the *señora* who will see if you understand what you'll be ordered. It's all right if you don't know everything, but you have to understand what they order." Then the *señora* said, "Yes, she understands," and so I worked there.

Her hours seemed endless—from the early morning to the evening. On top of this exhausting schedule, the maid did all sorts of things in her masters' home. According to an interviewee:

> I cleaned, ironed, cooked, went to the marketplace. More work, you get tired. That's why I left. At six o'clock I'd get up, prepared breakfast first because the boss had to have breakfast and go to work. I went out to get bread; after breakfast, I'd start to cook, and I did laundry at noon. On the next day I'd have to iron. I did everything. Yes, everything, and quickly. The day after ironing, I had to do laundry. As to cleaning, I had to clean the floor, wax, dust, clean the stairs. I was the only one working. Too much work. At seven p.m. the family had dinner, I'd go out with the girl, who had to be walked in the park, I came back and went to sleep, it was 9 p.m. already. I also had to wash the service dishes.

There were specialized roles in the bigger houses, such as the nanny, who took care of the children. She did not have to clean the house or cook. According to an interviewee, in this job

> one is enslaved by the children. Because in the houses where I have worked I have seen the enslavement of the maid who . . . takes care of that little girl. The baby's cradle is in her room, on one side the cradle, on the other the bed. Everything's spick and span. One had to shower and wash every day, change uniform, all your clothing had to be clean. The baby gets sick, and you have to step in for the mom, in the middle of the night, you get up, feed her medicine, very irritating.

The general consensus was that *cama afuera* (as opposed to "live-in") was much preferable, but the majority of those who worked in domestic service lived in the houses of their employers. This situation contributed to the exploitation experienced by the female domestic. According to an interviewed male:

> There were two kinds of arrangements: *cama afuera* and live-in, full-time service. Full-time live-ins do everything in the house and go out once a month. OK. But those in the other arrangement finished their things every day and went back to their homes.

Some women told me that they felt imprisoned in their employer's houses when working as live-ins. One woman said that what she found most galling about her job was her inability to go out on a daily basis:

> *No*, I have never liked it . . . staying there was like staying in jail, the despair at night, I can't, I can't, I never could.

As another woman put it:

> There isn't much freedom while working as a live-in. Sometimes you go out to the door and look at the cars, and then I'd go into my room and mend, iron, and fix my clothes, cleaning my stuff to keep my room clean, that sort of stuff. That was my life.

A woman who had come to Lima from the highlands—the most common case—could not see her family even on her day off. In one case, the only contact between a woman and her family was that she sent them cloth. Instead of visiting her family during her days off, this woman related that

> when the 15 days were up, I'd get paid a little money. She'd tell the cook "María, the *cholita* is going out. The *cholita* will go out tomorrow . . . María, go with her, take her to visit the coastline and streets, like that, make her visit." And she gave her a little money too, and me too. But I didn't go there, no I didn't. Do you know the Dos de Mayo plaza? That used to be very pretty, not like today. It was full of trees and flowers, such pretty flowers! And we'd go there, to the Dos de Mayo and we'd sit down. That was our day out. Instead of walking around, we'd sit down there, and there were ladies selling fruits. I liked sweets a lot, sweet I saw, sweet I'd buy. We would have some soda. We'd do that instead of strolling. Just sitting there, chatting. There weren't any cars and you could stroll. Afterward, I'd go back. I was a live-in. I went out after lunch. I'd serve the meal, and after that, we'd go out.

In terms of salary, work as a maid was very abusive too. They only rarely had a fixed salary; usually they only had room and board, plus a tip on her day off and, in the home of generous employers:

> During the holidays, July 28, she'd buy me a little bit of cloth. She measured me, sewed and gave me the dress as a gift, pleased with the work I did. Some people give gifts to their servants.

Besides being a tough, low- or nonpaying job with little freedom to go out, living with the employers could involve a slew of problems. The maid was subjected to her employers' control in many tangible ways, such as food. According to a woman:

They fed us miserably. The manservant had to eat eggshells. They simply did not feed me. I told my dear mother to save me some food for when I'd go out, to eat. My mother kept it for me and she fed me, because I couldn't eat there. I lasted five or six days and that was it. Was I to starve to death? How could I stay if they didn't even feed me?

But many women who worked as domestic servants were not allowed out nor did they have (as was the case with highland women) a mother in the neighborhood to bring them food.

As to their freedom to switch from one house to another, maids were severely restricted. She had to ask for permission from her employer, as exemplified by this woman:

I was asking the cook to find me a job to leave that house. Then the cook would say, "He won't let you," and I had to talk with Don Raúl. Because back then you couldn't just leave. The boss had to put up a sign saying that he needed a maid or a cook, and then the next one comes and you could go. You needed a replacement.

Maids also had to put up with the paternalism and racism of their employers on a daily basis. The common practice of calling their servants *cholita* or *negrita* not only showed a racism masked by supposedly "affectionate" terms, but also their sense of superiority over their servants. As one woman put it:

Then he'd call me, he didn't use my name, he said *"cholita."* The boss said, *"Cholita,* come," and I'd go . . . It was a term of endearment— *"Cholita." "Chola"*—now that's an insult, it's demeaning, but *"cholita"* isn't. Some people say, "That *chola"*—that is an insult. But saying *"Cholita,"* that's affection, affectionate. The lady would tell me, "Don't get angry, my child, if Señor Raúl calls you '*Cholita,'* no, that's affectionate." The wife of Señor Raúl told me so.

And according to a black woman:

The bosses called me *"Negra"* or *"Negrita,"* but with affection. You have to see how they pronounce the word, how it is said. If they say, "Go, *Negra"* (said with contempt) that is an insult.

In both cases, the women emphasized that the use of racial words was affectionate, but these words establish their subordinate position, not only due to their jobs, but also due to their race.

The interviewees showed a profound ambivalence vis-à-vis their employers. Beneath their portrayals of their bosses as kind and generous lurked the awareness of being exploited. A case that highlights the two sides of the maid-boss relationship is the story of a woman who at the beginning of her interview said that her boss

> was like my father . . . (He told me) "Hija, my child, if tomorrow or sometime in the future something happens to you, if he beats you or you suffer, come to my house" . . . and the señora said, "You are going to eat, *hija*, my child, for your health. Bananas, apples, oranges, those things you are going to eat, because it is a great thing, nutrition. But other things, no. There are other fruits that are full of worms. If you eat that, you'll get sick." She showed me all that. And that is why, when she died, I grieved.

Over the long process of interviewing this woman, however, another side of the maid-boss relationship came to light. Her boss's father believed that he had the right to use her to satisfy his sexual appetites. She said:

> I slept with the eldest daughter. She had a bed like this, and I had another bed next to the cradle for the boys. And right there, then, Señor Raúl's father scared me . . . he scared me. They say it was his habit, that's why the señora said: "Raúl, I can't have good-looking servants, because this happens. That old man is very lecherous." I was scared and had to go complain with my boss. That old man was used to living with one, having sex with the servants. They say that was his habit. And that is why the señora changed cooks almost every month. Her cooks didn't last. After that happened to me, that was it, there were no more live-ins. After lunch, the cooks went back to their homes. But I had to stay there.

This case exemplifies the intense exploitation to which the female domestic servant was subjected and showcases her lack of freedom. She had to ask for permission to go out, could not choose what she ate, and was also subject to be raped by her employers, powerless to defend herself or to switch jobs with ease. For all these reasons, domestic service was one of the jobs the interviewed women despised the most.

Translated by Jorge Bayona

Note

Suspension points (. . .) in this selection appeared in the original text and do not indicate an ellipsis.

V

Interlude

Nostalgia and Its Discontents

Since at least the second half of the nineteenth century, many writers and commentators as well as ordinary people constructed an idealized representation of old, colonial Lima as a city of beauty, charm, and prosperity. Even life among poor and working-class people, popular customs, and mischievous behavior were (re)imagined as part of a familiar, friendly urban space, one whose continuity was threatened by economic progress, urban growth, political changes, and the overall fascination with a "modern" lifestyle. Traditionalist Ricardo Palma has been singled out as one of the most effective "inventors" of the myth of the "old Lima," but he was certainly not the only one. An entire genre developed as a result of this nostalgia for times past. "La Lima antigua," "Lima de antaño," "La Lima que se va": this is just a sample of titles of the many books, pamphlets, poems, and songs written to express a sense of loss and melancholy for a Lima that, in truth, had never existed. Chabuca Granda, the most famous composer of Peruvian (criolla) music in the twentieth century, reflected in her lyrics this view of a "true Lima" that had (sadly) disappeared.

In his seminal *Lima la horrible* (1964), Peruvian writer Sebastián Salazar Bondy aimed at demolishing the myth of Lima as a "colonial Arcadia." The timing of his denunciation of this myth is very telling: the city had been radically transformed by the presence of hundreds of thousands of Andean migrants who, beginning in the 1940s, moved to Lima in larger numbers than even before seeking economic and educational opportunities. In addition, writers of the so-called 1950s generation (Oswaldo Reynoso, Enrique Congrains Martin, Julio Ramón Ribeyro, Mario Vargas Llosa, and others) had started to offer a view of the city quite different from that of nostalgic traditionalists, incorporating characters (marginal youth, urban gangs, prostitutes, beggars, and others) and social spaces (bars, brothels, urban slums) that projected a much more diverse and less idealized portrait of Lima's so-

Monument to Manco
Cápac, mythical
founder of the Inca
empire, in La Victoria
district, c. 1930. In
La ciudad virreinal
(Lima: Casa Baselli,
c. 1930). Photographer
unknown.

ciety. Almost twenty years later, historian Alberto Flores Galindo not only
challenged Salazar Bondy's claim that the past dwells over every limeño
or limeña, but also sought to identify the historical and cultural roots that
explain the generalized idea of the "decay" of old Lima.

This brief section allows the reader to capture and rethink the construction of one of the most powerful myths about Lima. Besides texts by Chabuca Granda, Salazar Bondy, and Flores Galindo, it features a short article
by acclaimed novelist Mario Vargas Llosa in which he attempts to deconstruct one of the (allegedly) defining features of Peruvian and limeño identity: *huachafería*. The behavior described, but also (and especially) the sense
of "authenticity" and at times superiority displayed by the observer, reveal
the cultural and social tensions generated by the social transformations that
Lima was undergoing.

Inauguration of the Monument to Francisco Pizarro, founder of Lima, 1935.
Photograph from the Archivo Histórico de la Municipalidad Metropolitana de
Lima, Perú.

Removing the Francisco Pizarro Monument, 2003. Photograph by Herman Schwarz.
Used by permission of the artist.

The True Lima

Chabuca Granda

One of the most recurrent topics in the imaginary of Lima's past is that of a beautiful, charming, and harmonious city where people of different backgrounds gathered to share in its striking architecture, its mixed culture, its music and food, and its traditions, many of which went back to colonial times. Whether or not people actually bought the notion of the beautiful city is hard to tell, but the cultural products stemming from this idealized view of Lima enjoyed (and continue to enjoy) wide popularity.

In popular music, the so-called Peruvian vals *(one of the key genres of the Lima-based* música criolla, *or creole music) was the genre that most popularized this romantic view of traditional Lima. Among the composers of this genre, none has projected that view with more poetic talent than Chabuca Granda (1920–83). The author of hundreds of songs, including the world-famous "La flor de la canela," Granda left unforgettable portraits of characters, scenes, and urban spaces that, in her view, represented "the true Lima," which was in the process of disappearing because of modernization, immigration, and foreign influences. Although she later embraced other, more socially and politically progressive themes, Granda will always be identified with the construction of the myth of Lima as a beautiful city of gentle and charming people. Here she refers to* la marinera, *a Peruvian coastal dance performed by couples.*

> Old city,
> becalmed illusion,
> beautiful truth,
> my inspiration:
> the ancient Lima
> that is departing.
> The majesty
> of your yesterday
> waves us goodbye
> from a balcony

concealing
its disdain.
Your cut-out silhouettes
obscure the thick wall
the decked-up little street
gives way to illusion;
shadows that conceal looks,
passionate pangs of jealousy,
outspoken flirtation
in *cajón*-driven *jaranas*.[1]
My Lady *marinera*,
how pretty is your little step
my mischievous *resbalosa*,
your chili is quite spicy;
with your figure-hugging skirt,
you reveal a little foot
sketching what they call
a most precious dance.
And such is the Lima I love,
such is the Lima I yearn for
the city of my chimeras,
of the charm I adore,
the Lady *marinera*,
who seems like a *resbalosa*,
why make her demure
if that is the true Lima?
When a rooster at sunrise
goes hoarse from a counterpoint;
when a rooster at sunrise
goes hoarse from a counterpoint;
Ay, I cried, I cried, I cried!
One awakens on the dot.

Translated by Jorge Bayona

Note

1. A *cajón* is a crate-like percussion instrument characteristic of Afro-Peruvian music; *jaranas* are musical celebrations; and *marinera* and *resbalosa* are music and dance genres popular among limeños and limeñas.

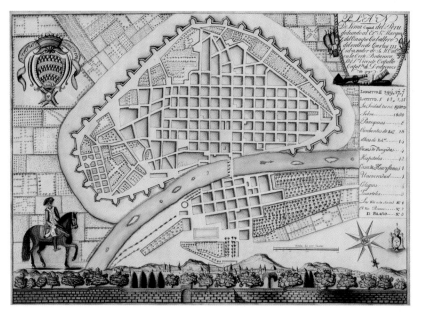

Map of Lima, 1790. Gift to Vicente Capello, army captain at a Spanish infantry camp, from the British court's ambassador to Peru. Available at https://www.historynyc .com/proddetail.asp?prod=97_l62R.

Lima's cathedral. In Theodore Auguste, *Voyage autour du monde execute pendant les annees 1836 et 1837 sur la corvette La Bonite*, Album historique, Fisquet (Paris: Arthus Bertrand, [184?]).

Cuadrilla de negros festejando el 28 de Julio de 1821

Blacks celebrating Independence Day, 1821. Peruvian and Argentine flags in background. Watercolor by Pancho Fierro. Colección Ricardo Palma, Municipalidad de Lima.

San Francisco convent, c. 1836. In Theodore Auguste, *Voyage autour du monde execute pendant les annees 1836 et 1837 sur la corvette La Bonite*, Album historique, Fisquet (Paris: Arthus Bertrand, [184?]).

Returning from the Amancaes Parade, a popular weekend entertainment for Lima residents of various social standings. Sketch by Leonce Angrand. Bibliothéque National de Paris, Cabinet des Estampes. In Léonce Angrand, *Imagen del Perú en el siglo XIX* (Lima: Editor Carlos Milla Batres, 1972), 141–42, fig. 120.

Cerro San Cristóbal, one of Lima's landmarks. Houses were painted with bright colors in the early 2000s. Photograph by Hans Kruse. Used by permission of the artist.

A mother of Andean origin crossing Abancay Avenue with her children, 2000s. Photograph by Fidel Carrillo. Courtesy of the artist.

A Lima seafood combo plate. Lima, La Muralla Restaurant, July 2015. A savory collection of popular dishes, including (from bottom, clockwise): *ceviche de conchas negras* (black shellfish ceviche), classic ceviche, *pulpo al olivo* (octopus in olive oil), avocado, and a *tiradito* (raw fish cut sashimi style with a spicy lemon sauce, a reflection of the Japanese influence on the cuisine), all surrounding a *causa*, with crab, avocado, and potato. Outside the frame are several pisco sours and *chicha morada* (made from purple corn). Photograph by Carlos Aguirre. Courtesy of the artist.

The so-called Wall of Shame, 2015. The poor live to the left, while Las Casuarinas, one of Lima's most upscale neighborhoods, is on the right. The wall was built by affluent neighbors of Las Casuarinas. Photograph by Joan Ríos. Courtesy of Oxfam.

Jirón Maynas, Barrios Altos, 2000s. Photograph by Marco Antonio Gamarra Galindo. Courtesy of the artist.

Solar El Suche in Rímac District, 2000s. Photograph by Marco Antonio Gamarra Galindo. Courtesy of the artist.

Inside a *callejón* or working-class tenement, 2000s. Photograph by Marco Antonio Gamarra Galindo. Courtesy of the artist.

Lima Gay Rights Parade, Plaza San Martin, March 7, 2015. Photograph by Jorge Alberto Chávez Reyes. Courtesy of the artist.

Lima from the air, with the Pacific Ocean and Miraflores district at the forefront and Cerro San Cristóbal in the rear. Photograph by Evelyn Merino-Reyna. Used by permission of the artist.

The Mislaid Nostalgia

Sebastián Salazar Bondy

Perhaps the most radical critique of the myth of the beautiful and enthralling "City of Kings" (what he called the "Colonial Arcadia") was penned by Peruvian poet, essayist, and playwright Sebastián Salazar Bondy in a pathbreaking book titled Lima la horrible. *In this essay, he scrutinizes nostalgic representations of Lima in the traditions written by Ricardo Palma, in valses, and especially in the imagination of limeños and limeñas, highlighting the tensions, contradictions, shortcomings, exclusionary practices, and social inequalities that have always characterized life in the Peruvian capital.*

The importance of this effort to deconstruct myths and historical lies about Lima was probably more relevant at the time of the publication of Salazar Bondy's essay: the metropolis had not yet exploded demographically and spatially to become the urban archipelago that it is today. It was easier for Lima residents, in the 1960s, to "imagine" the ancient splendor of Lima and to buy into the "mislaid nostalgia" of yesteryear Lima, for its convents and churches, its modernist buildings, and its promenades and alamedas were still part of the daily experience of a good portion of the Lima population. Salazar Bondy's radical (albeit not entirely new) departure from that pattern anticipated (and opened the way to) new approaches to understanding Lima as a complex, multifaceted, and ever-changing metropolis.

I have not learnt anything about Peru in Lima. Nothing pertaining to the public happiness of the kingdom is ever dealt with there. Lima is farther away from Peru than London is, and though no other part of Spanish America is guilty of excessive patriotism, I know not any city in which this feeling is more muted. A cold selfishness permeates everyone and that which does not concern one, concerns no one.
—Baron von Humboldt (Correspondence)

As though the future and present lacked any substance, Lima and its denizens wallow in the past. This has been imposed upon us by those who thought they were getting to the bottom of the enigma of our identity, an identity that has always eluded us, and about which—hoping to decipher our destiny—we always wonder. It has thus been established that our city is charged with *a kind of forlorn nostalgia* (Raúl Porras Barrenechea), an observation that is more valid insofar as it describes the hopelessness of the sensation rather than the sensation itself. Where do we look toward, historically? We observe the mirage of an age unfairly portrayed as idyllic, that was instead characterized by rigid castes and in which wealth and welfare were enjoyed by few and denied to the vast majority.

The colonial period, idealized as an Arcadia, has yet to meet the severe judge who will pass his scrupulous ruling. The image projected by columns, stories, and essays suggests abundance and peacefulness, overlooking the easily imagined tension between masters and servants, foreigners and natives, rich and poor, which must have set an undertone of social fragmentation. Yet nobody has any certainties about that probable class conflict, and those who suspect its existence barely have the chance to point it out. Debunking that colonial Arcadia will always be a painful and thankless task, since the masses have unwittingly absorbed more than a century's worth of pages written by nostalgic, hallucinogenic-dosed Doctors. Despite his liberal affiliation, Ricardo Palma was entrapped by its aura, and became the brightest producer of this literary opium. His formula, in his own words, was to *mix tragedy with comedy, history with lies.*

. . .

The past lives and persists in Lima, and draws you with undeniable force, wrote Porras Barrenechea quite accurately. We speak not about the survival of the monuments, which constitute concrete but impaired testimonies of yore, but that mind-set labeled—due to its regressive nature—*colonialismo* (José Carlos Mariátegui) and *perricholismo* (Luis A. Sánchez).[1] It is the veneration, to use such a term, of the palatial ostentation that limeños—be they of good stock or not—hope to achieve (as Miss Villegas did by lying on Viceroy Amat's sheets). Among us, the Court is brought back to life thanks to a lifelong semi-professional effort. Resembling *malinchismo*[2] on sweetener—due to its long-windedness and lack of passion—*perricholismo* appears to be the driving force of limeño individuals and society. Even though the House of Pizarro has been inhabited by presidents for the past 140 years, that does not preclude them from strutting around as though they were Spanish viceroys (as has been exposed by Héctor Velarde's sharp wit) or, if only for the sake of power sharing, some kind of hybrid Inca emperor.

Saying that the past attracts us is an understatement: we are alienated by it, not just because it is the source of all our popular culture, our national kitsch, and it sets the pattern of behavior to be followed by upstarts who want to become potentates, and that the present constitutes no more than a caricature of the order of the past; but because there appears to be no alternative to wearing our heads backward, mesmerized by the past and blind to the future. The past is ever present, encompassing home and school, politics and print, folklore and literature, religion and secularity. Thus, for instance, elders routinely tell colonial tales, Arcadian lies are spouted in the classroom, golden government carriages parade through the streets, and newspapers repeat, as though in a drunken tirade, the elegies of the lost Eden. We sing and dance *"valses criollos"* that still obstinately evoke *ye olde bridge and grove*, and books full of anecdotes and memories of what José Gálvez called *the Lima that slips away* are printed. Old processions march through the smoke of fried foods, and newer ones, among the same vapors, give a newer look to the age-old devotional gregariousness. And we attend—it cannot be helped!—weddings and funerals rife with useless rites and hypocritical conventionalism. The snares of colonial Arcadia befoul all our paths. Avoiding them is no easy task.

It is important to point out that, no matter how hard it tries, Lima is not Peru; but that is another matter altogether. There is no doubt, however, that it unfortunately irradiates the entire country with a nonenlightening sheen. Lima has long ceased to be—the enemies of modernity notwithstanding, even though it has blessed the nostalgic and past-obsessed with automobiles, transistors, penicillin, nylon, etc.—the quiet city marching to the rhythm of Matins and the Angelus, which so delighted the Frenchman Radiguet. It has become a metropolis where 2 million people, simply to survive, bash into each other while in a chaos of horns, loud radios, human congestion and other contemporary insanities. Two million people *abriéndose paso* ("making way for themselves"; Francisco Moncloa has underscored the selfish undertone of this colloquial expression) among the men transformed into wild animals by overcrowded underdevelopment. Civil chaos, the by-product of a half-starved urban settlement that grows like cancer, has become, thanks to the vortex of the capital, an ideal: the entire country is dazzled by it and hopes to dive into it, to help fan the flames of its spiritual holocaust. Traffic jams downtown and in the streets, the tough competition between peddlers and beggars, tired queues due to insufficient transportation, the housing crisis, bursting pipes that flood the streets, a faulty telephone network that feeds neurosis; they are all the result of improvisation and malice. These two vices shine brightly, like the eyes of a serpent, and seduce the candor of the inhabitants of the hinterlands, annihilating it with their filthy and cumbersome contradictions. The convent-like peace of Lima that was praised by nineteenth- and even early twentieth-century travelers was swept away by the demographic explosion, but the transformation was only quantitative and superficial: the urban roar has only veiled, but not suppressed, the melancholic tendency of limeños, because colonial Arcadia becomes ever more archetypical and desirable.

Therefore, a fleeting look may convince the tourist that the surviving colony has been, finally, superseded, but it's best not to trust the mistaken impression of the traveler. The past that drives us mad is in the peoples' hearts. Moreover, not only in the hearts of those who have lived here for many generations, but also in the *provinciano* and the foreigner who set their roots in Lima. Both arrive in the city full of thoughts for the future, but after a few years, the desire for progress that drew them evaporates. That original strength is substituted by the satisfaction of believing themselves assimilated into the colonial substratum of Lima society. This means that they built themselves a small private viceroyalty and that, due to it, marriage, association, connivance, or all those factors, they now partake in the power of masters and slumlords held by the Great Families. Subjected to the capital city, the rest of the country absorbs its ideals of nobility (with deeds handed out by all-powerful banks), and therefore in every city, town, or village, we witness the elaborate pantomime that is the dress rehearsal for the move to the capital.

. . .

The myth of colonial Arcadia has been successful—we have to admit— and even those of us who have, if not avoided being caught in its net, at least evaded partaking in its worship, find it difficult to completely free ourselves of being mesmerized by those fictional entities—viceroys, cardinals, oidors, *tapadas*, saints—which are all strategically placed in corners of old neighborhoods, in the catchy whims of a popular song, in a commonplace saying, in a gesture of habitual urbanity.

Translated by Jorge Bayona

Notes

Suspension points (. . .) in this selection appeared in the original text and do not indicate an ellipsis. On the epigraph see von Humboldt, "Impressions of Lima," in part II.

1. *Perricholismo* is a neologism coined by Peruvian literary critic Luis Alberto Sánchez, derived from Perricholi, the nickname of Micaela Villegas (1748–1819), the mistress of Viceroy Manuel de Amat y Juniet. It could be loosely translated as "courtism."

2. *Malinchismo* (derived from Malinche, Hernán Cortés's mistress in Mexico) refers to the attraction to things foreign that groups of natives have.

One of the Ugliest Cities in the World?

Alberto Flores Galindo

Alberto Flores Galindo (1949–90) was one of the most creative and prolific historians in twentieth-century Peru. He was also a committed public intellectual. The history of Lima was one of his many academic and political preoccupations. He authored an innovative study of Lima in the late colonial period and wrote numerous shorter pieces about its social and cultural history.

One of his targets was the romantic and idealized view of Lima as a beautiful, charming city that was ruined by a series of natural and human calamities. In this excerpt, originally published in 1985, Flores Galindo examines the notion of the lack of preservation of that "old Lima" and poses a very poignant set of interrogations: Why is that the case? Who is to be blamed? Does every resident in Lima have the same kind of nostalgia for what was lost? Flores Galindo invites us to move beyond competing intellectual and cultural representations of Lima and address the concrete historical and social factors that have shaped the history of the Peruvian capital.

Lima must be—in my opinion—one of the ugliest capital cities in the world. The downtown area lacks broad avenues and far-reaching urbanistic prospects. This could be compensated by the fortuitous human charm of the streets, but the lumping together of the most varied and conflicting architectural styles, the uneven size of its buildings, its grayness, the omnipresence of ads and billboards, its unkemptness and filth overwhelm whatever few pleasant places—such as balconies, churches, or old houses—still resist the encroachment of concrete.

The city's destruction cannot be blamed on earthquakes. According to César Pacheco Vélez, despite a handful of particularly devastating tremors, such as in 1940, its destruction was a human enterprise, executed by urbanists and engineers with the acquiescence or support from the city council or even the state itself. Thus, there is blame to go around. Some of the most moving pages in Pacheco's book[1] are devoted to describing the solitary effort of those who attempted to stall the "advance of progress" and who witnessed sadly the widening of streets or extensive demolitions prompted by new avenues (such as Tacna, Abancay, or Emancipación) and the search for straight lines and right angles. Pacheco bears witness to the destruction of what he calls "The Old Lima," but fails to ask the reasons behind it. Demolition is an obvious way of destroying the past. The owners of those abandoned houses—which end up being demolished and transformed into parking lots and subsequently into buildings—in addition to being completely indifferent toward the environs and devoid of any aesthetic sensibility, are people who, unlike César Pacheco, do not feel any connection with the past and would never admit to history being part of their personal identity. Demolition would belie Salazar Bondy's thesis that the past lords over limeños. This may be the case with readers of Ricardo Palma or creole music enthusiasts, but not with those who own the dilapidated houses, to whom a balcony or a fence are utterly meaningless. I believe that if there are those who perpetrated the destruction of the city, apart from pointing them out, we must ask about their motivations. Why has "The Old Lima" not been preserved?

Before answering that question we must first define what we mean by "The Old Lima." A thoroughly *hispanista* ideal, it does not grieve over the destruction of prehispanic *huacas* and shrines, only colonial buildings. The layout of the central streets and some temples goes back to the sixteenth and seventeenth centuries, but as a whole, colonial Lima—in recollection, remembrance, or imagination—is the city of [Viceroys] Amat and Abascal, rebuilt after the 1746 earthquake and whose borders were the *Alameda*, the *Plaza de Acho*, and the temple of *Nazarenas*. A 1.76-square-mile city that housed more than fifty thousand inhabitants. Its late eighteenth-century architecture is represented not by temples or public buildings, but by houses that have been named after the family that owned them: Torre Tagle, Riva Agüero, Osambela . . . These were mostly merchant families, with peninsular backgrounds, who had immigrated recently and whose wealth was built using ships, Pacific trade, Callao warehouses, and muleteers. These fortunes sustained a copious aristocracy, but we must be mindful of proportions: it was more powerful than the Chilean upper class, but less solid than the Mexican court (which lacked Lima's glitter). The Lima aristocracy also had to deal with the competition of a rival merchant nucleus in Buenos Aires. On the other hand, it lacked a prolonged history: Lima's merchant aristocracy was fledgling, still in formation, located halfway between Peru and Spain, and with scant connections to the domestic market. Perhaps that is why its members felt no need to build residences that would manifest their desire to last and endure. Geographic conditions led to adobe, cane, and wood being the building materials of choice, and though they were tremor-resistant, they required care and conservation. The aristocracy's fortunes were spent not on their dwellings but on paintings, carriages and, above all, silverware: the constant fear of rebellion prompted hoarding and an inclination for wealth that was easy to transport and hide.

This was the ruling class that collapsed with Independence. Its ruin was due to various circumstances: the decline of Pacific Ocean trade routes, the loss of Upper Peru, competition from Buenos Aires, the destruction of the merchant marine on the rebels' arrival, and the expense of drawn-out military campaigns. But there were choices involved as well: being or feeling Spanish, the merchants always sided with the losing Royalists and did not even understand the project of Independence. Thus, those who built "The Old Lima," the Lima of the eighteenth century, did not consider themselves part of the country but merely fleeting inhabitants of the City of Kings, which was but a corner of the Spanish Kingdom. This is the origin of the stereotype that portrays Lima as a foreign capital city with its back turned to the rest of the country, which like any other prejudice has some sprinkling of truth in it.

Translated by Jorge Bayona

Notes

Suspension points (. . .) in this selection appeared in the original text and do not indicate an ellipsis.
1. The author is referring to César Pacheco Vélez's book *Memoria y utopía de la vieja Lima* (Lima: Universidad del Pacífico, 1985), excerpted here in part I.

Understanding *Huachafería*

Mario Vargas Llosa

To identify the defining features of a given collective is never easy—actually, it can be misleading and dangerously close to creating stereotypes or engaging in absurd generalizations. Despite this, however, the temptation is always there to do so among not only writers and intellectuals but also ordinary people. Since the late nineteenth century a peculiar form of behavior came to be highlighted in Peru, especially in Lima: that of being a huachafo *or* huachafa. *The origin of the term is the subject of controversy, and its meaning is quite elusive, but there are certain aspects of* huachafería *that are more easily identifiable than others, such as bad taste or tackiness, lack of authenticity, florid language, and an appetite for upward mobility. Calling somebody* huachafo *or* huachafa *is meant to discredit his or her behavior or manners from a supposedly more "authentic," tasteful, or legitimate stand.*

Acclaimed novelist Mario Vargas Llosa sees in huachafería *an essential component of Peruvian identity. In the following article, published originally in 1983, he describes with humor and wit several cultural manifestations that allegedly shape the identity and behavior of important segments of the Peruvian population. Although* huachafería *is not exclusive of* limeños *and* limeñas, *it does help understand the social, racial, and cultural tensions that have shaped the history of Lima over the last century or so.*

Huachafería is a Peruvianism that dictionaries impoverish by defining as *tacky.* It is actually more subtle and complex, and amounts to one of Peru's contributions to the universal experience; whoever disdains or misunderstands it will remain bewildered by this country and the psychology and culture of a large number (perhaps a majority) of Peruvians. Huachafería is as much a worldview as an aesthetic; it is a way of feeling, thinking, enjoying, expressing oneself, and judging others.

Tackiness implies distortion of taste. A person is tacky when he or she unsuccessfully imitates something—sophistication or elegance—and, in so doing, debases and caricaturizes certain aesthetic paradigms. Huachafería does not pervert any models because it is a model unto itself. It does not degrade aesthetic patterns, instead it creates them, i.e., it is not an absurd copy of elegance and sophistication, but a distinct—Peruvian—form of being sophisticated and elegant.

Instead of trying to give huachafería a precise definition—a conceptual chain mail from which innumerable ingredients of that disseminated and protoplasmic entity shall inevitably escape—it would be preferable to show, with a few examples, its vastness and evanescence as well as the many areas where it manifests itself and on which it leaves its mark.

There is huachafería for aristocrats and proletarians, but its favorite milieu is among the middle class. Within the city, it is ubiquitous. In the countryside, however, it is nonexistent. A peasant is never huachafo, unless he or she lived in the city for a protracted period. In addition to its urban nature, it is antirationalist and sentimentalist. Huachafo communication between man and world is mediated by emotions and senses but not reason; ideas are decorative and superfluous, an obstacle to the free effusion of feeling. Creole waltzes are the expression par excellence of huachafería in the musical sphere, to the point that we may postulate a law that bears no exception: in order to be good, a creole waltz must be huachafo. All our great composers (from Felipe Pinglo to Chabuca Granda) perceived this, and so their lyrics—frequently esoteric from an intellectual point of view—are saturated with images of striking colors, shimmering sentimentalism, erotic malice, merry necrophilia, and other formidable rhetorical excesses that contrast, almost always, with intelligent thought. Huachafería may be brilliant but is rarely intelligent; it is intuitive, verbose, formalistic, melodic, imaginative and, above all, sentimental. A minimal dose of huachafería is required in order to understand and enjoy a creole waltz; *huaynos* are different, as they rarely are huachafos, and those that are, are usually bad.

However, it would be a mistake to deduce that there are only huachafos in the cities of the coast and that the highlands are immune from huachafería. *"Indigenismo,"* an ornamental, literary, political, and historical exploitation of a stereotypical and romantic pre-Columbian Peru, is the highland version of its equivalent coastal huachafería: *"hispanismo,"* an ornamental, literary, political, and historical exploitation of a stereotypical and romantic Spanish Peru. The feast of *Inti Raymi,* which is re-created in Cuzco every year with thousands of extras, is an intensely huachafo celebration, no more and no less than the Procession of the *Señor de los Milagros* that paints Lima purple in October (note that I write with huachafería).

Due to its nature, huachafería is more closely associated with certain tasks and activities than others, but there is no behavior or occupation that truly excludes it in essence. Speeches seduce our audiences only if they are huachafo. Politicians that steer clear of gesticulations, rhetorical curveballs, excessive metaphors and allegories, and roaring or chanting (as opposed to speaking) will rarely touch the heart of their listeners. In Peru, the phrase "a great speaker" describes someone who is luxuriant, florid, theatrical, and musical. In short, a snake charmer. Exact and natural sciences have only limited links with huachafería. Religion, on the other hand, is steeped in it constantly, while some sciences bear an irresistible huachafo disposition, such as the so-called—in huachafo fashion—"social" sciences. Are there "social scientists" or "political analysts" who do not indulge in some kind of huachafería? Perhaps, but they would make us feel swindled, much as when the bullfighter refrains from taunting the bull.

Literature may well be the best place to fully appreciate the infinite variations of huachafería, since the spoken and written word are its favorite haunts. Some poets, such as Vallejo, are huachafos at times, whereas others, such as José Santos Chocano, are huachafos all the time. Even others, such as Martín Adán, are immune from it when they write poetry but not when they write in prose. A case like prose writer Julio Ramón Ribeyro, who is never huachafo, is unusual, exceptional for a Peruvian writer. Writers like Alfredo Bryce Echenique and I are more typical. Despite our prejudices and cowardice with regard to huachafería, it sometimes appears in our work, much like an incurable secret vice. A notable example is Manuel Scorza, in whom even commas and accents appear huachafo.

A few examples of huachafería as practiced by the upper classes: challenging people to a duel, a penchant for bullfighting, owning a house in Miami, having a surname with a "de" or "y," using Anglicisms, and believing themselves to be white. Middle-class: watching telenovelas and playing them out in real life, hauling huge pots of noodles to the beach on Sunday and eating them among the waves, misspeaking Spanish and smothering everything in diminutives ("Would you like some *champancito, hermanito?*") and treating others as *"cholo"* (in the derogatory sense or not). And proletarian: wearing brilliantine, chewing gum, smoking marijuana, dancing rock and roll, and being racist.

Surrealists used to say that the prototypical surrealist act was going out to the street and shooting the first passerby. The emblematic huachafo act is that of the boxer who uses the television cameras to wave to his dear mother, who is watching him and praying for his victory; or that of the failed suicide who, upon awakening, asks for confession. There is tender huachafería (the girl who buys a pair of lacy red panties to unsettle her boyfriend) and viewpoints that, in their unexpectedness, evoke it: Marxist priests, for instance. Huachafería offers a tool to observe (and organize) the world and its culture. Argentina and India (judging by their movies) seem closer to it than Finland. The Greeks were huachafos, while the Spartans were not; among religions, Catholicism wins the gold medal. The most huachafo of the great painters was Rubens, the most huachafo century was the eighteenth, and, among monuments, nothing is as huachafo as the Sacre Coeur and the Valley of the Fallen.

Should I finish this article with a huachafo phrase? I have written these modest lines free from intellectual arrogance, armed solely with a most human warmth and sincerity, thinking about these wonderful creatures of God, my fellow beings: mankind!

Translated by Jorge Bayona

VI

The Many Limas (1940–)

In 1940 Lima had approximately five hundred thousand inhabitants. By 2010, the number was close to 8 million. Today some estimates put that figure at 10 million. This explosive demographic growth has been overwhelmingly the result of successive waves of migration from the interior, especially from Andean areas, rather than immigration. Urban growth, on the other hand, has not been the result of any centralized planning and has presented a real challenge—both for state or municipal authorities and for scholars trying to make sense of it. Terms like "invasion," "flooding," "anomia," or "conquest" have been used to describe the process, but they capture the process from an external point of view, not from the perspective of the migrants themselves.

It is undeniable that this urban growth presented a number of challenges —for those already living in Lima as well as for those newly arrived. Employment, housing, and educational opportunities were not always available; public services were lacking; cultural and social tensions were inevitable. We should also consider the various (and quite serious) economic and political crises that Peru has confronted over the last few decades, which increased the difficulty in addressing the challenges of rapid urban growth. Infrastructure and housing projects have been pursued from time to time to address demographic growth. These include initiatives favoring mostly the middle classes, such as the construction of *unidades vecinales* during the administration of Manuel A. Odría (1948–56), the San Felipe residential complex by President Fernando Belaúnde Terry (1963–68), the Paseo de la República highway (popularly known as the Zanjón or Big Pit) that connected Lima's downtown with the southern districts of Miraflores and Barranco by Lima mayor Luis Bedoya Reyes (1964–69), and the Torres de Limatambo and Torres de San Borja during Belaúnde Terry's second term (1980–85). Socialist mayor Alfonso Barrantes (1984–87) sought to improve infrastructure in Lima's poorest neighborhoods. These were all important initiatives, but they fell short of solving the problems that affected large sectors of the Lima population.

Shoppers and strollers at Jirón de la Unión, 1970s. Colección Lima Antigua, Archivo Vladimir Velásquez. Unknown photographer. Courtesy of Vladimir Velásquez.

Shoeshine boys, Plaza San Martín, 1970s. Colección Lima Antigua, Archivo Vladimir Velásquez. Unknown photographer. Courtesy of Vladimir Velásquez.

Plaza San Martín, 1980s. Colección Lima Antigua, Archivo Vladimir Velásquez. Unknown photographer. Courtesy of Vladimir Velásquez.

But focusing only on the negative effects of these transformations would be a great mistake. The influx of peoples of different backgrounds (social, ethnic, cultural) contributed, to a large degree, to breaking the (real or imagined) barriers that oligarchic Peru had imposed on those belonging to the most vulnerable sectors of society. Lima has become a much more plural, diverse, and even democratic society. Moreover, migrants brought with them energy, creativity, and ambition, elements that have had an enormous impact on the economic and social transformation of Lima. Some of the most dynamic areas of the economy in twenty-first-century Lima are in the hands of first- or second-generation migrants. Informality has been and continues to be part of this dynamic, with its pros and cons. If Lima today is a vibrant and dynamic city, it is because of a combination of factors, including the vigorous participation of those who used to be called "new limeños."

The transformation of Lima into an archipelago of multiple human and physical spaces occurred gradually, and this section attempts to offer a series of textual and visual vignettes that help us reconstruct that process. It contains descriptions of various neighborhoods in the 1950s and 1960s, the gradual occupation and expansion of urban space by scores of migrant peoples, the obstacles they faced in their attempt to assimilate into the social and human fabric of the city, the effects of various political processes (military rule, political violence, and others) over life in Lima, the persistence of various forms of discrimination and segregation, and the cultural mechanisms used both to cope with adversity and to create new spaces for the manifestation of values and traditions not always welcomed by those who claim "ownership" of the city. Andean migrants, street sellers, *chicha* and *huayno* performers, members of locally grown religious organizations, and radical political activists appear alongside aristocratic families, middle-class and privileged adolescents, and successful restaurant entrepreneurs.

The materials presented in this section will help the reader and traveler understand (and prepare for) the seemingly disparate and yet closely connected social, cultural, and ethnic groups that make up the city of Lima, their different patterns of socialization, their dreams and expectations, and the diverse ways in which all of them live the experience of being limeños.

Malambo, a Black Neighborhood

Hugo Marquina Ríos

Although slavery was abolished in 1854, its long shadow shaped life in Lima for decades and centuries. Blacks continued to be treated as second-class citizens and to perform low-status jobs. Access to education and opportunities was limited. At the same time, blacks were able to forge a relatively autonomous culture, which emerged and survived in neighborhoods and residential areas that came to be perceived as "black," such as the Rímac or La Victoria districts.

One distinctly "black" area of the city was Malambo, a neighborhood in the present-day Rímac district that grew out of the slave marketplace that had operated there since colonial times. Although it always contained a racially mixed population, by the early twentieth century it was considered a black (and thus allegedly dangerous) area. Many prominent criminals (such as Carita and Tirifilo, the protagonists of a famous knife duel in 1915) in fact came out of Malambo, but it was also the site of working-class activism and mobilization as well as a popular festive culture.

In this ethnographic account, Hugo Marquina Ríos offers a glimpse into the daily life of Lima's black population in the mid-twentieth century, focusing on both the challenges they confronted (poverty, overcrowding) and the ways in which they coped with marginalization and adversity.

Lima is a city of tradition and legend. The humblest of its corners preserves a memory or tells a story. Not in vain did arrogant viceroys and constables, parsimonious bishops and frugal Inquisitors walk its streets, nor *tapadas* showcase their mischievous and cajoling grace in the atrium of the church or the seigniorial balcony.

The district of Rímac is located "under the bridge" on the opposite bank of its namesake river. It is crisscrossed by numerous streets and alleys, the chief of which was the densely populated artery known as Francisco Pizarro Avenue.

Between 1850 and 1900, the main streets around this avenue comprised the neighborhood of "Malambo." It being a malaria-infested area, the Spanish planted a number of "Anti-Fever" trees known as "Malambos," hence its name.

. . .

Malambo Street was wide and well designed, and seemed even wider and more spacious due to the squat houses surrounding it and the almost complete absence of automobiles. It used to be one of the most beautiful streets of Old Lima before falling into disrepair, at which point there was nothing pleasant in that street, and one would go there only out of necessity. Its sidewalks, despite their width, forced people to walk in columns of one. Its trees were uneven, with scraps of paper, fruit peelings, pieces of string, shards of bottles, etc., piled under them.

Orchards and gardens surrounded the avenue. It was canalized in vain, however, since the ditches that watered the trees and crossed the *callejones* and orchards frequently became clogged. The resulting mud was left exposed to fetid vaporization and fermentation, making for a noxious atmosphere that was breathed in by hundreds of beings every hour. Children, along with skinny, hairy, hungry dogs, played joyously in its midst. Groups of criminals would gather under the cover of darkness to plan their robberies or other misdeeds. An endless supply of ruffians picked fights with any outsider they came upon.

. . .

Malambo was composed of callejones, shops, and empty lots, and was inhabited almost exclusively by blacks and mulattoes. There were a few inns, shabby and traditional, with rooms for guests and stables for the beasts. . . . Most of its black inhabitants were peons from haciendas, water carriers, cabbies, wet nurses, washwomen, and street vendors. . . .

Jovial black and *zamba* (African and indigenous mix) women watched over tables in the doorways of the callejones, thus helping their husbands make ends meet for their numerous offspring. Bowls with reasonably priced food were displayed on these tables. The *zambas* served their customers, who sat on benches and ate with their hands.

These blacks from Malambo lack any devotion other than that of Señor de los Milagros—which compelled them to parade over the bridge of La Palma on the way to Nazarenas in their traditional purple robes and white shoes, while hatless and displaying their curls—and one or two famous nativity scenes in the neighborhood.

. . .

This neighborhood's *jaranas* were renowned in Old Lima, and included guitar, *cajón*, and singing, the latter faithfully representing the spirit of these people, who were good people after all. Firewater, wine, beer, and some-

Emoliente vendor, Caquetá Street, 1992. *Emoliente* is the piping hot herbal mix famed for its curing abilities. Archivo fotográfico TAFOS/PUCP. Código: TA406-4. Photograph by Daniel Pajuelo. Used by permission of Archivo TAFOS.

times *guarapo* and *chinchiví* were lavished upon the guests; *chicha* was not popular, however, as the blacks argued it was a drink for *cholos*. The latter were rarely invited due to their cold, reserved, ungrateful character, which did not mesh well with that of the blacks, who are ardent, frank, talkative, and loyal to their masters. Venerable grandmothers who could no longer dance the *marinera* sat by the only table, or on a quilt-covered bed, and reminisced about the past, back when they excelled at dances such as the *escobilleo* and the *zandunga* and were experts with the handkerchief.

As previously mentioned, these neighborhoods—Malambo Street principally—are surrounded by callejones. Long ago, a *callejón* was property that belonged to a rich person who could not care less about the hundreds of people that inhabited them. "He has many callejones" was often said about great landlords; "he already has a little callejón," was said about an employee who had saved up enough to become the owner of one. A callejón guaranteed a steady income.

A callejón was a long and narrow alley that could extend anywhere from half to the full length of a block. It was arranged in two rows of little rooms, beyond which lay a half-roofed small pen, under whose shade they placed a stove and a grindstone. The tenant in the first room next to the doorway was the wife of a cobbler and she supervised the neighborhood. At the

Women at Señor de los Milagros procession, 1980s. Archivo fotográfico TAFOS/PUCP.
Código: SM66-37. Photograph by Walter Silvera. Used by permission of Archivo TAFOS.

far end of the callejón, a sink with a garbage pail below and a minuscule
trickle of water took care of the drinking, cooking, and cleaning needs of
the five hundred or more inhabitants of the callejón; that pail also collected
their daytime and nighttime discharges; this is where they washed their
pots, dishes, chamber pots, and other unmentionable pestilences. The far
end of the callejón also featured a small altar with the image of some saint
or a missionary cross, with the callejón often being named after the Saint.
Large callejones split in the interior and were known as *solares*. Some *solares*
were inhabited by an entire village, and several even included small grocery
stores for the convenience of the neighborhood.

Each room was populated by an entire family: grandmother, mother-in-
law, husband and wife, plus offspring from the eldest to the youngest, some
still breastfeeding, others crawling, some learning to stand, and five out of
six were involved in all sorts of mischief, playing with marbles or horsing
around constantly; there were also roosters, chickens, guinea pigs, and a
skeletal and shivery cat that languished next to the fireplace.

Behind closed doors, life was hard. One son went down with measles, another with smallpox, the wife suffered from tuberculosis, and the husband
was a drunkard; moans, weeping, blasphemy, humid days, a waterless faucet were constants. In public, the doorwoman would rudely insult a tenant,
or godmothers would quarrel among each other, or youths would fight each

other to exhaustion. The washwomen in the open area where they hung their clothes gossiped about their bosses.

When the festivity of the callejón's religious image came about, the door-woman would rouse the inhabitants and collect funds among all the tenants, with which she purchased rockets, candles, and colorful paper that were hung on the walls in strands or links. The rest of the funds were spent on *pisco*, a lot of *pisco* and fireworks, all to pray the Saint's novena and get drunk for several days.

Translated by Jorge Bayona

The Original Mansion

Alfredo Bryce Echenique

Lima's elites—first Spanish, later a mix of families of various European backgrounds —have always lived luxurious and even ostentatious lives in big mansions and surrounded by all kinds of foreign ornaments: paintings, statues, lamps, china, and so on. Elite families also sought comfort and reinforced their status by employing a number of domestic servants—male and female slaves, free blacks, or Indians, referred to as cholos *and* cholas—*a practice that has continued into the twenty-first century.*

Since at least the 1920s, the influence of U.S. culture (language, sports, social clubs, schools, and so forth) has been much more visible among Peruvian elites: they have given their offspring English names, for instance, or taken vacations in Miami or Disneyland.

Acclaimed Peruvian novelist Alfredo Bryce Echenique captured the daily life of the affluent classes of Lima through the eyes of a child, Julius (Bryce's alter ego). With humor not devoid of social criticism he offered a portrait of a class that would soon enter into a period of crisis and decline, but whose mentality and social practices would survive in the behavior of other groups of upper-class limeños.

Julius was born in a mansion on Salaverry Avenue, directly across from the old San Felipe Hippodrome. The mansion had carriage houses, gardens, a swimming pool, and a small orchard into which two-year-old Julius would wander and then be found later, his back turned, perhaps bending over a flower. The mansion had servants' quarters that were like a blemish on the most beautiful face. There was even a carriage that your great-grandfather used, Julius, when he was President of the Republic, be careful, don't touch! it's covered with cobwebs, and turning away from his mother, who was lovely, Julius tried to reach the door handle. The carriage and the servants' quarters always held a strange fascination for Julius, that fascination of "don't touch, honey, don't go around there, darling." By then his father had already died.

The Belle Époque–era Colón Theatre after its closing, at a time when Lima's downtown area had experienced a severe decline (1980s). Photograph by Herman Schwarz. Used by permission of the artist.

Famous painter Víctor Humareda in Barranco, 1970s. Barranco, a traditional artistic district, is now a bohemian hot spot. Photograph by Herman Schwarz. Used by permission of the artist.

Julius was a year and a half old at the time. For some months he just walked about the mansion, wandering off by himself whenever possible. Secretly he would head for the servants' quarters of the mansion that, as we've said, were like a blemish on a most beautiful face, a pity, really, but he still did not dare to go there. What is certain is that when his father was dying of cancer, everything in Versailles revolved around the dying man's bedroom: only his children were not supposed to see him. Julius was an exception because he was too young to comprehend fear but young enough to appear just when least expected, wearing silk pajamas, turning his back to the drowsy nurse and watching his father die, that is, he watched how an elegant, rich, handsome man dies. And Julius has never forgotten that night—three o'clock in the morning, a lit candle in offering to Santa Rosa, the nurse knitting to ward off sleep—when his father opened an eye and said to him poor thing, and by the time the nurse ran out to call for his mother, who was lovely and cried every night in an adjoining bedroom—if anything, to get a bit of rest—it was all over.

Daddy died when the last of Julius' siblings, who were always asking when he would return from his trip, stopped asking; when Mommy stopped crying and went out one night; when the visitors, who had entered quietly and walked straight to the darkest room of the mansion (the architect had thought of everything), stopped coming; when the servants recovered their normal tone of voice; and when someone turned on the radio one day, Daddy had died.

No one could keep Julius from practically living in the carriage that had belonged to his great-grandfather/president. He would spend the entire day in it, sitting on the worn blue velvet, once gold-trimmed seats, shooting at the butlers and maids who always tumbled down dead by the carriage, soiling their smocks that the Señora had ordered them to buy in pairs so that they would not appear worn when they fell dead each time Julius took to riddling them with bullets from the carriage. No one prevented him from spending all day long in the carriage, but when it would get dark at about six o'clock, a young maid would come looking for him, one that his mother, who was lovely, called the beautiful Chola, probably a descendant of some noble Indian, an Inca for all we know.

The Chola, who could well have been a descendant of an Inca, would lift Julius from the carriage, press him firmly against her probably marvelous breasts beneath her uniform, and not let go until they reached the bathroom in the mansion, the one that was reserved for the younger children and now belonged exclusively to Julius. Often the Chola stumbled over the butlers or the gardener who lay dead around the carriage so that Julius, Jesse James, or Gary Cooper, depending on the occasion, could depart happily for his bath.

And there in the bathroom, two years after his father's death, his mother had begun to say good-bye. She always found him with his back to her, standing naked in front of the tub, pee pee exposed, but she never saw it, as he contemplated the rising tide in that enormous, porcelainlike, baby-blue tub, which was full of swans, geese, and ducks. His mother would call him darling, but he never turned around, so she would kiss him on the nape of his neck and leave very lovely, while the beautiful Chola assumed the most uncomfortable postures in order to stick her elbow in the water and test the temperature without falling in what could have been a swimming pool in Beverly Hills.

And about six-thirty every afternoon, the beautiful Chola took hold of Julius by his underarms, raised him up and eased him little by little into the water. Seeming to genuflect, the swans, geese, and ducks bobbed up and down happily in the warm, clean water. He took them by the neck and gently pushed them along and away from his body, while the beautiful Chola, armed with soapy washcloths and perfumed baby soap, began to scrub gently—ever so gently and lovingly—his chest, shoulders, back, arms, and legs. Julius looked up smiling at her, always asking the same questions, such as: "And where are you from?" and he listened attentively as she would tell him about Puquio, a village of mud houses near Nasca, on the way up to the mountains. She would tell him stories about the mayor or sometimes about medicine men, but she always laughed as if she no longer believed in those things; besides, it had been a long time since she had been up there. Julius looked at her attentively and waited for her to finish talking so he could ask another question, and another, and another. And it was like that every afternoon while his two brothers and one sister finished their homework downstairs and got ready for dinner.

Those days, his brothers and sister already ate in the formal dining room of the mansion, which was an immense room replete with mirrors where the beautiful Chola would carry Julius, first, to give his father a sleepy kiss and then, after a long walk to the other end of the table, the last little kiss of the day to his mother, who always smelled heavenly. But that was when he was just a few months old, not now when he would go to the main dining room by himself and spend time contemplating a huge silver tea service, looking like a cathedral dome on an immense china cabinet that his great-grandfather/president had acquired in Brussels. Without luck, Julius tried over and over to reach that enticing polished teapot. One day, though, he did seize it; but he couldn't manage to stay on his tippy-toes nor let go of it in time, whereupon the teapot came crashing down with a big noise, denting its lovely shape and crushing his foot; it was, simply put, a complete catastrophe. From that point forward Julius never again wanted to have anything to do with silver tea sets in formal dining rooms in mansions. Along with the tea service and mirrors, the dining room had glass-paneled cabinets, Persian rugs, porcelain china, and the tea set that President Sánchez Cerro gave us the week before he was assassinated. That's where his brother and sister ate now.

Only Julius ate in the children's dining room, which was now referred to as Julius's dining room. It was like Disneyland: the four walls were covered with Donald Duck, Little Red Riding Hood, Mickey Mouse, Tarzan, Cheetah, Jane, properly dressed, naturally, Superman, probably beating up Dracula, Popeye, and a very, very skinny Olive Oil. The backs of the chairs were rabbits laughing raucously, the legs were carrots, and the tabletop where Julius ate was shouldered by four little Indians who were not related to the Indians that the beautiful Chola from Puquio would tell him about while she bathed him in Beverly Hills. Oh! and besides, there was a swing with a tiny seat when it was time for the bit about eat your soup little Julius (at times, even more endearingly, cutie pie Julie), a little spoonful for your Mommy, another for little Cindy, another for your brother Bobby and so on, but never one for your Daddy because he had died of cancer. Sometimes his mother would pass by the room while they swung Julius and fed his soup to him, and she would hear those horrendous nicknames the servants used that were ruining her children's real names. "Really, I don't know why we ever gave them such attractive names," she said. "To hear them say Cindy instead of Cinthia, Julito instead of Julius, what a crime!" she said to someone on the telephone, though Julius hardly ever heard her because, what with finishing his soup and that swinging motion embracing him like a somniferous plant, he would get drowsy, ready for the beautiful Chola to pick him up and carry him off to bed.

Diego Ferré and Miraflores

Mario Vargas Llosa

Miraflores is a district located south of Lima's downtown, alongside the Pacific Ocean. It began to acquire a distinct identity in the early twentieth century, as well-to-do families started to build homes so that they could be closer to Lima's beaches. For a few decades it was the quintessential bourgeois district of Lima, with comfortable and beautiful private homes occupied by professionals and businessmen, well-maintained yards, and nice social clubs. There were also more mesocratic areas in Miraflores, where aspiring employees and other poorer families owned or rented more modest homes. Diego Ferré Street was in one of those areas.

Around the middle of the twentieth century, several areas of Miraflores still had the feel of a barrio (neighborhood), that is, a space (physical and cultural) in which neighbors knew each other, their children played together, and a sense of belonging nurtured a sense of identity among them.

Peruvian novelist Mario Vargas Llosa lived in Diego Ferré Street in the 1940s and 1950s, and his experiences were transferred, in fictionalized form, to several of his novels, including Time of the Hero, *a novel about adolescents and masculinity from which the following excerpt has been taken.*

Diego Ferré Street was less than three hundred yards long, and a stranger to it would have thought it was an alley with a dead end. In fact, if you looked down it from the corner of Larco Avenue, where it began, you could see a two-story house closing off the other end two blocks away, with a small garden protected by a green railing. At a distance, that house seemed to end Diego Ferré, but actually it stood on a narrow cross street, Porta. Two other parallel streets, Colón and Ocharán, cut across Diego Ferré between Porta and Larco Avenue. After crossing Diego Ferré they ended abruptly two hundred yards to the east at the Malecón de la Reserva, the serpentine that enclosed the Miraflores district with a belt of red brick. It marked the farthest limits of the city, for it was built along the edge of the cliffs, above the clean, gray, noisy waters of the Bay of Lima.

There were half a dozen blocks between Larco Avenue, the Malecón and

Tragedy at the National Stadium. More than three hundred fans died in a stampede trying to escape from police tear gas, May 24, 1964. Photographer unknown. Courtesy of Aldo Panfichi.

Porta Street: about a hundred houses, two or three grocery stores, a drug-store, a soft-drink stand, a shoe repair shop half hidden between a garage and a projecting wall, and a walled lot that was used as a private laundry. The cross streets had trees along both sides of the pavement, but not Diego Ferré. The neighborhood lacked a name. When the boys organized a soccer team to compete in the annual tournament held by the Terrazas Club, they named their team "The Happy Neighborhood." But when the tournament was over, the name was not used any longer. Also, the crime reporters used "The Happy Neighborhood" to describe the long row of houses called Huat-ica de la Victoria, the street of the whores, which made it somewhat embar-rassing. So the boys simply called it the neighborhood, and when somebody asked them which one, they distinguished it from the other neighborhoods in Miraflores, like the 28th of July or Reducto or Francia Street or Alcan-fores, by saying: "The Diego Ferré."

Alberto's house was the third house on the second block of Diego Ferré, on the left-hand side. The first time he saw it was at night, when almost all the furniture from the previous house, in San Isidro, had already been moved. It seemed to him a lot larger than the other one, and it had two ob-vious advantages: his bedroom was further away from that of his parents, and since there was an inner garden they would probably let him have a dog. But the new house would also have its disadvantages. Every morning, the father of one of his friends had driven both of them from San Isidro to La Salle Academy. From now on he would have to take the express, get off at Wilson Avenue, then walk at least ten blocks to Arica Avenue, since La Salle, although it was a very respectable school, was located in the heart of the Breña district, with its *zambos* and its swarm of workers. He would have to get up earlier, and leave right after breakfast. And there had been a bookstore across from his house in San Isidro, where the owner had let him read the *Penecas* and *Billiken* behind the counter, and had even lent them to him for a day, warning him not to crease them or get them dirty. Also, the moving would deprive him of an exciting pastime: that of going up onto the roof to watch what went on in the Nájar family's yard. When the weather was good they ate breakfast in the garden under bright-colored umbrellas, and played tennis, and gave dances at night, and when they gave dances he could spy on the couples who sneaked off to the tennis court to neck.

On the day they moved he got up early and went to school in a good mood. When he got out he went straight to the new house. He got off the express at Salazar Park—he still had not learned the name of that grassy esplanade hung out over the sea—and walked along Diego Ferré, which was deserted at that hour. At home he found his mother threatening to fire the maid if she started spending her time with the neighboring cooks and chauffeurs the way she had in San Isidro. After lunch his father said, "I've got to leave. It's very important business." His mother cried, "You're lying again! How can you look me in the face?" And then, with the help of the servant and the maid, she began a very careful inspection to make sure that nothing had been lost or damaged by the movers. Alberto went up to his room and stretched out on the bed, aimlessly doodling on the jackets of his books. A little later he heard the voices of boys through the open window. The voices stopped, there was only the sound of a kick and the hum and slap of a ball as it bounced against the door. Then the voices again. He got up from the bed and looked out. One of the boys wore a flaming shirt, red and yellow stripes, and the other wore a white silk shirt with the buttons open. The former was taller, with blond hair, and his voice and looks and gestures were insolent. The other was short and stocky, with curly black hair, and he was extremely quick. The blond boy was playing goalkeeper in the door of a garage. The dark boy kicked the brand-new soccer ball at him, shouting, "Stop this one, Pluto!" Pluto, with a dramatic grimace, wiped his forehead and his nose with the back of his hand and pretended to fling himself at the ball, and if he stopped a goal he laughed uproariously. "You're an old lady, Tico, I could block your kicks with my little finger." Tico stopped the ball skillfully with his foot, set it, measured the distance, and kicked, and almost every kick was a goal. "Butterfingers!" he jeered. "Fairy! Look out for this next one. It's going to the right, and boom!" At first Alberto watched them without much interest, and apparently they had not noticed him. But little by little he began to study their styles, and when Tico kicked a goal or Pluto intercepted the ball, he nodded without smiling, like a veteran fan. Then he began to pay attention to the jokes the two boys were making. He reacted the way they did, and at times the players gave signs that they knew he was watching: they turned their heads toward him as if they had appointed him as their referee. Soon there was a close exchange of looks, smiles and nods. Suddenly Pluto kicked one of Tico's shots and the ball went sailing down the street. Tico ran after it. Pluto looked up at Alberto.

"Hi," he said. "Hi," Alberto said.

Pluto had his hands in his pockets. He was jumping up and down in the same place, like one of the professionals loosening up before a game.

"Are you going to live here?" Pluto asked him. "Yes. We moved in today."

Pluto nodded. Tico had come back. He was holding the ball on his shoulder with one hand. He looked up at Alberto. They smiled. Pluto turned to Tico.

"He just moved in. He's going to live here." "Oh?" Tico said.

"Do you fellows live here?" Alberto asked.

"He lives on Diego Ferré," Pluto said. "In the first block. I live around the corner, on Ocharán."

"One more for the neighborhood," Tico said.

"They call me Pluto. And this here is Tico. He's an old lady when it comes to soccer."

"Is your father a good guy?" Tico asked. "I guess so," Alberto said. "Why?"

"They keep running us off the street," Pluto said. "They take our ball away. They won't let us play here."

Tico began to bounce the ball up and down as if it were a basketball.

"Come on out," Pluto said. "We'll kick some goals till the others come. Then we'll get up a game."

"Okay," Alberto said. "But I'd better tell you I'm not very good."

The Banquet

Julio Ramón Ribeyro

Julio Ramón Ribeyro (1929–94), considered one of the most important writers in twentieth-century Peru, published numerous novels and short story volumes. He is mostly remembered and praised for the rather dark and murky portraits he offered of lower-class people in Lima: poor, hard-working, ordinary people who struggled to find a voice in a city that seemed forever divided between the very rich and the extremely poor. In Ribeyro's stories failure, frustration, and boredom are constantly invoked to draw a collective portrait of a group that no other Peruvian writer had ever taken seriously. His characters include obscure state employees, recent migrants from the interior, retired and solitary elders, and individuals struggling to find love and success in the midst of a rapidly changing society.

The Lima that appears in Ribeyro's stories is one in which nothing extremely terrible or extremely uplifting ever happens, and whenever there are dreams and illusions, they reflect the misguided aspirations of frequently unscrupulous individuals who, nonetheless, almost always end up failing. In "The Banquet," a short story written in 1958, Ribeyro added another element to his gloomy portrait of limeño society: the corrupt and unpredictable nature of the political system.

Don Fernando Pasamano had begun planning in great detail this major social event two months ahead of time. For starters, his home would have to be completely renovated. Since it was a big, outdated structure, several partitions had to be torn down, windows enlarged, wooden floors replaced, and all the walls repainted. These changes made others necessary, of course— like when someone buys himself a new pair of shoes and decides that, if he's to show them off properly, he'll also need new socks, shirt, suit, and finally new underwear—Don Fernando felt compelled to replace all the furniture, from the living room consoles to a bench for the pantry. Then came new rugs, lamps, draperies, and paintings to cover the walls that somehow seemed larger and bleaker after the paint job. Finally, he would have to add a garden, since an outdoor concert was listed on the program. In just fifteen days a team of Japanese gardeners transformed what used to be a wild orchard into a fabulous rococo garden with sculptured cypress trees, intricate little pathways, a pond stocked with goldfish, a grotto for the goddesses, and a quaint wooden bridge spanning an imaginary brook.

The most troublesome detail, however, was deciding on a menu. Like the majority of Peruvians born and raised in the nation's interior, Don Fernando and his wife had only attended large, rural feasts where *chicha*,[1] the traditional drink, was mixed with whiskey and where hands, instead of forks, were used to finish off portions of the guinea pigs that were always devoured at these events. That's why Don Fernando was confused about what to serve at the banquet he would be giving in the president's honor. All his relatives who gathered to discuss this matter only added to the confusion. Finally, Don Fernando decided to poll Lima's finest hotels and restaurants. That's how he found out about presidential cuisine and, of course, the fine wines that he would need to have flown in from the southern vineyards.

When all these details had been worked out, Don Fernando nervously had to confess that he had invested his entire fortune in this banquet which would involve 150 guests, forty waiters, two orchestras, a ballet troupe, and a movie cameraman. But in the long run, the expense would seem insignificant compared to the enormous benefits he would receive by hosting the elaborate affair.

"With an ambassadorship in Europe and railroad service to my property in the sierra we will rebuild our fortune in the wink of an eye," he would tell his wife. "That's all I ask. I'm a modest man."

"We don't even know if the president will come," his wife replied.

The fact is, Don Fernando had not yet invited him. He felt fairly certain for now that he would accept his invitation, reassuring himself with the knowledge that he, after all, was kin to the president, one of those rather vague kinships so common in mountainous regions, and yet, somewhat difficult to prove for fear of discovering in the process some evidence of illegitimacy. Nevertheless, just to be sure, he found the opportunity—during his first visit to the presidential palace—to take the president aside and humbly tell him about the invitation.

"I'd be delighted," the president responded. "It's a wonderful idea. I have a busy schedule right now, but I'll confirm my acceptance in writing a little later."

Don Fernando began waiting impatiently for the letter of confirmation. Meanwhile, he ordered some last-minute touches that gave his mansion an unnatural, garish look, like a palace decorated for a masquerade ball. His last idea was to commission a portrait of the president—painted by an artist from a photograph—which he made sure was hung in a prominent place in the house.

The letter arrived at the end of four weeks and transformed Don Fernando's growing doubts into overwhelming joy. It was a day to celebrate, and just the beginning! Before going to bed, he and his wife stepped out on the balcony to view the luminous garden and savor the pastoral vision that would be forever etched in their memory. The countryside, however, almost seemed to exceed the bounds of ordinary sensibility. Everywhere Don Fernando looked he saw himself in a cutaway coat, smoking cigars against a background that looked a lot like travel posters, where monuments of Europe's four most important cities all begin to look the same. In a distant corner of this vision, he could see a train returning from the tropics with a cargo of gold. He saw himself surrounded by sensuality itself in the form of an elusive, transparent feminine figure with long, sexy legs, a regal hat, and Tahitian eyes—not at all like his wife.

On the day of the banquet the first to arrive were the presidential body-guards. From five o'clock that afternoon they posted themselves outside, making every effort to hide their identity. This was impossible, of course, because their hats and exaggerated look of indifference gave them away, especially the disgusting display of shiftiness often acquired by detectives, spies, and others who perform undercover operations.

Later, cars started to arrive from which emerged heads of state, members of parliament, diplomats, businessmen, and intellectuals. An attendant received them at the gate, an usher announced them, a valet took their wraps, and Don Fernando, in the middle of the hall, shook their hands while murmuring polite words of welcome appropriate for such an occasion.

When all the local bourgeoisie and people from the tenement houses had crowded in front of the mansion and were getting caught up in the luster of this unexpected event, the president arrived. Escorted by his military aides, he walked immediately into the house, causing Don Fernando, who was suddenly moved by the intimacy of that moment, to lose control and forget protocol; he threw his arms around the chief executive with such fervor that he crushed one of the epaulets on his uniform.

The guests, who were scattered throughout the spacious rooms, hall-ways, terraces, and gardens, discreetly consumed—between exchanges of wit and humor—all forty cases of whiskey. Later they gravitated toward the tables and chairs that had been reserved for them and made themselves comfortable. The largest table, decorated with orchids, was occupied by the president and other important figures who began to eat and boisterously talk while, in one corner of the hall, the orchestra was making a futile attempt to perform a Viennese waltz.

Halfway through the meal, after white wine from the Rhine region had been raised in a toast and the Mediterranean red wine began to fill the glasses, a round of eloquent speeches began. The oratory broke off, however, when the pheasant was served and didn't start up again until after the champagne was poured; the final eulogies trickled on through the after-dinner coffee and finally evaporated altogether, much like the cognac.

Through all this Don Fernando couldn't help anxiously noting that the banquet was in full swing, charting its own course, and that he had not yet had a chance to bend the president's ear. Although he had again botched the rules of protocol by seating himself to the left of the honored guest during dinner, he never found the right moment to bring up his plans. What's more, after dinner, people began to get up and form drowsy, listless little groups among which he, as host, felt obligated to circulate and enliven with liqueurs, cigars, mindless chatter, and a friendly pat on the back.

Finally, around midnight, when one of the cabinet members, thoroughly plastered, left in a great deal of commotion, Don Fernando managed to steer the president toward the parlor. There, seated on one of the sofas that in the Versailles court someone probably used to propose to a princess or break an alliance, Don Fernando made his modest requests known.

"No problem at all," responded the president. "In fact, right this minute there's a vacancy in the Rome Embassy. When I meet with my cabinet tomorrow I'll recommend you for the post. Better yet, I'll appoint you. And about the railroad, I can tell you that a congressional commission has been discussing that project for months. Day after tomorrow I'll call a meeting of its members, and you come too so you can help them work out something to your liking."

An hour later the president left after repeating the promises he had made earlier. His cabinet members, the congress, and so on, followed behind him in the customary order.

At two o'clock in the morning there were a few audacious ciphers still hanging around the bar hoping that another bottle of champagne would be uncorked, or that they would have a chance to pilfer a silver ashtray when no one was looking. It was three o'clock when Don Fernando and his wife finally had the house to themselves. They stayed up until dawn sharing impressions and making ambitious plans for the future amid the remaining bits and pieces of their fabulous feast. At last they fell asleep, knowing that never before had someone from Lima thrown a more lavish bash nor so shrewdly risked everything he owned in order to pull it off.

At noon the following day Don Fernando was awakened by his wife's scream. As he opened his eyes he saw her rush into the bedroom with a newspaper spread between her hands. Snatching it from her, he read the headlines, and without uttering a word, he fell back onto the bed in a dead faint. Just before daybreak, a government official, taking advantage of the reception, had led a coup d'état, forcing the president to resign.

Note

1. *Chicha* is an alcoholic drink made from maize.

A *Serrano* Family in Lima

Richard W. Patch

Massive migration from the highlands in the 1940s and 1950s changed the cultural and social landscape of Lima. These migrants created shantytowns (barriadas), but some of them also found housing in the poorer areas of the city, like La Victoria, El Porvenir, and other traditional working-class districts. Life was much harder than the newly arrived migrants had expected. Jobs were not easy to find, linguistic and cultural assimilation proved to be difficult, and racial discrimination kept them on the margins of mainstream society. With few exceptions, Lima was not the city of opportunities that they had dreamed of.

Anthropologist Richard Patch conducted extensive fieldwork among migrant families in the 1960s, trying to understand their strategies of survival and the obstacles they faced in Lima. La Parada, a conglomerate of wholesale retail shops, informal restaurants, and precarious housing units, was the location for some of Patch's research. The following portrait of the Punarejo family, based on interviews with its members, takes us into the daily struggles of Lima's migrant population.

Don Valentín Punarejo was a *serrano* and a man of parts in Puno, a department and town in southern Peru on the altiplano (twelve thousand feet above sea level) bordering on Lake Titicaca. He was forty-six years old, married to Doña Lorenza Rodríguez de Punarejo, and the father of two daughters, Susana, eleven years old, and Consuelo, two. He owned land, a house with the customary crosses on the rooftree, and a herd of twenty cattle. His was a worldly life in that high outpost of desolation. With twenty-five thousand soles (nearly a thousand dollars) of capital, he would buy cattle from his neighbors and acquaintances in Puno, giving them only a first payment down and paying the rest after he had sold the cattle. He would drive the cattle to Lima in fifteen or sixteen days and sell them there at the slaughterhouse of the Terminal.[1] In the Terminal, Don Valentín would buy clothes for himself and his family, absorb something of the wonders of Lima, and then return to Puno via a two-and-a-half-day bus trip.

On return, he was a center of attraction in Puno, completing payment

Children inside a *callejón*, 1970s. Archivo fotográfico TAFOS/PUCP. Código: GA09-3. Photograph by Daniel Pajuelo. Used by permission of Archivo TAFOS.

for the cattle, distributing small items he had been commissioned to buy in Lima, and dedicating himself to his wheat fields as the rains closed in, turning the roads to mud and making the rivers unfordable. For the family's provision there were sheep, hogs, chickens, ducks, and guinea pigs. Since Don Valentín belonged as much to the Spanish-speaking town of Puno as to the society of neighbors around his land, he was able to play something of the *gran señor*. Sometimes he would put on a suit and boots, and in bad weather he would wear a raincoat and a rainhat—all marks of the "White Man." Often he would invite his neighbors in to eat and to drink the distillations he had brought from the Terminal, telling them all the while of his travels and the splendors of Lima.

Perhaps he convinced himself of the city's advantages; at any rate he decided that since he spent so much time in Lima it would be better to move his family there. In El Porvenir, a section of Lima near the Terminal, he rented a house with four rooms and a closetlike kitchen for four hundred soles (less than sixteen dollars) a month, and returning to Puno, he put him-

Street vendors in the Gamarra garment district, now one of the most economically dynamic areas of Lima. Colección Lima Antigua, Archivo Vladimir Velásquez. Unknown photographer. Courtesy of Vladimir Velásquez.

self and his family aboard the train for the coast. Doña Lorenza and the children—having lived all their lives at twelve thousand feet—became ill during the trip, and even more so when they reached sea level. It was a reverse *soroche*, the illness produced by altitudinal change. (Usually the victims of *soroche* are coast-dwellers traveling into the sierra). It took a week for Doña Lorenza to recover after arriving at the house in El Porvenir.

Don Valentín had not foreseen the problems of residence in Lima. The language of the family was Aymara, and his wife spoke practically no Spanish. The elder daughter, Susana, spoke Spanish, learned in the school of Puno which she had attended through the third grade. Thus, at first the father and daughter had to do the marketing, and when the mother did go out of the house she was frightened by the automobiles, trucks, and buses, and would lose herself in the unfamiliar streets. Don Valentín, going in search of her, would usually find her in a police station where she had been taken for safe-keeping.

After a month, affairs began to go more smoothly. Susana could go alone to buy a few things at a Chinese store nearby, and her mother learned her way about the Terminal, where she would go every two or three days to buy food. Fortunately, she found stalls operated by persons from Puno with whom she could speak Aymara.

With the family somewhat settled, Don Valentín went back to Puno to buy cattle. There he discovered that his old friends and associates would no longer accept just part-payment for their animals. They wanted the full amount because they felt that, having moved away from Puno, he could now decide at any time that he would not return. Forced to raise more money, Don Valentín gave a five-year mortgage on his house and land to a member of the town council for five thousand soles (less than two hundred dollars). Driving twenty-five head of cattle, he returned to Lima and sold them at the Terminal.

The children of the Terminal had begun to shout insults at Doña Lorenza and Susana, calling them *serranas* and *cholas*. *Serrana* is a colorless word, referring only to origins in the sierra, but *chola* is an emotion-charged word, carrying the meaning of a low background in the sierra.[2] It is as near a racial insult as appears in the interviews in the Terminal, where great care is used to make racial allusions matter-of-fact and without grounds for injured feelings. Don Valentín took the only possible course in telling his family to ignore the taunts. Living in their own house rather than in a collective dwelling, the family was able to insulate itself more than most of the sierra people of the Terminal.

Doña Lorenza suffered in the new surroundings—from the "heat" of Lima, which is certainly warmer than the high-altitude chill of Puno, from separation from her family and friends and the animals she had cared for in her old home, and even from the frustration of radio programs in a language which she could not understand. Susana, on the contrary, enjoyed her new life. She no longer had to carry water in buckets from the well, she did not have to search for stove wood, and she did not have to take the sheep out to pasture. The house in El Porvenir had a kerosene stove, electric lights, and running water. Other needs could be satisfied by going a short distance to the Terminal or to the Chinese store on the corner. She enjoyed going to the Coliseo Nacional (a large tent where the management provided sierra residents in Lima with hours-long performances of sierra music and dances), to the movies, and to the street carnivals. She was even more enthusiastic about her enrollment in school, where she was placed in the fourth grade.

Once again Don Valentín traveled to Puno to buy the cattle which supported his family. But drought had come to southern Peru, many cattle had already been sold or slaughtered, and he was unable to buy the livestock he sought. In his search he was forced much farther afield, to Huancavelica and to Cerro de Pasco, and there he found prices higher because of the large number of cattle buyers already combing these parts of the sierra. He returned from Huancavelica to the Terminal with only fourteen head of cattle on which he could expect to make little profit.

Arriving home, he found that his wife was pregnant—yet working harder than before because Susana was in school and of little help to her. Susana, in turn, recounted that her first days in school had been hard—her schoolmates had called her *serrana* and accused her of "smelling of llamas" (an animal seen by coastal Peruvians only in zoos). She continued, however, to take her father's advice to ignore the insults, and indeed her schoolmates soon tired of the game. (The *criollo* interviewer commented that "*criolla* girls in the schools are not so bad with *serranas* as *criollo* boys are with *serranos*. The girls only put on airs and do not accept the *serranas* into their group of friends. The *criollo* boys, on the other hand, continually abuse the *serranos*, insulting them and hitting them.")

Eight months after having moved his family from Puno to Lima the father faced up to impending economic disaster. He was spending all of his income on immediate family needs; his wife was about to have another child; and summer rains made the roads to Puno impossible for driving cattle. In the hope of holding on to some of his capital, Don Valentín asked several of the men from Puno whom he knew in the Terminal how he might best invest his hard-earned soles. One of them was eager to return to Puno after having spent a hard and unprofitable time in the Terminal, where he had a licensed retail stall stocked with small food staples. This man spoke to Don Valentín with all the eloquence he could summon, painting his little business in brilliant colors ("que le pintó pajaritos"). Don Valentín had ten thousand soles (nearly four hundred dollars), and he paid this for the transfer, the license, and the stock. The seller, well pleased, left immediately for Puno, while the unfortunate buyer soon found that the stall had practically no business—yet required his presence from six o'clock in the morning until four in the afternoon. Susana had to bring his lunch to him there.

Don Valentín also found that the buyers of his wares in the Terminal were mainly women who preferred to buy from women. Doña Lorenza, however, had entered the maternity clinic to give birth to a son, and afterward she was hospitalized. During this time Don Valentín attempted to sell his recently acquired stall, but he was offered only half the price he had paid for it. At last he opened the stall for only moments each day, closing it afterward and cursing the *paisano* who had sold it to him and used the money to leave the Terminal forever. His wife's hospitalization and convalescence took the rest of the family's money.

Once again Don Valentín went to Puno, this time to try to recover the house and land which he had mortgaged for five years to the member of the town council. His former friend, now living in Don Valentín's house, pointed to the fields which had been newly planted and refused to return the house and land, offering instead to purchase them outright. Don Valentín, desperate for money, accepted an additional 5,000 soles and the promise of 7,000 soles more in a year (a total purchase price of 17,000 soles [$634] for the homestead, trees, gardens, and small fields). He was soon to feel that by this act he had sealed his fate.

In Lima, Susana was on vacation from school, helping both her mother in the house and her father at the market stall. Don Valentín decided that he could no longer afford the rent for the house and moved the family into a single room on the Avenida Humboldt in the Terminal itself. The following year Doña Lorenza bore yet another son in this room—making a total of six members of the family—and the two younger children were often ill. Economic catastrophe became imminent.

Although she made no complaint, Doña Lorenza was quite aware of the situation, and she decided to prepare and serve meals for the people of the Terminal. Don Valentín was opposed at first, but she convinced him, and he bought a small cart, a primus stove, and other small necessities for the business. Thus, the mother became the main source of the family's income. By this time, Consuelo was four years old and taking care of her baby brothers, and Susana had finished grade school and entered an "academy for accounting." Don Valentín was proud of his eldest daughter, believing that Susana would become an accountant and the pride of the family. She was thirteen years old. (The *criollo* interviewer conceded that she had become *acriollada*—that is, nearly indistinguishable from the coastal-born *criollas*.) Thus more years passed—Susana sometimes helping in the stall, her father sometimes hiring himself out as a peon in construction work.

Jobs were few. With Susana helping in the stall, Don Valentín bought a hawker's cart for himself and began to sell potatoes in the market of La Victoria (a section of Lima). This venture came rapidly to an end, however, because he was only an itinerant street seller (*ambulante*) with no license, and the police had begun a campaign against such vendors. He returned with his cart to the Terminal, where he tried to sell fruit. By this time Susana was eighteen years old and very *criolla* ("ya era bien criolla"). A coastal-born *criollo* was courting her. The second daughter, Consuelo, was ten, in the fourth grade, and intelligent. The young brothers, however, were "a pair of demons" who stayed in the family's room only to sleep. "They paid no attention to their mother, who had aged greatly. The father took little interest in correcting them, saying they had been born on the coast and were destined to have no respect for their family."

Susana married her *criollo* suitor. The bridegroom, Ángel Castañeda, was the watchman for a walled enclosure stacked high with thousands of empty

wooden boxes. There he made his living repairing the boxes used for transporting fruit and vegetables, and for his watchman's duties he had free use
of two rooms in the enclosure. Water had to be fetched from a spigot in the
street, and as the spigot served the majority of persons in the Terminal who
were without running water, and since it was turned off in the afternoons,
two metal drums were filled each morning and kept in the rooms. Light
was provided by kerosene lamps and candles. Here her bridegroom brought
Susana and all her family to live.

Susana and Ángel remained for eight months in these surroundings, but
life there was difficult for them, being two among eight people in the two
small rooms. The two young boys, for instance, would rob Ángel of money
whenever they had a chance, although Ángel said nothing to his mother-in-
law, who had again become ill. Finally, Ángel turned over his watchman's
job to Don Valentín and, with three thousand soles which he had saved,
made a down payment on Don Valentín's market stall. He made some further monthly payments of five hundred soles each. Then the two young
people went to live in La Victoria. Susana continues to work in the stall at
the Terminal, which she has stocked and where she is popular with many
buyers.

Consuelo studies in the afternoon and spends the rest of the time helping
her mother. The two young sons, Felipe and Alfredo, shine shoes and sell
newspapers, using the money for their own needs. They publicly make fun
of their father and mother, calling them *serranos* and trying to disassociate
themselves as much as possible from the family. They spend their time as
"fruit birds,"[3] reading the comic books which are rented out in the Terminal and looking at television. (Several entrepreneurs of the Terminal have
bought television sets and easily pay for them by putting them in rooms
which are filled with people in the evening, each paying from fifty centavos
to one sol to watch the programs.) Occasionally the father must retrieve the
boys from the police station, where they have been held because they are
minors and there are too many such aspiring hoodlums in the Terminal for
the police to handle.

Don Valentín is now fifty-eight years old and looks much older. He has
not perfected his Spanish; Aymara obviously remains his first tongue. He
has reverted to sierra-style clothing, except for his shirts and a hat, which
are like those used by the *criollos*. He no longer wears boots or even shoes,
having gone back to the cheap sandals made from truck tires. His teeth are
green from chewing coca and his main pleasure is to drink with a friend.
His clothes are no longer kept clean. He makes no attempt to attract customers to his fruit cart, saying, "If they want to buy they will, if they don't

they won't." If a comment is made in his vicinity which he does not quite hear, he interprets it as a criticism of his drunkenness. His friend is an old man who spends his days carrying sacks of produce on his back. Every time he passes Don Valentín's fruit cart he asks, "Brother, shall we go have a little one?" ("Compadre, vamos a echarnos unita?") Don Valentín invariably accepts and goes off, leaving his cart in the care of the vendor beside him.

Notes

1. "El Terminal" and "La Parada" were colloquial ways of referring to the large market-place built in the 1940s in La Victoria district. The terms refer to the fact that it was the last stop for trucks coming from the interior with produce to be sold in Lima.

2. Actually, *serrana* does carry a racial connotation in the Peruvian context. It is almost synonymous with "Indian."

3. In Spanish, *pájaros fruteros* or petty thieves.

The Great March of Villa El Salvador

José María Salcedo

Poor, working-class, and migrant populations in Lima have always faced a seri-ous problem with regard to adequate housing: in the colonial and early republican periods they lived mostly in callejones. *With the arrival of tens of thousands of migrants in the 1940s and beyond, the demand for housing increased dramatically. For many, the only solution was to occupy empty private or state-owned land. Land invasions began in the 1950s and (not before violent confrontations with police forces) eventually led to the formation of* barriadas, *urban shantytowns composed of precarious homes generally occupied by poor families. In the 1970s, during the period of military nationalism, land occupations took a step forward in the midst of important social reforms implemented by the Velasco Alvarado regime and the increasing organization of grassroots movements.*

The largest slum born out of this process was Villa El Salvador, which would eventually reach the status of a district. What made Villa El Salvador special was its communal form of organization, which is described in this piece written in 1985 by José María Salcedo, a Spanish-born journalist who has spent more than six de-cades of his life in Peru chronicling social and political change.

Epifanio Pérez Yarasca is one of the historical founders of Villa El Salvador. He makes a living driving a heroic blue Volkswagen cab with an overheat-ing engine. His home is already entirely made of brick and mortar. His two-story home is—rather aptly—accessed through a huge garage that doubles as an old-fashioned gateway.

Today, don Epifanio sweats profusely in his white sleeveless shirt while the faucets of his house run dry. "The water mains in the district," he points out, "aren't as wide as they should be. Many community leaders have been venal, making money off our needs and hopes."

In 1970 he was the director of La Nacional, a school for drivers. "Señor Pérez," a student asked him, "are you a homeowner? I ask because there is about to be an invasion." Epifanio had an epiphany: his landlord had sued him, and he was surely going to be evicted.

Urban dwellers, many of them migrants from the interior, invading vacant land to build housing units, 1970s. Archivo Fundación José Matos Mar. Photograph by José Matos Mar. Courtesy of the artist.

Lower-class women's protest, including a group from Villa El Salvador, 1980s. Archivo fotográfico TAFOS/PUCP. Código: VES26-35. Photograph by Donatilda Gamarra. Used by permission of Archivo TAFOS.

"And so, on February 19, 1970, we invaded Ollantay, across from Pamplona Alta. They beat us with sticks, forcing us to pull down our poles and straw mats, but we were promised lots within three months. We labeled and numbered all our straw mats and poles. But the months went by and we were forced to act again."

Thus, they founded the Asociación Padres de Familia Pro Vivienda Propia, Delfín Lévano [The Delfín Lévano Association of Parents for Homeowning]. Delfín Lévano's name had prevailed over other contenders: Carlos Barba, Nicolás Gutarra, and Adalberto Fonkén.[1]

A worker's name for a worker's day: a few minutes before May Day, 1971, Pamplona was invaded. Things were better organized this time: every family had straw mats, whistles, and Peruvian flags. Epifanio can still recall the shrill pierce of those nocturnal whistles in the silence of the desert.

The rest of the story is well known: the death of Edilberto Ramos, the incarceration of Monsignor Bambarén, the Velasco administration's quick intervention to grant lots, the dismissal of hot-headed General Artola, and the massive and immediate exodus of thousands upon thousands of the disenfranchised toward the desert already referred to as Villa El Salvador. Villa El Salvador, now Lima's newest district, has issues in common with all the *pueblos jóvenes* [new towns, a euphemism for shantytowns] of the great city—it even has above-average unemployment rates—but it boasts sixty thousand students enrolled in twenty-eight educational centers, a hundred preschools, many communal centers, and half a million planted trees. From the heights of the famous Lomo de Corvina hill, the green blotches appear to have almost won the battle against the desolate desert. But above it all, Villa El Salvador has a system of neighborhood organization that sets it apart from other popular neighborhoods, *barriadas*, shantytowns, or whichever term one may wish to use.

It all began as a utopian dream.

The settlement consolidated itself between May 1971 and November 1973. The Office for Pueblos Jóvenes, and then SINAMOS,[2] pushed forward the lot-plotting and registration processes while the heavy machinery of the Ministry of Housing made their first treads in the desert. Those may have been Juan Velasco Alvarado's finest days. Why not aim for a model city, a laboratory of sorts that would herald a new and beautiful society?

A blackboard under a temperature-magnifying corrugated iron roof displayed the master plan of what might become a socialist island surrounded by a sea of voracious capitalism, as drawn by Antonio-Chango-Aragón. Utopian or not, nowadays nobody doubts that the efforts of people like Aragón were decisive in laying the foundations of the social organization of Villa El

Salvador, as were those of parish Christian groups that assembled the youth and encouraged the Salvadorean passion for education.

Anyhow, in July 1973, an assembly of residents green-lit a project that would make the efforts of the most ambitious city planner pale in comparison: a grouping of manufacturing, commercial, and service-related enterprises, along with an industrial park, and complemented by a block-based local organization concerned with political, educational, and services issues. In sum: a new local power, a self-governing city that questioned the received wisdom of individual title deeds.

And thus was born CUAVES: Comunidad Urbana Autogestionaria de Villa El Salvador [Self-Governing Urban Community of Villa El Salvador]. It was to be bankrolled by a communal fund, with contributions from all residents.

But reality was, is, and shall be harsh.

How would they escape from the economic laws of "the rest" of society? In the early days they were definitely favored by the political environment promoted by the more progressive sectors of the Velasco regime, but the new military administration[3] grew less interested in their self-government, prompting CUAVES to recast itself into a more militant entity, similar to those of other *pueblos jóvenes* of Lima: battling perennially for electricity, running water, sewers, and transportation.

That being as it may, Roger Muro, one of CUAVES's current leaders, says: "Although there may no longer be a project of economic or entrepreneurial self-government, we must redeem its social and organizational dimensions."

Although it has known moments of decline, leadership squabbles, and undemocratic manipulations in the recent past, CUAVES is the sole organization of the people of Villa El Salvador.

Every two years, everyone over eighteen votes to elect a block committee. After that, an assembly comprising the inhabitants of an entire residential grouping—spanning sixteen blocks—nominates a central board. Finally, their representatives elect a Communal Executive Committee, which is the highest executive organ of CUAVES.

Their main areas of concern are health, education, manufacturing, services, and commerce, all of which are controlled by an Oversight Council and a General Assembly. With the recent creation of the district of Villa El Salvador—on June 1, 1983—CUAVES appears to enter a new and more dynamic era. By means of a written commitment—endorsed by Municipal Decree 001—CUAVES and city hall committed to a holistic development project, establishing Mixed Working Commissions with representation from CUAVES and municipal power.

Translated by Jorge Bayona

Notes

1. These are the names of prominent labor leaders in early twentieth-century Peru.

2. SINAMOS was a government-controlled organism to mobilize labor, peasant, and other sectors of the population behind the military government led by General Velasco (1968–75). Its acronym means National System of Support toward Social Mobilization.

3. Velasco was ousted in August 1975 by more conservative sectors of the Peruvian armed forces.

Being Young and Radical
(Late 1960s and 1970s)

Maruja Martínez

The 1960s was a decade of radical political and social change, mobilization, and utopian dreams in large portions of the globe. The impact of the Cuban Revolution, the decolonization process in Africa, the anti–Vietnam War protests, Che Guevara's call for revolution, and the civil rights movement in the United States were felt throughout the world. In Peru, a new generation of young people joined the ranks of multiple, divided, and often dogmatic and minuscule leftist political movements. They were Maoists, Trotskyists, Castroists, or Guevaristas; they all felt the call for action to end social injustice and imperial domination.

The process of reform started in October 1968 by the Peruvian armed forces left the radicalized youth—but not only them—perplexed: the guardians of the old order had become agents of social change.

Maruja Martínez (1947–2000), a leftist militant and cultural activist, was part of the generation that dreamed with socialist utopias, embraced (and were confused by) gender role and generational changes, suffered from state repression, and eventually dealt with disillusion and frustration. Her vivid account of those years of love, rage, and militancy illuminates the political and cultural environment in which thousands of young students and workers lived in the 1960s and 1970s, when revolutionary change seemed so close and ultimately proved to be so elusive and unattainable.

April 9, 1970. A great rally of miners is coming to Lima to insist that the military dictatorship respect their union and resolve their list of demands. The leaders of the CGTP [Confederación General de Trabajadores del Perú— General Confederation of Peruvian Workers] are—as expected—claiming that it is actually a rally in support of the "Peruvian Revolution" [the Velasco Alvarado military regime]. The majority of people attending the public meeting are miners themselves. There are also many students, and I am glad to realize that, despite classes having only just begun, the entire FRES

[Frente Revolucionario Estudiantil or Student Revolutionary Front] is present. I am no longer in college, so I see them from afar. I am in the party delegation, along with my cell. The Dos de Mayo plaza is packed full of miners.

1957. My mother says that this is where the miners live, they who produce a good part of the country's wealth. I pay attention through the train's windows. How can people live in these glacial, lifeless expanses? They sometimes cover themselves in plastic to protect themselves from the rain and cold. And the children run around in the grimy soil or by the shore of some dead lagoons, unable to fish or roll around in the grass, like us.[1]

This is La Oroya, she tells us. Look at that chimney: it is the tallest in the world. And that fence, mommy? My mother lowers her eyes, ashamed. The Americans live on one side, the miners on the other, and you need company permission to cross it. And she changes the subject. Misunderstanding, we insist. That's how it is, girls. But some Peruvians live among the Americans, and she mentions some acquaintances of ours. They can even go into the Inca Club, she says, remembering with some relief.

I have heard that the government has removed the fence, and I have trouble believing it: for so long it was a symbol of Yankee power and of the clear division between those who command and those who obey. Has that already changed in La Oroya? I do not quite understand the ideology of the military dictatorship.

And now, on seeing those thousands of miners here in Lima, I feel closer to their sun-toasted skins. I show off a bit in front of my comrades: as soon as I hear the miners speak I immediately—almost without realizing it—switch my accent to that of the people from the Mantaro Valley, my Mantaro Valley.

I make my way among the throngs to reach our delegation's designated spot. I suddenly feel a hand fondling me lasciviously. I immediately slap the face of a miner who despite the blow does not cease to look at me and grin. I feel a mix of rage and despondency as I keep on walking. I am supposed to overlook these things. I am ashamed to speak of them. It would amount to tarnishing the day's heroics.

I finally make it there and I stand next to Modesta, my cell leader. Some strange movements interrupt my thoughts. Suddenly I notice some fingers pointing at us from the far end. I had already recognized some students from the university, both Christian-Democrats and militants of the Communist Party, combing the rally with some obvious agents of the investigative police. But I didn't think that we would be involved, us harmless students, still wet behind their ears, attending a workers' rally. I have not even finished my thought when I feel my arms being grappled from behind.

"Let me go, *carajo!*" I shout. But when a small crowd has gathered, I hear, "They're *apristas*, they're *apristas*, and they've come here to act as provoca- teurs!" I cannot believe my ears. Accused of being an *aprista!*[2] The miners who had surrounded the incident withdraw because they feel it is not their problem. I am taken to El Sexto security jail in a patrol car, and on entering I see a line with many people from my class in the social sciences depart- ment and comrades from La Molina University. I am a little relieved, for once there I find out that the one targeted had been Modesta, who was "tall and wore glasses" like me. They order me to sit in a couch with another girl, whom I believe is from La Cantuta University. *Are you a virgin?* She asks me. And before I can reply, she goes on: *Thankfully I'm not and I could hide some notes that I had. That's fortunate*, I say, although I am still bewildered.

We were released at 11 p.m., and they only wrote down our names. But the next day, students from the social sciences department are fired up. They are waiting for me, as I am to address the assembly: among the stu- dents, I saw the person who had been singling us out. The meeting is about to begin, but they summon me, as something is going on behind the first- year classroom: Cucho has removed his leather jacket—his trademark that makes him recognizable anywhere—and his glasses. *I'll take him*, he says, *I'll kill him.* I'm touched by the gesture, but am also amused by his short- sighted expectation that the informer should be brought to him for punish- ment. *Let's go to the assembly*, we persuade him, *we'll see about that later.* The assembly begins, and I'm given the floor. *I saw Pibe*, I say, *and people from the Communist Party.* Manano wants to defend them, rallying the Christian- Democrats and looking for support. But even the professors are incensed. Many ask for their expulsion and nobody stands up for them. I only want the truth to be known. I also have to set straight that my voice is breaking from all the shouting at the rally and the cold of El Sexto, not from being close to tears, like many remark compassionately. On leaving the assembly, Manano shouts that this is slander. But nobody pays any attention. Plus, Christian-Democrat support for the government makes them even guiltier.

We exit the assembly with satisfaction: it is a political victory against the military dictatorship and against the remnants of Christian-Democrats in the university. FRES is bolstered.

We gather in the Centro Federado [Student Union] once more. Up till last year we spent more time there than at classroom lectures, which I found increasingly uninteresting. It is just that so many things have happened in the last two years, since we started studying social sciences.

And not just in Peru. I am reminded of the day that Carmen María came, in August 1968. She had experienced May 1968 in Paris and had much to tell us. We decide to meet in the Centro Federado so that she could tell us her experiences. A kind of collective hypnosis sets in. She is a very pretty girl, thin and with very short hair, and without a drop of makeup. Corduroy pants, a dark sweater with a very high neck, wool socks within a pair of shoes sporting thick medium-height heels. There is a certain charm in that mix of elegance and lack of care for appearances, a certain Bohème that I'd never seen up close. (By the guys' stares, I suspect their interests lay not entirely in the Parisian political experience.) *Thousands of students*, she says, *and workers, and even policemen. Sartre and Simone were there too. Red and black flags. Marx and Mao, Trotsky and Lenin. And Che, Che was in the hearts and shouts of everyone.* It is a peculiar revolution. In the end, I think that even those who went solely to gaze upon Carmen María are entranced by the story. And only after a brief moment of silence do the questions start to overwhelm our new codisciple.

How exciting. And I don't miss the Beatles as much as when I first arrived in Lima. I have instead grown used to another kind of music: Paco Ibáñez, Los Chalchaleros, Jorge Cafrune. Atahualpa Yupanqui, and Violeta Parra captivate me.

Or recordings like Che's farewell speech, which was ingrained in my memory almost from the first time I heard it: "Fidel, I remember that day, when we met at Maria Antonia's house . . . Other lands require the aid of my modest efforts . . . I can do that which is forbidden to you . . . I resign my commission as *comandante* . . ." When I heard it for the first time, I could not hold back the tears. Fidel Castro's voice sounds moved in this small record I received as a gift. The applauding crowd is moved too, and mourns Che. His face in that photograph in an old issue of *Life* is burned into my mind's eye, lying there in a remote Bolivian locale. His face, his sweet eyes open, his mouth that is almost smiling. Like a dead but happy Christ. For he died fighting for what he believed in.

Hardly two months have gone by since Carmen María's arrival that we hear that in Mexico students have also taken to the streets, with shouts and flowers. But Mexico is not Paris, and on October 2, hundreds of them died in Tlatelolco Square. I have mixed feelings, because other tanks, Soviet tanks, have gone into Czechoslovakia, threatening the people who faced them with flowers. In the meantime, we are moved every day by the people of Vietnam: invaded, besieged, and fighting on despite the napalm. *And us*, I think, *what about us?*

The next day, as I am calmly arriving at school, I come upon a General Assembly and discover that classes have been suspended. A general has overthrown Belaúnde: a military coup. Knowing Latin American history, we believe that fascism is upon us, and that we have to do something. *Organize the resistance*, we say. Javier and Cucho try to out-radicalize each other in their speeches in the assembly. A few professors too. The visiting professors from Holland observe us silently. We declare ourselves in a state of permanent assembly. *This is fascism*, we say. Joselo García Belaúnde is detained and beaten by the police, and we feel somewhat uneasy at having something in common with the right-wingers: they had been our adversaries back in our early years in the university.

However, within a few days, the government carries out a military occupation of the Talara oilfields, and national jubilation ensues. Everyone remembers the issue of the missing page 11 of the contract signed with the International Petroleum Company. Just a few months ago we were marching in defense of our dignity against North American imperialism. Now, none other than a military dictatorship recovers the oilfields for Peru. We are even more confused now.

Translated by Jorge Bayona

Notes

Suspension points (. . .) in this selection appeared in the original text and do not indicate an ellipsis.
1. Martínez grew up in the beautiful Mantaro Valley in the Andes to the east of Lima.
2. Apristas were the militants of the APRA Party. APRA had a great rivalry with leftist groups and was seen by the latter in the 1960s as pro-imperialist and right-wing.

The Day Lima Erupted

Enrique Zileri

The military regime led by Juan Velasco Alvarado (1968–75) attempted to radically transform Peruvian society by embarking on a series of reforms such as land distribution, the nationalization of foreign-owned companies, and the creation of collective forms of property. By early 1975, however, Velasco Alvarado's health problems, accusations of communist infiltration, and protests deriving from the 1974 expropriation of privately owned media led to increasing discontent among the population.

On February 3, 1975, an unexpected challenge threatened to shake the military regime: a strike was declared by an important sector of the police forces in Lima. That day, the city woke up without policemen in the streets, and to guarantee public order the government resorted to the army. On February 5, politicized groups of opponents organized demonstrations and attacked governmental and military buildings, while scores of vandals used the opportunity to loot and sack businesses, sending Lima into a state of mayhem.

Enrique Zileri (1931–2014), director of the weekly Caretas *and one of the most prominent Peruvian journalists of the second half of the twentieth century, was a vocal critic of the military regime.* Caretas *was censored and closed on several occasions, and Zileri deported, because of his criticism of the military. What follows is his personal account of what he saw during one of the bloodiest days in the history of Lima.*

For me, February 5, 1975, began with a phone call at five in the morning:

—Did you know there's a revolution going on?—asked the anonymous woman. And that the army is attacking the Radio Patrulla police headquarters in La Victoria right now?

I dressed hurriedly and drove my run-down jalopy to 28 de Julio Avenue, hearing gunfire as I approached. Every now and then the roar of a heavy machine gun drowned out everything else.

The sun was rising when I joined the excited crowd on the corner of Andahuaylas Street, from where I saw the wall of the barracks and a crushed patrol car in front of the main gate.

A tank had rolled over it, knocking out the gate and ending all resistance.

I saw a puddle of blood next to the bullet-pocked perimeter wall, and the neighborhood was flush with rumors about a massacre within the barracks, and the flight of the policemen to the surrounding houses.

Reuters would later report thirty dead in the Radio Patrulla barracks, while the government lowered the death toll to six.

With the newspapers being confiscated, and radio and television stations under the control of the military government, the majority of the population was unaware of the police strike. It had begun with demands for higher wages, but what had sparked the confrontation was an incident at the Presidential Palace: a general had slapped a policeman for allowing a journalist to get too close to the presidential car.

On the previous day, around one thousand policemen had gathered at Radio Patrulla, the headquarters of the Forty-First Precinct, as a gesture of rebellion and protest, leaving the city police-less.

Overnight negotiations failed, and at three in the morning troops and armored vehicles surrounded the barracks. They attacked after a peremptory ten-second ultimatum delivered by a colonel by megaphone ran out.

A *Caretas* photographer, Juan Vilca, had managed to sneak into the barracks the previous day, and tried to gather information. Further inquiry was impossible, and those of us who tried to cross the street were driven away with warning shots. Such was the jumpy aftermath of battle (it later turned out that Vilca was under arrest in the prefecture).

A group of surrendered policemen were escorted out the exit on Bausate y Mesa, but they were gone by the time I walked around. Newspapers were published without a word on the events, and thus people indignantly ripped copies in the street.

I then heard the first rumors about shops in Plaza Manco Capac being looted, and I walked over through a vehicle-free stretch where many people were running.

I witnessed some of the pandemonium before becoming alarmed by the first columns of smoke in the city center, and hastily headed that way. A traffic booth had been hurled from a bridge into the Vía Expresa, the city's lone expressway.

I observed the first scene of mass looting upon arriving in the Plaza San Martín, on Jirón de la Unión. Apparently caught by surprise, the merchants had been unable to lower their metal curtains. Men and women ran laden with clothes, electric appliances, edibles, and all sorts of goods, and sometimes some of the looters were in turn plundered by others. A helmeted motorcyclist stopped next to me to watch as well, and zoomed off after uttering a strangely enthusiastic "Terrible, huh?"

I arrived at the magazine's offices planning to muster reporters and photographers (the issue had closed the previous day), but all had come and were already at work. I left again.

Bedlam was on the rise and was becoming more destructive. A huge cloud of smoke loomed over the city. It came from the fire in the Centro Cívico, where the minister of commerce, General Luis Arias Graziani, had tried to thwart the vandals with a machine gun.

The Círculo Militar facilities in the Plaza San Martín were gutted, and someone stormed the Club Nacional with a torch, but had to leave in utter bewilderment after running into the then-president of the institution, Miguel Mujica Gallo. "Gaviota" allegedly browbeat him: "Young man! Smoking is not permitted in the premises!" The offices of *Correo*, *Expreso*, and *La Crónica*—all newspapers under government control—were attacked, but wanton looting is not necessarily political in nature, and neither is vandalism.

The government reacted at two in the afternoon, when a column of tanks from the Armored Division and troops from other barracks started to patrol the streets.

A threatening mob had approached the US Embassy when warning rounds were fired by the armored vehicles, prompting an American diplomat to coin a remarkable phrase: "Thank God for Russian tanks!"[1]

An Él clothing store on Emancipación Avenue was being looted. A corpse and a hemorrhaging man lay on the sidewalk, but the mob simply went over them to pillage what was left. Every now and then a light tank would show up and drive them off, fire into the shop as if fumigating for insects, and then continue its patrol.

Both the dead man and the wounded man remained there, and the looters returned to plunder the leftovers: an ashtray, a toilet. Off in the distance, we saw a helicopter that seemed to fire toward Chacra Colorada.

The government ordered a curfew starting at eight in the evening. I recalled that I had left my car in La Victoria, but with so much looting going on I reckoned nobody would pay any attention to that wreck. And I was right.

The "Limazo" left a toll of more than a hundred confirmed fatalities, and at least one thousand wounded by gunfire, as well as vast material damage.

The curfew was enforced for months. It was the death knell for the Velasco regime.

Translated by Jorge Bayona

Note

1. During the military regime, Peru increased its purchases of Soviet military equipment.

A City of Outsiders

José Matos Mar

During the 1980s the combination of political violence in the countryside and a severe economic crisis forced hundreds of thousands, mostly people of Indigenous background, to leave their communities and relocate in Lima, following on the steps of previous migratory waves. The social, cultural, demographic, and economic impact of this migration is discussed in this excerpt by renowned anthropologist José Matos Mar.

Matos Mar (1921–2015) began to study urban changes in Lima in the 1950s. In 1984 he published a pathbreaking volume—from which this excerpt has been taken—in which he coined the expression desborde popular *("popular flood," a title that some critics found unfortunate, a reflection of Lima's fear of Andean immigrants) to describe the ways in which lower-class immigrant populations were modifying Lima's human landscape. They imposed new cultural and social patterns that contributed to the democratization of social life and the consolidation of informal practices, processes that have exerted an enormous influence on the way Lima society is configured in the twenty-first century.*

The population of Lima is split along social and economic lines. On one side, close to 80 percent live in popular urban settlements. And, on the other, over 20 percent is concentrated in the residential areas of the middle and upper classes.

Of the 80 percent comprised by the so-called lower classes (*sectores populares*), almost 37 percent live in *barriadas* (shantytowns), 23 percent in popular neighborhoods, and 20 percent in slums, *callejones*, and *corralones*. This means that the barriada is the most common urban residence for the lower classes.

The growth rate of barriadas over the past twenty-eight years—1956 to 1984—has been astounding. When the first general census was carried out in 1956 by students from the Universidad Nacional Mayor de San Marcos, they recorded 56 of them, with 119,886 inhabitants, that is, 9.5 percent of the total population of Metropolitan Lima, then estimated at 1,260,729

Mother and children in Cerro El Pino, one of many hills in Lima where lower-class people built their homes, 1980s. Archivo fotográfico TAFOS/PUCP. Código: EP05-11. Photograph by Daniel Pajuelo. Used by permission of Archivo TAFOS.

Crossing the bridge over the Rímac River, with Cerro San Cristóbal in the background, 1990s. Archivo fotográfico TAFOS/PUCP. Código: TA350-39A. Photograph by Daniel Pajuelo. Used by permission of Archivo TAFOS.

Jilguero del Huascarán, Andean folk singer, portrayed on a wall in Quilca Street, 2013. Photograph by Carlos Aguirre. Courtesy of the artist.

inhabitants. It practically doubled to 316,829 inhabitants in 1961 (17.2 percent). By 1972, they housed 805,117 people (24 percent). The census of 1981 recorded 408 barriadas, accommodating 1,460,471 people (32.5 percent). By the end of 1983, when a team from the Instituto de Estudios Peruanos (IEP) carried out a survey focusing on community leaders and longtime dwellers of the Lima barriadas, it revealed that there were 598 *pueblos jóvenes*,[1] housing 2,184,000 residents, 36.4 percent of the total population of Metropolitan Lima. In less than thirty years, the previously inexistent barriada has become characteristic of a transformed Lima.

In the past forty-four years—1940 to 1984—the population of the capital of Peru has increased tenfold. In fact, according to the 1940 census, Lima had 645,172 inhabitants; it tripled twenty-one years later (1961 census), reaching 1,652,000 inhabitants; according to census figures, by 1972 it had quintupled to 3,302,523, to multiply sevenfold by 1981, amounting to 4,492,260, and subsequently reaching 6,000,000 in 1984, thus matching the entire country's 1940 population. This huge demographic leap constitutes one of the greatest transformations in Peru. The physical and human geography of the capital has undergone serious realignments, along with the great transformation of a country that was rural (65 percent) in 1940 and is now urban (65 percent).

Cement stairs in one of Lima's hills that became lower-class residential areas, 1986. Archivo fotográfico TAFOS/PUCP. Código: EA29-8A. Photograph by Daniel Pajuelo. Used by permission of Archivo TAFOS.

Scoring a goal in a sandy field, 1994. Archivo fotográfico TAFOS/PUCP. Código: CHU5-34a. Photograph by José Chuquiure. Used by permission of Archivo TAFOS.

The capital's growth rate is higher than the national one. While the former had a mean annual growth rate of 3.7 percent in the period between 1972 and 1981, the latter only reached 2.5 percent over the same interval. This means that Metropolitan Lima harbored 41 percent of the country's urban population and 27 percent of the total population. As of July 1984 close to 50 percent of the national urban population, as well as more than 30 percent of the total population of Peru, lives in the greater Lima area. Limeño centralism, harking back to the sixteenth century, now acquires a new character and a new dynamic. This massive concentration subjects the spatial and social structures of the urban milieu to historically unprecedented tensions.

Greater Lima absorbs the largest share of migrants in the country, those who, tired of provincial poverty, leave their places of origin and search for a better future. According to the 1981 national census, 41 percent of the Lima population, which in absolute terms amounts to 1,901,697 inhabitants, was of migrant background; of these, 54 percent came from the highlands. Of the migrant population that flowed from the twenty-four departments in the country, the biggest portions came from Ancash (10.6 percent), Ayacucho (8.38 percent), and Junín (8.11 percent) and the lowest from Madre de Dios (0.13 percent). More than 10 percent of these immigrants came from the other provinces of the Department of Lima, especially the highland districts. In 1984, Lima is a city of outsiders. The provincial masses, having overwhelmed the city, impose profound changes in the lifestyle of the capital and give it a new face.

The city that incorporated the valleys of Chillón and Lurín into the metropolitan area tends to expand northwards toward the rural regions from the border of the valley of the Rímac to Ancón, and southward to Pucusana. It forays eastward to Ricardo Palma and to the northeast forms the pocket of San Juan de Lurigancho. This trend shows that the greater part of the migrant population has occupied new areas, and a good portion of the natives have tended to leave the central areas. The pressure exerted by the new population has not only provoked the displacement of the former occupants but has also led to a spectacular expansion in the old borders of the metropolitan region.

. . .

The spatial and demographic overflow of a considerable sector of low-income population is turning out to be the most important phenomenon of the present decade. The invasion of new areas—such as the banks of the Rímac River, the skirts of the hills, and deserts—plus the taking of the traditional core of the city have isolated the middle and upper sectors in their residential neighborhoods. The enormous displacement of the provincial masses to the capital has transformed it into the melting pot and cross-section of all the ongoing social changes in Peru. This major migrant concentration in shantytowns and popular neighborhoods has led to them becoming the key factor in the new metropolitan social dynamic.

Translated by Jorge Bayona

Note

1. *Pueblos jóvenes* (literally, "young towns") was the official euphemism given to urban slums (formerly *barriadas*) during the military government led by General Velasco Alvarado.

The Israelites of the New Universal Covenant

Peter Masson

Changes in the human landscape in Lima have affected not only the economy, the social structure, and cultural manifestations such as music or gastronomy, but also the realm of religion and faith. If Catholicism had been the dominant religion since colonial times, the second half of the twentieth century, and particularly its last two decades, witnessed significant transformations. On the one hand, there was substantial growth among evangelical churches, which even had a political manifestation with the election of one of its members as vice president in 1990. On the other hand, a remarkable homegrown cult created in 1955 by an Indigenous shoemaker who claimed to have been chosen by God to restore his divine pact with mankind took root and expanded. As Peter Masson discusses in this text, the "Israelites," as they are commonly referred to, recruited their followers mostly from among peoples of Indigenous descent. Migrants from the interior found in this cult a response to their spiritual and, to a certain extent, material needs as they confronted the challenges of adjusting to life in Lima.

The Asociación Evangélica de la Misión Israelita del Nuevo Pacto Universal (AEMINPU—Evangelical Association of the Israelite Mission of the New Universal Covenant), who are colloquially known as "Israelites," is set apart from numerous other "new churches" and fundamentalist denominations by (a) integrating some of their own—very general—understanding of several Andean traditions into their ethical message, (b) successfully proselytizing among the many Andean migrants who are marginalized from the social life of the city, and (c) the south Andean rural background of its founder, Ezequiel Ataucusi Gamonal. These three factors make us describe AEMINPU—much like anthropologist Manuel J. Granados—as Andean and indigenous. Even though most of their parishioners have been recruited from the *pueblos jóvenes* of Lima, this religious movement is not an exclusively urban phenomenon. Their eastward expansion toward several jungle colonies reveals a new, mostly agrarian, communal life, which they extol in their own publications. Led by a charismatic and prophetic leader, the messianic-apocalyptic movement of the Israelites wants to give clear and concise answers to the miserable living conditions prevalent in the countryside and in the *pueblos jóvenes* of the great city, the violent social conflicts in Peru, the deeply ingrained social inferiority complex, the loss of ethical guidelines, and the desired "contractual" relationship between human beings and divine power.

Religious services carried out in tunics and clothes that match the illustrations featured in fundamentalist editions of the Bible (men sport beards and tousled hair; women wear head scarves reminiscent of those of the Near East) and rituals of burnt offerings of "unblemished" animals (the "holocaust") are two of the most remarkable traits of their upper- and mid-level officials. Saturday services and the prophecies of their founder and other high-ranking male members of this group's hierarchy (although there are also female prophetesses) are other elements that underscore their supposedly Old Testament orientation, which does not exclude the New Testament, thus making them not quite so "exotic" for our times. Their religious hymns are accompanied, nevertheless, by "celestial music," which tends to be a mix of *huaynos* and *yaravíes* with *chicha* and rock music. On the other hand, their efforts at establishing healthy, community-based economies with common recreational activities, such as, for instance, the "bingo-lotto," prove their concern for "this life." The "reverse side of the same coin" seems to be comprised by those many men (mostly young, and in modest yet relatively well-cut clothes) who are devoted to the material well-being and economic progress of the religious movement.

Their "exotic" behavior is not the only reason that the Israelites have garnered enmity and hatred. Their rejection of many aspects of creole urban life and modern Western life in general, in addition to their attempts at creating islands of a new life, both urban and rural, have attracted suspicion and criticism. From the outside, a negative image prevails, which has taken the shape of numerous accusations by the Lima media. Several leaders of the movement have been accused of robbery, rape, sexual molestation, exploitation of free labor by followers, the collection of high fees, and the accumulation of large sums of money for social, ritual, and missionary duties (but, at least in part, also for personal enrichment). This has coalesced in a constant stream of accusations and allegations, not only in Lima, but also by Andean peasants and Amazonian "natives." Andean rejection of the Israelites is similar to that aroused by plagues, terrorist guerrillas, and the punitive actions of security forces; they are also blamed for causing natural disasters.

From a general and comparative point of view from the perspective of the sociology of religion, the parallels it bears with several fundamentalist Protestant denominations and churches is not surprising: an emphasis on biblical study; Bible-based ethics; a positive view of work discipline; satisfaction in the success of individual effort; a "puritan" prohibition of alcohol, tobacco, and all kinds of stimulants and drugs; the moralization of private sexual life (negative outlook on abortion, adultery, divorce, and "free unions"); a high importance placed on family; and, above all, an emphasis on the moment of spiritual and moral conversion.

Translated by Jorge Bayona

María Elena Moyano

Robin Kirk

Beginning in the 1970s, ample sectors of the Peruvian population, especially from lower- and working-class backgrounds, had begun to establish democratic and participatory grassroots organizations to address critical issues such as housing, education, food supply, and safety. One of the most salient examples of this trend was the case of Villa El Salvador, a shantytown that became a model of collective effort and self-government (see the Salcedo essay above). When Shining Path started its insurrection in 1980, it clashed against popular and democratic forms of political participation, such as the Villa El Salvador community. During the same period, a new generation of grassroots leaders, including many women, came to the forefront. These organizations and leaders confronted the state for its lack of attention to their needs but also resisted the imposition of Shining Path's authoritarian project.

One of the brightest and most courageous such leaders was the Afro-Peruvian María Elena Moyano, who paid with her life for her defiance of Shining Path's methods and whose life and legacy is summarized in this excerpt by human rights advocate and writer Robin Kirk.

One afternoon, I went to Villa El Salvador to interview the vice mayor, María Elena Moyano. I was doing a story about a new generation of Peruvian politician—not white, sometimes female, with a solid constituency in the impoverished neighborhoods their families had helped build. A black woman with an electric, gap-toothed smile, Moyano was twelve years old when her parents took part in the land takeover that led to the creation of Villa in 1971. As a girl, she had been part of a church-organized youth group heavily influenced by liberation theology. After finishing high school, she held a series of posts until being elected president of the Villa Women's Federation. In 1989, at thirty, she won the vice mayor's seat on a ticket sponsored by the United Left coalition.

Although both men and women built Villa, it could be said that women raised it much as they raised their own children. Women defended their *iglus* from police while the men were at work. Even as they spent long hours as washerwomen and market vendors and maids, and caring for their own families, they devoted time to getting electricity and water, establishing bus routes, grading roads, building schools, establishing cooperative businesses. By the time Moyano took office, Villa was considered a model city. Every time American politicians came to visit Peru, Agency for International Development vans ferried them to Villa, where they were received in busy workshops, fed in communal kitchens, and shown new project plans. It was a tour designed to showcase hard work, perseverance, and the essential goodness of the poor. The message was simple: release them from the bondage of dependency and they will help themselves. *Autogestión* (self-help) was the key. The Americans inevitably came away impressed and showed it by directing more development cash to the Villa accounts.

There was truth to the message. There was also careful editing. By the time Moyano was elected, the Shining Path had mounted a determined campaign to win Villa. The leaders of the United Left dismissed it, sure that Villa's heroes, those noble *cholos*, were already theirs. But not all of them were. In community meetings, *senderistas* would stand and say their piece, identifying themselves as clearly as if they had worn a conventioneer's hat. They also set off bombs, pressured drivers to honor armed strikes, and slipped death threats under doors. For them, all of Villa's advances amounted to a gigantic trick. The goal of the dark forces behind it—the political parties, the pope, the imperialist U.S.A.—was to keep the masses in misery and exploit their labor.

Moyano was one of the few leaders on the left who recognized the strength of the Shining Path message. Unlike others, what she saw was that it was not directed at the noble *cholos* who had built Villa, but their children: the ones who didn't have jobs, the ones crowded into the inadequate schools, the ones who saw their futures opening before them like the vast desert south of town. Villa was failing them not because of an internal flaw, but because Villa was no island. Villa was part of Peru and Peru was a mess.

"Our youth are rebellious, impulsive," she once told an interviewer. "In the Shining Path, you see expressed their doubts and frustrations about their lack of a future. It is a mystique, a total commitment, that seems to answer their hunger for complete change."

Moyano made the Shining Path crazy. After guerrillas blew up the warehouse that supplied ninety-two Villa soup kitchens and killed and threatened local leaders, Moyano led the first-ever march against them. They vowed to annihilate her. She gave the press long interviews in which she rejected their terror tactics. Guerrillas called her leftist beliefs "revisionist" and claimed she had stolen soup kitchen money. Moyano made the soup kitchen accounts public to show there had been no wrongdoing. To keep guerrillas from attacking soup kitchens and individual leaders, she supported organizing neighborhood watch committees to walk the streets at night. The Shining Path accused her of joining forces with the army. She replied that to defeat the Shining Path, "we must root out fear."

Moyano never showed up for my interview. Protected by four bodyguards, she had been varying her schedule so much, to throw off a potential attempt on her life, that it had escaped her control entirely. As I waited that gloomy morning, her secretary pointed out for me the rickety shacks, high in the dunes, where the guerrilla columns moved at night. "The poorest of the poor," she said.

On February 15, 1992, Moyano was shot as she chatted with people attending a chicken barbecue fund-raiser. Some inside knew what would happen, but no one warned Moyano. They were too frightened. The assassins had been there for hours, eating chicken, waiting.

Among her attackers was another black woman. I would bet Moyano knew her as the woman forced her down, then shot her in the temple and dropped five pounds of dynamite in her lap. To me, this encounter is fully as mysterious—and charged—as another encounter commemorated in 1992, that of the Inca Atahualpa with the conqueror Pizarro almost five centuries earlier. As they stood face to face, Inca and Spaniard, they must have been impressed by their physical differences. One was burned red and covered with hair. The other was dirt-brown, smooth as an egg. They gazed across culture, indeed a kind of historical chasm. But Moyano and her attacker could not have been other than struck by their similarities. Both black, both female, both poor. They lived the same culture, shared history. Yet the political choices they had made turned them into enemies to the death.

Four years after killing Moyano, to commemorate International Women's Day, the Shining Path killed Pascuala Rosado, the former mayor of another Lima shantytown. Rosado had recently returned to Peru after several years away, a precaution against their threats. They shot her as she was leaving her home. Just so no one would have any doubts about the message they intended to send, they killed her as they had killed Moyano—with a bullet and a lapful of dynamite.

We'll get you, no matter how long we have to wait, they meant. We are waiting. And we see.

The Tarata Street Bombing: July 16, 1992

Peruvian Truth and Reconciliation Commission

Daily life in Lima in the 1980s was constantly disturbed by both Shining Path's actions (blackouts, the detonation of car bombs, terrorist attacks against governmental and other buildings, and selective assassinations) and the state's violent response, although for many Lima residents the war seemed like a distant conflict whose reverberations only occasionally threatened their livelihood.

On April 5, 1992, President Alberto Fujimori suspended the constitution, closed the Congress, and began to rule as a dictator. One of his first decisions was to intervene in Lima's prisons, where Shining Path inmates enjoyed a great deal of autonomy and controlled the internal space of the prisons. Nearly forty of them were killed.

In response, Shining Path launched a deadly series of bombing attacks in various parts of Lima, including the residential and commercial district of Miraflores. The bombing of a building on Tarata Street was something of a shocking wake-up call for many people in Lima: probably for the first time they felt that the war was knocking on their door. Fear and a sense of vulnerability rapidly spread through different spaces and social groups, although it also fueled the decision to mobilize and resist the imposition of Shining Path's violent project.

In 2001 a Truth Commission was formed to shed light on the period of violence that plagued Peru between 1980 and 2000. The Tarata bombing was one of the many episodes discussed in the commission's final report, issued in 2003.

On July 16, 1992, a Shining Path squad detonated a car bomb on Tarata Street in the district of Miraflores, killing 25 people and wounding 155.

Between January and July 1992, thirty-seven car bombs were detonated in the Lima Metropolitan Area, inflicting approximately fifty fatalities. Shining Path was stepping up its offensive in the capital, which also included the assassination of community leaders such as María Elena Moyano. According to Abimael Guzmán, the war had entered the phase of "strategic equilibrium" that would precede the overthrow of the state and the final

The aftermath of the July 16, 1992, car bomb placed by the Shining Path on Tarata Street in Miraflores. It killed 25, injured at least 155, and destroyed or damaged 180 homes and 400 businesses. Archivo Caretas. Photograph by José Vilca. Used by permission of Marco Zileri.

takeover. The "Fifth Military Plan"—known as "Advancing the Conquest of Power"—was launched, guiding subversive operations in Lima.

The escalation of violence and terror was furthered by the undemocratic coup d'état carried out by President Alberto Fujimori on April 5, 1992. The struggle against subversion had been put forward as an argument for breaking constitutional order. The political class's loss of prestige and the population's desire for more security made the self-coup a popular measure. Despite the ensuing international pressure, the political-military leadership that had taken power effectively ruled the country.

One of its first measures was to crack down on a mutiny in Castro Castro Prison. This resulted in the death of thirty-five people convicted of terrorism and treason who had refused to be transferred. Fujimori thus announced the rigors that the penitentiary system would acquire over the course of his administration.

Planning of the Attack by the Leadership of Shining Path

According to testimony given by Juanito Guillermo Orozco Barrientos, alias Franco, the leadership of Shining Path decided to detonate a car bomb in the district of Miraflores, and assigned the mission to squad 12, led by Daniel (identified as Carlos Mora La Madrid). Mora and Nicolás decided to target the Banco de Crédito located on the corner of Larco Avenue and Schell Street. Behind it ran Tarata Street.

This version is corroborated by a prisoner who, in an interview with the Truth and Reconciliation Commission, stated the following: "Word in Shining Path [. . .] was that the car bomb attack in Tarata Street was aimed at the financial entities located on Larco Avenue in Miraflores, such as the Banco de Crédito and others, but that the excessive activity in the neighborhood prevented them from reaching their objective; as a result, they took the car bomb to Tarata Street, where they let it roll and blow up."

The attack was scheduled for July 16, 1992. Tasks were assigned as follows: Nicolás, Arturo, Manuel, and Lucía (subsequently identified as Cecilia Rossana Núñez Chipana) were to reconnoiter the area, while Percy, Antenor, and Rosa would steal the vehicles necessary for the attack. Finally, Daniel was in charge of planning the route the attack would follow.

Execution of the Attack on Tarata Street

On the same day as the Tarata Street bombing, Shining Path attacked the San Gabriel, José Carlos Mariátegui, and Nueva Esperanza police stations located in the district of Villa María del Triunfo, as well as an agency of the Banco Latino located in the district of La Victoria. These were diversionary attacks aimed at spreading the police thin.

From the early hours of the 16th, Carlos, assisted by Lucía, Antenor, and Franco, mixed ammonium nitrate with fuel oil and packaged it. At 4 p.m. they began installing the explosives into a Datsun vehicle. Nicolás and Arturo rode in it; the former carried a firearm and small bombs (*contes*) to distract security personnel around the location.

At around 7 p.m. they were joined by a second vehicle, which would serve as an escort for the car bomb and getaway vehicle for the subversive operatives. This car was crewed by Percy and Manuel.

The two vehicles arrived in the vicinity of the Banco de Crédito on the busy Larco Avenue in the Miraflores district. According to them, security guards prevented them from parking in the planned spot in front of the bank, prompting them to decide to go into Tarata Street.

The driver of the bomb-packed vehicle slowed down and bailed out, letting it coast along Tarata Street toward the residential buildings located on both sides. The automobile exploded at around 9:20 p.m. at the second block of Tarata Street, where the El Condado, San Pedro, Tarata, Residencial Central, and San Carlos buildings were located.

The cherry-colored licenseless Datsun contained approximately four hundred kilograms (almost nine hundred pounds) of dynamite and ANFO. The attackers got away in the other vehicle, a Toyota with license plate LQ-3655, which they abandoned at the sixth block of Larco Avenue.

According to the census carried out by the Centro de Investigación de Proyectos Urbanos y Regionales (CIPUR—Center for Research of Urban and Regional Projects), the bombing of Tarata Street caused the death of 25 people, of whom 3 women and 2 men were never identified. Additionally, 5 people disappeared and 155 were wounded.

. . .

The blast affected a radius of three hundred meters, inflicting considerable material damage as well. Residential buildings, commercial establishments, and banking and financial entities in the area were partially destroyed.

Material losses were estimated at $3,120,000, and the Institute for Civil Defense assessed that 360 families had suffered the effects of the attack.

. . .

The impact of the attack was felt throughout the country, especially in certain sectors of limeño society that had hitherto remained distant from the subversive violence that had claimed the lives of thousands of their countrymen in the Andes and the Amazon area. There was a growing feeling that Shining Path was invading Lima and that their advance could not be curbed. The citizenry, however, also closed ranks in self-defense, and condemnation of Shining Path grew manifold.

Translated by Jorge Bayona

Shining Path: A Prisoner's Testimony

Peruvian Truth and Reconciliation Commission

When Shining Path began its violent actions in 1980, it initially seemed like a distant annoyance for Lima. Vague newspaper articles about death and destruction in far-off Ayacucho appeared next to texts about bus accidents and natural disasters. Even when concern grew (sparked above all by violence in Lima), major political groups in the capital showed little concern about events in and the people of the Andean highlands. This indifference as well as the atrocious human rights abuses by the Shining Path and the Armed Forces led the Peruvian Truth and Reconciliation Commission (CVR) to begin its 2003 report with the following: "The report we hand in contains a double outrage: that of massive murder, disappearance and torture; and that of indolence, incompetence and indifference of those who could have stopped this humanitarian catastrophe but didn't."[1]

The Shining Path, however, acted in and marked Lima in the 1980s and 1990s: car bombs, blackouts or apagones, *assassinations, and curfews By the late 1980s there was growing concern that they were effectively expanding into Lima and posed a national threat. In addition, the brutal war forced more than five hundred thousand people to relocate, the vast majority to Lima. New residential districts such as Huaycán and Manchay arose on Lima's outskirts.*

The CVR archive contains thousands of testimonies from participants in the war. Those by Shining Path veterans underscore the will to use violence to advance their cause, but also shine light on militants' doubts and suffering within the party. Testimonies such as the recent memoir by Lurgio Gavilán have broken the myth of the disciplined, fanatic Shining Path members who never doubted their mission.[2] This account by one prisoner, a participant in the socorro popular *or popular aid groups that provided medical assistance to Shining Path members, highlights the enormous personal cost that her militancy inflicted, the guilt she carries, and her mistreatment by both the state armed forces and the Shining Path.*

We have changed the name and other specific details to protect the identity of the individual and excluded some paragraphs. We have followed the testimony's structure, a narrative with interspersed quotes from the prisoner. Most section headlines are from the original, but we have added a couple to help organize the material.

Testimonio # 70 . . .
Date and location of interview: 2002, Lima

1. *Context and Antecedents*

DETENTION AND SENTENCE

Around 1995, when she was detained, Jennifer Vilca Neri, native of Lima (born in 1966), lived in a working-class district of Lima with her partner and child.

She has currently been in jail for seven years, having been sentenced to twenty for the crime of terrorism.

HER INVOLVEMENT WITH THE SHINING PATH

At the end of 1982 she found out (through her aunts and uncles) that her grandfather and two of his brothers had been killed by the "Sinchis" [Police Special Forces] alongside other peasants in their community. She comments, "This made me furious against the Sinchis," while at the same time she saw the hard time people were having. This fury led her into the Shining Path, also because they told her what they had was perfect.

In 1985 she found out that an uncle had been picked up in a raid when leaving the San Cristóbal University in Ayacucho and taken to the Los Cabitos military base (this she learned from another relative who was a general) and that they had beaten and even raped him. After a few months they went to his house and took his money and possessions. She and her family never heard what happened to him.

In May 1986 she went to El Fronton Island to see if her uncle had been taken there. She was surprised to learn that the people detained there didn't have names, just pseudonyms. No one gave her information about her uncle. When she was there, navy soldiers (*la marina*) began to shoot. A month later the prison massacres took place and she had no further contact, as all the prisoners died.[3]

In 1986 she was studying at San Marcos University. In 1988 other people from the university asked her to collaborate and to aid the sick. She says that she helped them with clothing from her parents' store and other tasks. She took a first aid course from N.N., who invited her to join the Shining Path.

In 1988 she became more seriously involved and aided students who had been wounded in confrontations with the police. She did this in operating rooms, "anywhere, in whatever house." She went where they sent her.

As far as the work she did, she comments, "There was a lot of pressure, and the individual in us disappeared completely. The group existed, but not the individual. I had to help a lot of people."

Shining Path inmates in El Frontón in the midst of the June 1986 prison uprisings. Shining Path had taken hostages in three jails in protest of prison conditions and the government's plan to move them to a new high-security prison. The armed forces struck back brutally; at least 224 inmates died. Archivo Caretas. Photographer unknown. Used by permission of Marco Zileri.

She also went to shantytowns (*asentamientos humanos*) to aid children and pregnant women, which made her "feel good." She began doing this part time, but then they asked her to give up her studies and do it full time.

"I left the university because 'they' didn't want me to study; I was no longer free; I was also a prisoner." After some time, she realized that "I was being forced." The time came when she wanted to leave the party but she was scared: "I had heard that they killed whoever left." She remembers that "a girl in medical aid in Socorro Popular," also in the organization (and also later arrested), was looking for a pill to give to someone who "was causing problems." Jennifer realized that they could also do this to her—eliminate her. This scared her.

She decided in 1993 to give up her militancy. From that point she lived looking over her shoulder. She was worried that they would take her child away from her: "I knew that both the Shining Path and the police were following me."

"When I left the party my life was hell. I always had to be on the lookout to see if I was being followed. I had lost my studies; I had nothing." She and her husband had to flee. They moved to different districts in Lima, but they always had someone searching for them.

As far as her life as a Shining Path militant, she says, "It's not heaven." She also witnessed terrible things within the organization [against] "the people who disagreed. For example, the Felicianos [followers of Óscar Ramírez, Comrade Feliciano, who took over the Shining Path after Guzmán's capture in 1992] killed the people from Socorro Popular. They killed Pedro" (she doesn't know his last name).

2. Development of the Facts

She was arrested in September 1995 in her house, when she was returning from shopping. She asked the police that she be allowed to leave her child with someone, but they didn't let her. She was taken with her child, who was later handed over to his father. She thinks they took her to a police station in an area unknown to her.

When they took her to DINCOTE [the National Counterterrorism Agency] they told her she was fortunate the navy, the army, or the Shining Path didn't pick her up because "they would have disappeared her." They told her she had been arrested because of her participation as a terrorist. They even called her by the pseudonym she used in the party.

She said that they knew this name because others had turned themselves in under the Ley de Arrepentimiento [Law of Repentance, a 1994 measure that softened sentences for Shining Path militants who turned themselves in and provided information] and given her name. When they arrested her they also picked up many others, mostly people who had previously surrendered. She said, "These are operations done by the police." Most of those people are free because they denied their participation. She says, "It's not clear whether it's better to tell the truth or lie; if she hadn't admitted her participation, she would be free in her house."

They showed her a photo album with the pictures (ID size), names, and pseudonyms of the entire health apparatus (of Socorro Popular). She couldn't deny anything because the police had information about what she had done and where, how she had moved about. Later it came to look like she had turned in the others.

In the afternoon they took her to her house to register it. They didn't find anything. They threatened to arrest her family.

"I acknowledged my participation. The fact of accepting it was a way to take revenge on the organization, even if Shining Path always taught us its golden rule, 'I know nothing, I have heard nothing, I have done nothing.'"

She said that she also agreed to give the names of all the people who participated in the health aid groups under Socorro Popular.

She was there for two months. She was sentenced to twenty years. In her
trial, she declared, "I have never made an attack on anyone's life." This did
not affect her sentencing.

"In jail I have been threatened and harassed by Shining Path prisoners."
She says that because she capitulated, they treat her badly. She says that
"for them [referring to Shining Path militants] I'm a squealer, a repentant.
Once they called me 'a damned squealer.'" She has also been reproached by
the police. They asked how could she have turned in individuals who were
innocent.

3. Consequences

"It's not only the seven years in jail. I've been in this hell for more than
twelve years." She still worries about getting out and that the Shining Path
will take revenge for her repentance. "Nobody knows what I feel. All this
time has been a hell and it still is. I managed to waste my life."

"I brought others into the movement. I feel guilty because my husband
is incarcerated. He was detained just because he is my husband and lived
with me. My sister was also detained and spent six months in prison. After
her release she found a job but lost it because both the military and the civil
courts reopened her case."

4. Final Reflections

"I was a very good student. I got good grades. I ended up studying at two
universities simultaneously, La Cantuta and San Marcos." She examines this
and asks herself, "Why? Why did I get into this? I've always been the person
that my family taught me to be, that is, to be correct." She thinks that perhaps she did it to take revenge on her family: her father separated from her
mother and began another family. The disappearance of her uncle still pains
her, especially because he was like a father to her. Her pain is enormous because he doesn't even have a tomb where he can be mourned.

Editors' Note: Jennifer Vilca Neri was released from jail in 2009 and currently resides in Lima.

Translated by Charles F. Walker

Notes

1. Comisión de la Verdad y Reconciliación, *Informe Final*, vol. 1 (Lima: Comisión de la Verdad y Reconciliación, 2003), 11.

2. Lurgio Gavilán Sánchez, *When Rains Became Floods: A Child Soldier's Story*, trans. Margaret Randall (Durham, NC: Duke University Press, 2015).

3. On June 18–19, 1986, over two hundred Shining Path inmates were killed by state forces in their attempt to put down three coordinated riots at the El Frontón, Lurigancho, and Santa Bárbara prisons.

Twenty-First-Century Feudalism

Wilfredo Ardito Vega

Lima, like the rest of Peru, is a society sharply divided and even segregated by class, race, culture, and social status. Despite various decades of social mobility, economic growth, modernization, migration, and racial miscegenation, Lima still shows powerful signs of an apartheid-like mentality and behavior. Public spaces such as restaurants, clubs, schools, and even entire neighborhoods continue to function as de facto instruments of social discrimination and reproduction of the privileges enjoyed by the social and economic elites.

The economic and commercial boom that Peru has experienced since the turn of the twenty-first century brought immense benefits for those sectors of the Lima population connected to the import/export economy and the international financial system. The increasingly more affluent middle- and upper-class limeños began to look for new areas to occupy and enjoy the privacy and social privileges that the overcrowded city was making more difficult to find. Oceanfront areas south of Lima were radically transformed from fisherman towns into expensive beach resorts with all the amenities found in big cities, such as shopping malls, restaurants, or movie theaters.

Emblematic of this move was Asia, a beach town about one hour south of Lima that—as described in this piece by Wilfredo Ardito, a human rights activist, lawyer, and journalist—came to represent some of the most clamorous forms of discrimination that continue to tarnish Peru's modernization process.

"This is not your country, ma'am, you have to abide by Peruvian law here," the ambassador of a European country was told.

By going into the sea to play with the rest of the family, her children's nanny had violated one of the beachside condominium's regulations. Naturally—and despite what the administrator said—the rule is illegal, as are the checkpoints that prevent common citizens from reaching those beaches. In the beaches of Asia [sixty miles south of Lima], Peruvian laws go unenforced.

The ambassador and his wife had faced trouble since they first set foot on the beach house they had rented for the weekend, since security had warned them that their nanny wore shorts and T-shirt instead of the mandatory uniform. The ban on light clothing or swimming clothes reflects not only a segregated view of humankind, but also a perverse pleasure—frequent in some Peruvians—in not allowing subordinates even the smallest comforts.

Asia is completely unlike other summer destinations in Latin America, such as Punta del Este, Cancun, and Viña del Mar. In these places, hotels or restaurants may be expensive, but the beaches and ocean are accessible to everyone. The condominiums of Asia, however, are frequented by Peruvians who would feel offended if they sunbathed next to a countryman of Andean or African traits.

In the early twentieth century, the grandparents of the current vacationers enjoyed La Punta, Chorrillos, or Barranco without fear of such contamination. They posed and smiled for *Variedades* or *Mundial*, the trendy magazines of the day. From the 1940s onward, however, the trickle of Andean immigrants became a veritable flood, which in turn accelerated Lima's own inner migration.

Residential neighborhoods sprang up, far from the areas occupied by immigrants; nevertheless, the latter's offspring would move there too in the ensuing decades. In the beaches, the newcomers advanced farther every year: they reached Chorrillos and Barranco, occupied La Punta, and enjoyed Ancon, the nearest thing to the beach resorts in other countries. Old limeños fled to the beaches of San Bartolo or El Silencio but were caught up with shortly thereafter. In a catchy tune, the "Los no sé quién y los no sé cuántos" band impishly mocked the ethnic coexistence in the beaches, concluding that "all are equal under the sun."

But not everyone found this coexistence enjoyable and thus, simultaneous to the appearance of the racist discos in Miraflores or Barranco, "exclusive" beach condominiums arose: these were the Fujimorista times, when "neoliberalism" *à la Peru* was based on the presumption that physical traits were more important than economic ability.

In Asia, the usurpation of public spaces manages to affront even many people of the middle classes. "Camping is becoming harder every year," says an economist working in a ministry, "because they take over the beaches."

The European ambassadors mentioned in the beginning of this article were outraged too, and decided to leave the condominium. The gesture carries a certain symbolism, since a few years back, the country they represent, as well as a few others, decided to terminate many aid programs in Peru. "After seeing those luxurious beach houses, they simply realized that there are plenty of resources to tackle the problem of poverty with—a friend involved with international cooperation tells me—and they believe it is absurd to continue to invest in problems that Peruvians could fix themselves, if only they had the political will to do so."

A few weeks ago, the nightmare of some Asia vacationers was that should the bitter [Ollanta] Humala win the elections, he would carry out a Velasco-style "beach reform," confiscating the beach houses and turning them over to *provinciano* clubs in Lima.[1] However, even the most neoliberal regime ought to guarantee free access to beaches and the ocean, resorting to public force should it prove necessary. Furthermore, in many countries beach houses are heavily taxed, which nobody considers totalitarian or socialist.

As to forbidding a person (domestic maids are people too, should there be any doubt) from swimming in the ocean, that is no more than a pathetic feudal relic that is unacceptable in a country that considers itself democratic. The abuses that are committed in these beaches are a symbol of everything that we must change in Peru in order to build a more just and caring society. I can only wish we could believe—whoever the next president may turn out to be—that the last racist summer in Asia is coming to an end.

Translated by Jorge Bayona

Note

1. When this article was first written, Ollanta Humala was running for president as candidate for the Nationalist Party. He lost that election but would eventually become president of Peru from 2011 to 2016. He did not "reform" the beaches.

Chicha and *Huayno*: Andean Music and Culture in Lima

Gisela Cánepa

One of the most important changes brought about by the massive migration to Lima was the emergence of new cultural manifestations and new forms of socialization. Migrants and their children assimilated certain aspects of limeño culture, but they also forcefully and creatively brought forward their own forms of music, art, celebration, and religious practices. Some attempted to re-create the cultural forms and events they had enjoyed while living in their hometowns and cities: the massive success of "Andean folklore" festivals and artists is evidence of this. Others, especially the younger and mestizos, produced culture that reflected the influence of both their Andean roots and the new environment in which they were now living.

Chicha music is probably the most conspicuous product of this syncretism. For more than four decades it has been a massive cultural, social, and economic phenomenon, and it now occupies a central space in the life of the city. But, as anthropologist Gisela Cánepa discusses in this text, the term chicha *came to represent in the imaginary of many Lima residents everything that was disorderly, anarchic, and inauthentic. A true cultural and representational battle has been fought during the last few decades around the value and legitimacy of chicha music and culture.*

On the other hand, huayno *music, arguably a more "traditional" expression of Andean culture, has also gone through drastic changes, including the emergence of female practitioners who have come to dominate the genre, and its presence, after decades of semiclandestine existence, in mainstream media.*

Chicha is a musical genre that emerged in the late 1960s. It resulted from the fusion of the Andean huayno with the Colombian *cumbia* and diverse tropical rhythms, and after its introduction to the radio and record companies it was disseminated throughout the nation. Chicha not only combines distinct musical rhythms but has also evolved while moving between Lima and the Andean provinces. It is an "itinerant" musical expression because, unlike the huayno and other Andean genres, it is no longer a purely regional

Los Shapis, Peru's most famed *chicha* group, 1984. Photograph by Carlos Domínguez. Courtesy of Mary Domínguez.

manifestation, nor is it ascribed to a particular territory. Chicha has evolved into an expression of migrants, especially initially, when themes such as migration, nostalgia for the "place of origin," and hopes for a new city life were central in the lyrics of its songs.

Later on, in the mass media, and even in academic debates, the term *cultura chicha* (chicha culture) was popularized. This expression was introduced to describe all the cultural manifestations that cross regional borders, particularly those of Andean origin that claim to reproduce or emulate urban modern culture, resulting in the end in hybrid forms. But from the point of view of hegemonic discourses, such hybridity is signified as a bad copy, a misguided effort to be modern, a simulation—what limeños call *huachafo*. Huachafo refers to someone who is "posing," also implying a lack of ability in mastering urban distinctiveness and specifically not knowing how to act as an actual limeño. Huachafo and chicha have the connotation of a mediocre copy, which is a way of delegitimising new popular urban practices by making them improper in the city. In sum, chicha is identified with being "out of place." Chicha is then further used to refer generally to all negative features of urban life. So the heavy and chaotic traffic, street commerce, and bureaucratic inefficiency are labeled as chicha.

The label *chicha* has become a way to reinforce the displacement of the new limeños of Andean origin, and therefore to question the legitimacy of their status as limeños and actors of limeño culture. The notion of chicha culture is already established in the public debate and is shared by those who apply it to others, as well as by those who assume or reject it. In that sense, chicha culture constitutes a space for debate and resignification. In other words, chicha should be seen as the result of the struggle over representation between the different migrant communities and the hegemonic groups in the city, and a site where discourses about culture and place and the location of the *nuevos limeños* are at stake.

According to the testimonies of some chicha musicians, they rejected the label, since the media imposed it on what they called *cumbia andina*. Nevertheless, others, instead of rejecting it, opted to resignify it. At the same time that an Andean heritage was claimed through lyrics, melodies and performative features, other topics besides that of migration and nostalgia were introduced, such as the self-ascription of a proletarian and popular identity, and a capacity for hard work. It can be argued that this latter turn in the poetics of chicha music contested a negative image of Andean migrants, but at the same time it aligned it with the public discourse on Andean migrants that saw them mainly as an economic force. It is through figures like Dina Páucar, a key figure of huayno, that slight changes get introduced.

When a TV series on the life of Dina Páucar broadcast on Channel 2 at prime time (9:00 p.m.) in 2004 and became an enormous media hit, folklore entered the space of the official and hegemonic culture. Her success was due to the fact that she already existed as a principal figure within the world of folklore music. She was certainly not the product of the media, but of an alternative circuit and field of cultural production. In other words, the TV series succeeded because it was able to talk to a public that had already been configured by a marginal cultural industry.

The huayno genre had an initial period that was mostly characterized by regional markers that were encoded in the musical style, the instruments, the content of the lyrics, and the costume of the singers. Later music, lyrics and costumes developed into more pan-Andean styles. In these huaynos other topics predominate, such as love, and female singers become the main figures, which marks an interesting difference from the chicha genre, which is totally dominated by men. What is rather projected here, through the figure of the migrant women, is the image of the woman who, despite economic and social difficulties as well as the cultural burdens of a *machista* society, is able to succeed economically, as mother and as reproducer of a cultural heritage.

The trajectory of Dina Páucar told in the TV series presents her as the embodiment of success, professionalism, and stylistic sophistication, which adds a class dimension to her Andean and provincial identity. The image as a whole challenges the notion of being just *emergente* and invests her with a moral status. Her moral status is based on the fact that she did not allow her lover to cheat on her and beat her, although she had to face the social price of being a single mother. And finally, she can prove that the representation of her music as the legitimate artistic expression and sentiment of an Andean and provincial identity is based not just on authenticity—an argument evoked by folklorists—but on three decades of endurance in the music industry, the latter being an argument that defines huayno music as a modern cultural product and a means for economic development.

That Sickly Applause

"El cholo Juan"

In recent decades, and partly as a by-product of mass urban unemployment, street comics have increasingly plied their trade in Lima. Central plazas (San Martín, Dos de Mayo) are the usual locations for these popular artists' work, although they are found throughout the city. Many have loyal followers and attract large crowds. They both ridicule and boost the morale of those around them and poke fun at politicians, celebrities, and themselves. They also explore collective frustrations and poverty.

In this excerpt (slightly modified from the original), one such comic known as "el cholo Juan" cajoles people to stay and listen, insisting that they don't need to have lots of money in their pockets to enjoy his street theater. He notes the presence of people from large, working-class districts such as Comas in the north and Villa Salvador in the south as well as from settlements on the hills around Lima and the desert-like shantytowns on the distant outskirts ("on the way to Arabia"). He makes fun of his "provincial" (i.e., Indigenous) face, comparing it to that of the famous Inca leader Atahualpa. No doubt he would close by passing the proverbial hat.

Why are you so mean? / if you don't have any money, stay here / no one's going to make you pay / this is the popular theater of the street / all kinds of people stop here / if you've got something to give, give it / if you don't have anything, don't give anything / we'll see / OK, here I go / hopefully, I'll be lucky / now / so I can also earn something today / I'm going to ask you all for some strong applause / no, wait, sorry / only the poor people / if there's a millionaire here, please don't clap / we'll see how many millionaires have come today / give me some applause, all you poor people / give it to me strong, brother

[applause]

thanks for that sickly applause [*aplausos tuberculosos*] / that was bad, listen / that one over there isn't clapping / how much would it cost you to clap? / listen, sit down, shit / sit down / I'm talking / the kid cuts in front of me / interrupts me / oh, it's tough / do you know why I say that the poor should

Famous mime Jorge Acuña performing at Plaza San Martín, 1980s. Photograph by Herman Schwarz. Used by permission of the artist.

clap? / because here, everybody's poor / who's a millionaire here? / maybe one / two / three with me here / there are people who've come a long way, here / there are people who've come from Comas / "the eighth millionth kilometer on the way to the far side [*pal fondo*]" / "hill number 98" / the human settlement "three blocks on the way to heaven" / that one over there lives in Villa el Salvador "on the way to the far side" / the last stop / a pure sandy spot / on the way back it's Arabia / he lives near Arabia / I'm going to make you laugh / I'm the shit / today I'm going to make you laugh until your belly button shrivels up with laughter / you don't believe me? we'll see / look at my face / hey buddy, a little silence / I'm from the provinces / I'm not from Lima / I'm provincial, look at my face / ugly / an Atahualpa face / an *olluco* [a lumpy Andean root vegetable] nose / but who told you that a face matters [*que la cara vale*] / a face doesn't matter / what matters is what you know [*lo que vale son tus conocimientos*].

Life among the Pirates

Daniel Alarcón

Although there has always been an "informal" sector in Lima's economy (street vendors, contrabandists, makers and sellers of fake merchandise), it was in the early 1980s that the phenomenon both took a major step forward and began to attract the attention of economists, anthropologists, and policy makers. Economist Hernando de Soto, for instance, depicted informality as the response by creative and industrious people to the obstacles and traps placed upon them by a paternalistic and hyperbureaucratic state.[1] But informality is not always synonymous with heroic entrepreneurship or resistance against an intrusive state; in many cases, it is just people (not necessarily poor) taking advantage of loose controls and socially acceptable unlawful practices.

That is the case with book piracy, a multimillion-dollar business that satisfies the appetite of the population for cheap books by breaking all the regulations and challenging the formal book industry. Best-selling international authors (from Mario Vargas Llosa to Isabel Allende) as well as successful local writers and scholars find their books sold for two or three dollars in the form of copies that quite frequently miss a few pages, are hardly legible, or break apart as soon as you open them.

Writer Daniel Alarcón (b. 1977), the author of novels such as Lost City Radio *and* All Night We Walk in Circles *as well as short stories and chronicles, offers this vivid account of book piracy in Lima. Needless to say, his own books have been pirated and sold in the streets of Lima for a fraction of their legal retail price.*

In March of last year, Rodrigo Rosales, the director of the Peruvian offices of the international publisher Planeta, got an urgent call from Madrid. Paulo Coelho's people were upset. It seems the Brazilian writer's latest novel, *O vencedor está só* (published in English as *The Winner Stands Alone*), had been seen on the streets of Lima in an unauthorized edition. Rosales was taken aback. Coelho is a steady bestseller in Peru (and everywhere), and any new title by him is certain to be pirated almost immediately upon publication, but this one wasn't scheduled to be released until July. In fact, it hadn't even been officially translated into Spanish.

Though book piracy exists all over Latin America and the developing world, any editor with international experience in the region will tell you that Peru's problem is both unique and profound. According to the International Intellectual Property Alliance, the local publishing industry loses more money to piracy than any other South American country, with the exception of Brazil—whose economy is more than eight times the size of Peru's. A 2005 report commissioned by the Cámara Peruana del Libro (CPL), a national consortium of publishing houses, distributors, and booksellers, came to even more alarming conclusions: pirates were employing more people than formal publishers and booksellers, and their combined economic impact was estimated to be 52 million U.S. dollars—or roughly equivalent to 100 percent of the legal industry's total earnings. The pirates operate in plain sight: vendors ply the streets of the capital, carrying heavy stacks of books as they drift through stopped traffic, or spreading a torn piece of blue plastic tarp on a sidewalk, laying their wares out hopefully for all to see. You can find them in front of high schools, institutes, and government buildings, or wandering the aisles of the markets where most limeños do their shopping. One Saturday, I came across a man selling pirated law texts (cloth-bound, official-looking copies so well made I had a hard time believing they were fake) who told me that on weekdays he rented a stand at a local university, inside the law school—where presumably Peru's future lawyers are taught about copyright law, intellectual property, and other fantastical, irrelevant concepts. On summer weekends, these salesmen work the beaches south of the city, or congregate at the tollbooths on the way out of town. On the margins of this business are the thieves, bands of skilled shoplifters who specialize in stealing books, trolling all the major fairs, hitting all the official bookstores, and supplying a vibrant resale market with their so-called *libros de bajada*. Then there are the pirates themselves, the informal book manufacturers whose overworked, antique presses are hidden in nondescript houses in slums all over the city. The larger of these operations can crank out some forty thousand volumes a week, and because of their superior distribution, the pirates can sell three times as many copies of a book as the authorized publishers can. For a bestseller like Coelho, the figure could be even higher.

It didn't take long for Rosales to confirm the story. He went out to look for Coelho's unpublished book and found it at the first major intersection. Something had to be done. Peruvian book pirates are among the world's quickest and most entrepreneurial, some would say most treacherous—a reality Coelho and his handlers are well aware of. At the start of this decade, the pirates had nearly killed the Peruvian publishing industry; its survival and subsequent resurgence are seen by many as something of a miracle. Counterfeit books printed in Lima have been known to show up in Quito, Ecuador; in La Paz, Bolivia; in the towns of northern Chile; as far east as Buenos Aires, Argentina. This same Coelho edition, if it were to be imported, could conceivably nullify the sizable investment Rosales's house had made to publish the novel in the Spanish-speaking world. Coelho's people demanded action.

So began the latest skirmish in the on-again, off-again battle against Peruvian book piracy. The CPL registered a formal legal complaint, an investigation began and a few months later, on June 23, after failing to find the presses where Coelho's book was being printed, the CPL helped organize a police raid on the points of sale instead. The chosen site was Consorcio Grau, a market on a busy avenue in central Lima notorious for its counterfeit merchandise. The operation seized a million soles' ($348,000 U.S.) worth of pirated books, nearly ninety thousand volumes in all. All the major networks covered the story, though few noted the fact that within twenty-four hours the stands were open again, fully restocked. Perhaps this wasn't news. Book pirates, like drug traffickers, always assume a certain percentage of their merchandise will never make it to market. These losses are budgeted for, part of the accepted cost of doing business.

But there was still one more surprise. In July, when Planeta finally published the official version of Coelho's novel in Peru, Rosales decided to compare the two texts. He went through line by line, page by page, and discovered that the translations were essentially the same. The Peruvian book pirates hadn't commissioned their own translation, as Rosales had previously assumed. Instead, they had infiltrated Planeta in Spain and stolen the official translation before it was complete.

New books in Peru—new, legally produced books, that is—are often sold bearing a sticker that reads "Buy Original," just one of the small ways the publishing industry has responded to the threat from book pirates. The fact is, though, being pirated is the Peruvian equivalent of making the bestseller list. One writer I know ends all his readings by urging those in attendance to "buy my book before it gets pirated." When I asked him about it, he confessed he hadn't actually been pirated yet, but hoped he would be soon. The award-winning novelist Alonso Cueto told me he receives unsolicited sales reports from the man who sells pirate novels in his neighborhood. At first it made him angry, but by now Cueto has learned to tolerate it. Less tolerable

is that the same vendor feels authorized to give the writer advice on potential subject matter that might be more commercially successful.

. . .

If there is a certain allure to book piracy, it is only because we imbue this
business with the same qualities we project onto the book itself. We focus
on what is being manufactured and sold, as opposed to the fundamentally
illicit nature of the enterprise. There are many reasons for this, of course.
As a cultural artefact, the book has undeniable power, and the idea of a
poor, developing country with a robust informal publishing industry is, on
some level, romantic: the pirate as cultural entrepreneur, a Robin Hood figure, stealing from elitist multinational publishers and taking books to the
people. The myth is seductive and repeated often: book piracy in Peru, the
story goes, responds to a hunger for knowledge in a country that throughout its history has been violently divided between a literate upper class and
the poor, unlettered masses. Literacy grew dramatically through the last
century—nearly 60 percent of Peruvians were illiterate in 1940, compared
with only 7.1 percent in 2007—and along with this progress came a desire
for books and all they represent. Still, millions of rural Peruvians are mono-
lingual speakers of indigenous languages, and remain politically and economically marginalized as a result. In a country divided by race, ethnicity,
and language, acquiring fluency and literacy in Spanish has often been seen
as an important first step toward socioeconomic advancement.

Still, original books remain a prohibitively expensive luxury item, out
of reach for most of the population. There are vast swathes of the country
with no formal bookstores. Iquitos, the largest city in the Peruvian Amazon, with nearly four hundred thousand residents, has only two, and had
none as recently as 2007. Trujillo, the country's third largest city, has only
one. School libraries, if they exist at all, are usually nothing more than a
few dozen moldering titles of little literary or historical value. More often
than not, the only significant collections are housed at private universities, where neither students nor faculty are permitted to roam the stacks,
where checkout privileges are limited to twenty-four hours—that is, just
long enough to photocopy (read: "pirate") a book and return it. Nor is this
bleak situation confined to rural areas or the provinces. An estimated 85 to
90 percent of books are sold in the Lima metropolitan area, but for a city
of nearly 9 million, there are relatively few formal bookstores, the majority concentrated in the upper-middle-class districts of San Isidro and Miraflores. North Lima, for example, comprising eight districts of the Peruvian
capital, home to roughly 2 million people and half the city's middle class,
has none. The wealthiest of these eight districts, Los Olivos, has a municipal

library of only fifteen hundred most donated volumes, including, naturally, a few counterfeit editions. On a larger scale, the National Library suffers the same neglect. For some thirty years its acquisitions budget remained unchanged—zero—and it too relied on donations to build its collection.

Given this context, is it any wonder that books are pirated? You can lament the informality of it, you can call it stealing, you can bemoan the losses incurred by the publishing industry—but if you love to read, it's difficult to deny the hopeful logic: if someone is selling books, someone must be buying them. And if someone's buying them, someone must be reading them. And reading, especially in a country as poor as Peru—isn't that a good thing?

. . .

The book market known commonly as Amazonas is a few blocks east of Abancay, one of the main avenues that leads to Lima's old city center. It sits on a sliver of land on the southern bank of the Rímac, a murky, polluted river that neatly divides the capital into north and south. The wall on the far bank is decorated with a mural—a painting of green hills, bright blue skies, and palm trees, a verdant, inviting scene that contrasts starkly with the actual view—a dusty, monochrome slum beneath a hill hidden in thick fog.

At Amazonas, you will find more than two hundred vendors of used, antiquarian and pirated books, most of whom have known each other for twenty years. They formed a loose cooperative in the 1980s, when thirty or forty booksellers began congregating on the median strip of a downtown avenue called Grau. They sold secondhand books, were inoffensive and not particularly prosperous. In those days, the old center of Lima had been overrun by informal commerce, an unsightly by-product of the social disarray and economic turmoil. The stately, colonial-era buildings, once the pride of patrician Lima, had been taken over by merchants and transformed into dense black-market labyrinths. Trade spilled outdoors, over the sidewalks and into the streets. In some areas, six lanes of traffic had been reduced to one in each direction, the rest given over to the informal economy. These vendors are known as *ambulantes*, which literally means "wandering" or "itinerant," but they had become a permanent part of the urban landscape. When they were finally moved from the major avenues, it was discovered that some carts had been there so long, their owners had affixed them with metal plates and screws to the very sidewalk. In the case of the Grau booksellers, the long-term urban plan for the city included an expansion of the avenue (which, eleven years later, is only now under way), and finally, in 1998, then-mayor Alberto Andrade convinced the booksellers to relocate to an empty lot along the Jirón Amazonas. They were joined by 160 more book vendors scattered throughout downtown and formed what is now the Cámara Popular de Libreros—which, not coincidentally, also uses the abbreviation CPL, like its official rival, the Cámara Peruana del Libro.

You can find almost any book or magazine at Amazonas, provided you are willing to wander its aisles and search amid the stacks of moldering volumes spread out on wobbly tables or crammed into rusting metal bookshelves. There are many original books, but counterfeits aren't hard to find. If you don't see what you want right away, just ask for "the Peruvian edition" or "a more economical version," and most booksellers will get the hint. Alongside books, some vendors have begun selling grade-school science projects—Styrofoam monstrosities representing the water cycle, the greenhouse effect, or the vascular system. While you look for, say, a readable edition of Victor Hugo's *Les Misérables*, you might see a young woman behind a counter, hard at work on a diorama of Machu Picchu, a look of grave concentration on her face, as she glues a plastic llama to a green, spray-painted mountainside. These projects sell for twenty soles, less than seven U.S. dollars, a price that includes a lesson on the topic, so the student can be prepared to present his or her science project in class. Some might consider this cheating, but all the students I spoke to said it was their teachers who had sent them here.

Science projects are a lucrative but relatively new product at Amazonas —and a controversial one. For more than a decade, Amazonas has been synonymous with books, and some vendors told me they were concerned about diluting the brand with these school projects. To be sure, books still make up the bulk of what is sold: secondhand volumes, stolen originals, and counterfeits, along with the sorts of oddities a culture of piracy will inevitably produce—an unauthorized edition of Dostoevsky's *Crime and Punishment*, for example, its cover emblazoned with a drawing of a revolver, smoke rising from its barrel; or a hundred-page, abridged version of a much longer Bryce Echenique novel, a few chapters excised arbitrarily to save printing costs. It was Bryce himself who told me he'd once seen a pirated edition of *La palabra del mudo* (literally, *The Word of the Mute*, though it sounds much better in Spanish), a famous story collection by Peruvian writer Julio Ramón Ribeyro, now out of print because of a dispute with the author's estate. The pirates had made one important alteration in order to maximize sales: instead of Ribeyro's name, they'd printed Mario Vargas Llosa's on the cover.

. . .

The authorized Peruvian edition of my new story collection was published in late July, with its blue "Buy Original" sticker in the upper-right-hand corner. I did a bunch of interviews, gave a few readings; the hubbub of the fair came and went. Suddenly it was August and I still hadn't been pirated. I was starting to get nervous. There is great vanity in this concern, of course, but so much of publishing is vanity—why should this be any different? I couldn't help it. Then, on the morning of August 14, my last day in Lima, my editor called with the good news. He'd seen the book for sale in San Isidro, on the corner of Aramburú and Vía Expresa. I happened to be downtown when he called—at Amazonas, actually. I'd decided to squeeze in one more visit before leaving town, hoping I could talk to some more booksellers, maybe find my new collection, but I'd had no luck. My editor's tone was congratulatory. I was frankly relieved. I spent the next few hours downtown, and every time I came across a bookseller—five or six between midmorning and lunchtime—I stopped to ask.

No one had it.

But all of them could get it.

By tomorrow, they promised.

It was late afternoon before I made it back to San Isidro. The Vía Expresa is a sunken eight-lane highway that connects Lima's southern districts to the colonial centre; above, at street level, two lanes on either side feed cars into the highway. Backups are common on this narrow frontage road, so naturally the area is crawling with *ambulantes*. About half a mile from Aramburú, traffic just stopped. We inched forward, braked, lurched ahead, then stopped again, until the waiting was too much. I decided to walk.

It's not an area designed for pedestrians. To be more precise, the only people not in a car are selling something: DVDs, batteries, fans, combs, brushes, model planes, potted plants, sponges. I teetered along the side of the highway, hugging the railing, watching the peddlers filter through the traffic. The air was acrid and dense. Every few yards, I saw a backpack tied to the railing, lying on the grassy slope along the side of the highway. It was the extra inventory each of these salesmen and women might need in the course of a day, bags bulging with fruit, CDs, even books—all invisible from the street, hidden from view unless you happen to be driving very slowly on the highway below. I kept walking. A hundred yards before the intersection, I saw the first book pirate. I asked him. He shrugged. Nothing.

But at Aramburú there would be another. I knew that. I knew they probably had a gentlemen's agreement not to poach one another's clients—one man gets Vía Expresa heading north, the other gets Aramburú heading west. Perhaps they even worked for the same distributor. I saw him from a distance and recognized my book's white back cover. I waited for the traffic cop's signal, and meanwhile I watched the vendor as he went up the line of idling cars. His books hung from a wire in four rows of three, covers out. He had two of these wires, one for each arm, and a backpack too, tied to a post, where he could keep an eye on it. As soon as I could, I crossed the street and called out to him, pointing at my book.

"How much?" I shouted.

He looked surprised—he most likely didn't sell to many people on foot.

"Twelve soles," he said.

"Ten."

"Don't be greedy. It's new. I just got it today."

"I know it's new," I said. "I wrote it."

He looked at me like I was crazy. We stood in the narrow median strip, afternoon traffic blurring past us. He put his books down, leaning the wire contraptions against his leg. I took out my wallet and showed him my ID. He held it in his hand, inspecting my name and the photo, glancing back and forth, at the ID, at the book, at me.

"What's your name?" I asked.

"Jonathon," he said.

"Jonathon, you really should give me my book for free."

He smiled nervously. I could see the very idea made him anxious. He was short, dark-skinned, and young. His black hair fell into his eyes, and his jeans were too big for him. He shifted his weight from one leg to the other.

"Do you know how long I spent writing that book?"

"No," he said.

"Three years."

He didn't respond.

"How many have you sold?"

Jonathon gave me a confused look, as if trying to guess what answer I'd most like to hear. "People ask about it," he said finally, "but they don't buy."

He took the book out now and let me hold it. The cover image, which my editor and I had argued about for days, was the same, but there was something wrong with it, a slight greenish tint. The paper size was different, making the book shorter, wider, thinner. Less substantial. I found it upsetting.

"You're stealing from me," I said.

It was more complaint than accusation.

To my surprise, Jonathan nodded. "I know." His voice was barely audible above the noise of the street. "But I'm small."

Somehow it was a crushing admission. I felt awful. By the looks of him, Jonathon did too. His shoulders slumped. His books leaned against his leg.

I took out my money, a ten-note.

He smiled.

Of course, this being Peru, the first thing he did was hold it up to the light.

Note

1. Hernando de Soto, *The Other Path: The Invisible Revolution in the Third World* (New York: HarperCollins, 1989).

How Food Became Religion
in Peru's Capital City

Marco Avilés

Lima is the center of the global boom in Peruvian food. Culinary tourism now at-
tracts people from abroad to check out Chinatown, hidden ceviche joints, and res-
taurants featuring new takes on old Peruvian classics. New places pop up seemingly
every day, and nothing pleases a limeño more than showing off his or her favorite
huarique, *or hidden spot. Twenty years ago it was difficult to find quinoa or other*
"Andean food" in upscale neighborhoods; now restaurants feature it across the globe
as well as in swanky Lima establishments. The September food fair Mistura at-
tracts tens of thousands of people who sample a variety of food, from guinea pig and
beef heart to high-tech concoctions.

Of course, the culinary boom has its critics. Many ridicule the high prices paid
for items sold for next to nothing in market stalls or the exaggerated rhetoric about
certain potatoes or other tubers, a phenomenon also found in the United States,
where quinoa has been granted almost divine powers. Others lament the constant
increase in prices and remember with nostalgia when lines were short and prices
low. Nonetheless, limeños love their food passionately and, as this essay underlines,
are proud of the well-deserved attention it is receiving.

The first time I went out to eat in Lima, it was in secret. It was the start of
the 1980s, and Peru was in the midst of a civil war. There were blackouts and
curfews—and very few people went out after dark. At the time, I was four
years old, and my only friend was a man who worked as a sort of assistant to
my father, who was raising four of us alone and needed the help. The man's
name was Santos. Santos was about thirty, and he had a huge appetite. Like
millions of other Peruvians who'd fled the violence unfolding in the countryside, we'd recently migrated to Lima from a town deep in the Andes. We
all missed home. But at night it was Santos who always seemed most heart-
broken. When I asked him why, he said that he no longer savored his food.

Santos soon discovered that the remedy for his sadness was the street food being served up by other migrants, and as he got to know his way around Lima, he turned into a different person. He became animated when he told me about all the delicious things you could eat in the capital. But for my sisters and me, going out there was still off-limits; the streets were a place where bombs exploded and people died. They were a place that my father—like many parents then—had forbidden us from visiting, especially after dark. But one evening when my father wasn't around, Santos decided to sneak me out.

The Lima I saw that night was almost completely devoid of streetlights: a world of empty avenues and concrete apartment blocks, without a real restaurant in sight. It was nothing like the city that three decades later we'd be calling the culinary capital of Latin America—a city that journalists, chefs, and visitors from all over the world would travel to in search of new dishes and chic places to dine. That night, Santos parked our car, then carried me in his arms to a dark corner draped in a cloud of fragrant smoke. A woman stood over a small grill covered in the skewered pieces of beef heart that we call *anticuchos*, a recipe first invented by slaves who seasoned and cooked cuts of meat that their owners refused to eat. While today *anticuchos* are a staple in restaurants all over the city, in the '80s it felt crazy to be eating them out there on the street. Nonetheless, what I most remember about that night is not a sense of danger but the perfume of the marinade hitting the grill. Even if Lima was a sad shadow of a city, that smell was joyful.

I think about that scene—and the city we once lived in—each time I go with my sisters to eat *anticuchos* at a working-class restaurant called La Norteña, tucked away in a neighborhood of family homes and office buildings near the airport. The owners started out in the 1990s, selling skewers in the street to whatever brave customers were venturing out. When the war finally ended and Lima became more prosperous, their business grew. At first it occupied the patio of the owners' house. Then it expanded into the dining room and, later, through the entire first story of the house. Now it's normal for a family to wait ten or twenty minutes to get a table at La Norteña.

The Lima of the twenty-first century is a relatively comfortable place, with plenty of jobs and an optimistic middle class. Yet in many ways it retains the spirit of the somber, deeply introverted city I came to know as a child. It doesn't have great architecture. It's not designed for walking. There are very few parks or public squares. The beaches often look abandoned. And the traffic is terrible. To put it bluntly, it's not the sort of city you fall in love with at first sight. Most limeños won't ask travelers what sights they've seen or suggest a stroll; they'll ask what dishes they've tried or invite them to have a meal. The tables we eat around aren't just social spaces. In Lima, food has long been its own landscape, a haven of beauty and comfort.

This gives coherence to a city that, at first, can seem utterly incoherent. One of Lima's most celebrated ceviche spots, for instance, is found on a noisy avenue surrounded by car repair shops. Al Toke Pez is a fast-food restaurant with the spirit of a neighborhood bistro; it has a single counter open to the street, half a dozen stools, and six options on the menu. Everything is served as takeout, yet most customers eat ceviche or stir-fry nestled along the bar, or standing, quietly relishing their food as they watch an enormous wok throw off flames. The place is run by chef and owner Tomás Matsufuji, a slight, serious guy. Matsufuji was trained as an engineer and has a doctorate in supramolecular chemistry; he also comes from a long line of *nikkei* chefs. (*Nikkei* refers to the large community of Japanese immigrants in Peru and their descendants, as well as the fusion created by mixing Japanese and Peruvian cooking. The Japanese immigrated to Peru in several waves, beginning in the nineteenth century, when industrialization in their homeland displaced agricultural workers.)

Matsufuji's ceviches and stir-fry highlight fresh, humble ingredients from the sea, which Matsufuji picks out himself at the fisherman's wharf in Villa María del Triunfo. At Al Toke Pez, people who don't normally cross paths—manual laborers, businesspersons, artists, yuppies, teenagers, and tourists—somehow all end up at his narrow counter, eating elbow to elbow. It might be the most democratic experiment to come out of the huge, multifaceted movement known as Lima's culinary boom.

In postwar Lima, we constantly use the word "boom." We say there's a musical boom, a publishing boom, a design boom. While the word smacks of commercialism, it also reflects a sense of national pride. But nothing compares with the pride we feel for our biggest boom, the one in cuisine. The great Spanish chef, Ferran Adrià, put it best: food is a religion in Peru. Cooking professionally has become something to aspire to, and about eighty thousand young people from every social class are currently studying to be chefs, in schools scattered across Lima.

It all took off in the mid-1990s, during the war, back when Peruvian food was seen as something you ate only in your house or, if you were a risk taker, out in the street. The shift happened at a small restaurant called Astrid & Gastón. The owners of the restaurant were a young couple—she (Astrid) is German; he (Gastón) is Peruvian—and they had studied cooking in Paris. So Parisian food was what they made, until one day when they tired of serving standard French dishes on white tablecloths. They decided to serve Peruvian cuisine, with the same respect and care afforded European cuisine, if not more. The decision would inspire an entire generation of young chefs, and eventually help elevate Peruvian cuisine across the world.

Astrid & Gastón recently celebrated twenty years in business by moving into a former palace in the heart of San Isidro, Lima's financial district. The space has a regal aura and a futuristic electricity. Each day chefs harvest vegetables from their own gardens, which are adjacent to the building and are referred to as "Eden"; carry out culinary experiments in a workshop-laboratory; and offer public conferences and cooking classes in an open-air patio. Astrid & Gastón is now as much a cultural center as it is a restaurant. The new space cost $6 million to renovate, itself a clear sign of changing times in Lima. Now middle-aged, Gastón Acurio oversees an empire of about fifty restaurants all over the globe. But nothing compares with the tasting menu offered at his flagship restaurant in Lima. That menu is called Virú (an indigenous term that is said to refer to modern Peru) and con-sists of twenty-eight to thirty small plates served over the course of three hours, showcasing ingredients and techniques from all over Peru. One dish is a hunk of earth and straw that contains three cooked potatoes. Diners are supposed to dig out the potatoes using their hands, to mimic the way people live and eat in the Andes, where more than four thousand varieties of potatoes are grown and often cooked in the ground. At Astrid & Gastón, a successful dish is one that tells a story about Peru. And increasingly, a suc-cessful chef is an ambassador who shows us the world outside the walls— real and imagined—of Lima.

My first trip outside Lima got cut short. It was 1995; the army and the guer-rillas of Shining Path were still fighting in the Andes. I was sixteen and far more ignorant than intrepid. I hitched a ride on a cargo truck on its way to the Amazon, with the idea that I'd turn around when the driver kicked me off or my money ran out. The army was stationed at the entry to a town called Pichanaki, where a soldier who looked about my age glanced at my documents, then told me to go back to the city. The guerrillas had attacked just a few days earlier. I did as I was told.

About twenty years later, chef and traveler Virgilio Martínez invited me to visit his office on the second floor of Central, a discreet restaurant just a few steps from the ocean, on a tree-lined street in the Miraflores district of Lima. It's decidedly exclusive, a place where you should make a reserva-tion at least a month in advance. Yet Martínez's office looked more like a biologist's lab or an art installation. It was filled with glass vials. Each one contained a seed, a root, or an herb that Martínez had brought back from his adventures. He showed me photos from his most recent trip into the Andes. There was an image of a frigid lagoon perched at an elevation of more than thirteen thousand feet, where he'd collected sphere-shaped edible algae. And there was one of him cooking beet soup in the home of some local farmers. His cuisine was a reflection of all the time he'd spent traveling across the country: since peace was established, it has become infinitely easier to get on a bus or a plane and see Peru.

The country's geography is like a staircase in the form of a letter *A*. You begin at the Pacific, ascend to the highest peaks of the Andes, and then descend the other side into the Amazon jungle. The full journey passes through eighty-four different ecological zones, each one with its own species of plants and animals. The tasting menu at Central reflects that diversity and is organized by altitude. "Bivalves and corals. Lima Ocean. 10 meters." "Different varieties of corn. Low Andes. 1,800 meters." "Frozen potato and algae. Extreme altitude. 4,100 meters." Not so long ago, when the city was locked away and absorbed by the war, this kind of diversity would've been impossible to imagine. Today, even though most limeños now go out to bars and restaurants, many people remain frightened by the thought of traveling outside the city. Yet young chefs like Martínez are helping to break that taboo.

Chef Pedro Miguel Schiaffino runs Malabar and Ámaz, which both specialize in Amazonian cuisine. Schiaffino is a friend, and a few years ago I accompanied him on one of his monthly trips to the jungle. (Full disclosure: I occasionally consult for Schiaffino on social media strategy.) On that trip, we started out at the Belén market in the river city of Iquitos, where it was about 100 degrees Fahrenheit. Stevedores unloaded rodents the size of small pigs off ships, as well as lizards and monkeys. Local delicacies such as piranha and edible larvae called *suri* are cooked on grills. Fruit sellers showed off products like *caimito*, a citrus fruit nicknamed the kissing fruit, because eating it is supposed to be like getting kissed. By afternoon, we'd left the market, and Schiaffino was submerged in a lake, along with a group of local men who were casting for *paiche*, a prehistoric-looking fish that can weigh over four hundred pounds and is often called the king of the Amazon. Everyone was surprised when Schiaffino managed to get his arms around an adolescent *paiche* and hoist it gently to the surface. He showed us the fish with a quiet sort of pride, as if he and the creature were old friends.

Schiaffino started to travel to this region in 2003, when many of his colleagues in Lima were still hung up on the idea of molecular cooking, mimicking European chefs by transforming local ingredients into foams, gels, and other novelties. Eventually Schiaffino moved to the Amazon for about six months, and what he learned there changed everything for him. After returning to Lima, he opened Malabar and, ever since, it's been considered a kind of secret gateway into unknown culinary territory. Today you can see his love of experimentation in little details, such as how the fish in his ceviche isn't marinated in citrus but in *masato*, a fermented yucca beverage that indigenous Amazonians have been drinking for centuries. Everyone knows that in Lima you can find thousands of delicious riffs on the city's ceviche, but Malabar's version will take you the farthest away from the city.

I never wanted to leave Lima until I fell in love with my wife, who's from the United States. Over the past few years, I've learned firsthand what a radical change it is to be away from the city's food; in some ways it feels more drastic than speaking a different language. Now whenever I go back, the most important part—after seeing my family, of course—is deciding where to eat. A new tradition is to have our first and last meal at El Timbó, a roast chicken joint that my father always loved. (While the Lima of my childhood had few restaurants, places offering rotisserie chicken or Chinese food were the rare exceptions.) Timbó still bravely hangs on to an aesthetic straight out of the 1970s—wood paneling, faux-crystal chandeliers, and plenty of mirrors—and it has perfected the art of rotisserie chicken, which a Swiss immigrant is credited with introducing. The classic dish is a quarter chicken browned over a wood fire, plus french fries and salad. Though it doesn't sound like much, Timbó uses a marinade that borders on magical, and the plates come out with a whole palette of bright, delicate sauces that complement the dish perfectly.

When we're in Lima, my wife also makes sure we get to Kam Men, a Chinese restaurant in Miraflores that she sweetly refers to as "our *chifa*." Chifa is the word Peruvians use for Chinese-Peruvian fusion, mixing local ingredients with Chinese recipes and cooking techniques collected over about two centuries of immigration. Like Timbó, Kam Men is an old-school spot that hasn't yet been touched by the purposefully cool aesthetic of the culinary boom. Much of the dining room is made up of private booths cordoned off by pomegranate-colored curtains. When my wife and I lived in Lima, we marked important occasions there, always with the same dishes: dumplings, roast duck, and a platter of curried noodles with beef.

But the most important place to eat in Lima is at home with my family. Back when Lima was a city in the midst of one long blackout, when restaurants were few and far between, and eating out was considered danger-ous, this is what we did. All over the city, we hid in our houses with our families and prepared variations of recipes now served in the thousands of restaurants that have made Lima famous as a culinary destination. Ceviche. *Ají de gallina. Arroz con pollo. Tacu tacu. Papa a la huancaína. Lomo saltado.* In Lima, these dishes are our monuments, the closest we'll ever get to an Eiffel Tower or a Statue of Liberty. So when you taste them at one of Lima's sleek, energetic restaurants, try to imagine for a moment a different city, where millions of people savored meals with their families in quiet, dark apartments, thinking about homes they had recently left. Then you might understand where the culinary boom really began.

Green Vultures

Charles F. Walker

Few would deem Lima a green city. The traffic and air pollution continually worsen as open spaces disappear and diesel-spewing cars clog every street, and the Rímac River contains toxic runoff from mines and residential sewage. Some nearby beaches are closed in the summer due to the contamination. Nonetheless, there are signs of improvement or at least resistance. Neighborhood groups have organized to demand parks and trees and to defend open-air markets, while the city has finally moved on various mass transit projects. Some neighborhoods to the north and the east have put up massive sheets to collect humidity at night, taking advantage of Lima's odd climate as a "humid desert" and providing much-needed drinking water. Recent efforts to combat trash piles have gained international attention.

Lima's 9 million people produce nearly ten thousand tons of trash a day, and far too much is never collected. Large trash piles pose health threats and contribute to the city's air and water pollution woes. Planners have found an ingenious way to attack the problem.

Vultures, or *gallinazos*, have always been part of the city's fauna, and the Ministry of the Environment, with support from USAID, has placed solar-powered GPSs and GoPro cameras on ten of them and trained them to return to their handlers. The vultures have extraordinary sense of smell and eyesight and can spot the piles from high in the sky. These scavengers circle the city and descend on trash piles, their natural feeding grounds. With the images and maps authorities can then send trucks to clean up. The maps of the cleanups indicate that the piles have been found in the poorer areas near the outskirts of the city but also closer to the historical downtown and in some upscale neighborhoods.

The scavengers have not only detected a great deal of organic trash but have also turned people's attention to the pollution crisis. "We had to do something innovative, since publicity campaigns compete with one another with too many messages. We drew the conclusion that the answer was in

This map of where vultures have found their feasts shows that trash piles up across Lima. In this case, they led cleanup crews to the Jorge Chávez International Airport; the Catholic University; the banks of the Rímac River; neighborhoods to the south; and the Andean foothills in the east. Project Gallinazo Avisa: http://www .gallinazoavisa.pe.

the sky," says Flavio Pantigoso, creative director at FCB Mayo PERU, the PR firm in charge of the campaign.[1]

Gallinazo Avisa, or Vultures Advise, has been a popular program, with thousands following the scavengers' progress online and many followers contributing their own pictures of trash piles. The ten birds have received the names of mythical flying creatures and now have their own fans. Followers are calling for more vultures and more garbage trucks, stressing that

(*above, left*) The vultures have their fans. Bennu, who covers the southwest, was named
after an ancient Egyptian deity associated with the sun, creation, and rebirth, in this case
the conversion of trash into food. Project Gallinazo Avisa: http://www.gallinazoavisa.pe.
Courtesy of USAID Peru.
(*above, right*) Captain Huggin works in the north and carries the name of a mythological
Nordic raven that brought ideas to the god Odin. Project Gallinazo Avisa: http://www
.gallinazoavisa.pe. Courtesy of USAID Peru.

only creative programs that gain widespread support can confront Lima's
multiple problems. Representatives from the Ministry of the Environment
recognize that the program has only made a small dent in the huge trash
problem, but they also underline that the publicity around the vultures has
prompted people to talk about the trash problem and to contribute to the
search for solutions.

Note

1. Jacqueline Fowks, "Vultures Help Track Garbage in Lima," *El País* (English), December
18, 2015, http://elpais.com/elpais/2015/12/18/inenglish/1450441371_105314.html. For more
information and vivid images, see http://www.gallinazoavisa.pe/.

Suggestions for Further Reading and Viewing

More books have been published on historic Lima than the contemporary city. Colonial Lima, second only to Mexico City in terms of size and importance in Spanish America, attracted the eye of contemporary writers—travelers, scientists, poets, and chroniclers—and subsequently historians. In recent decades, the nineteenth century has been the subject of much scholarly debate while archeologists have also excavated in and around the city. This focus on the past is changing, however, as Lima's cuisine, music scene, population growth, ethnic diversity, and complex social divisions attract growing attention.

We have included only works in English and movies available in the United States. The list in Spanish would be considerably longer. Works excerpted in the book are not listed here. For those interested in literature and culture, James Higgins's informed treatise on Lima is highly recommended. The indispensable source on the Shining Path, the MRTA, and violence in Peru from 1980 to 2000, is the final report of the Peruvian Truth and Reconciliation Commission. Parts of it have been translated into English: http://www.cverdad.org.pe/ingles/paginao1.php.

General

Higgins, James. *Lima: A Cultural History.* New York: Oxford University Press, 2005.

Hünefeldt, Christine. *A Brief History of Peru.* 2004. 2nd ed., New York: Facts on File, 2010.

Klarén, Peter. *Peru: Society and Nationhood in the Andes.* New York: Oxford University Press, 2000.

Pike, Frederick. *The Modern History of Peru.* New York: Praeger, 1967.

Pre-Hispanic, Conquest, and Early Colonial Lima

Bowser, Frederick. *The African Slave in Colonial Peru, 1524–1650.* Stanford, CA: Stanford University Press, 1974.

Charney, Paul. *Indian Society in the Valley of Lima, Peru, 1532–1824.* Lanham, MD: University Press of America, 2001.

Cussen, Celia. *Black Saint of the Americas: The Life and Aftermath of San Martín de Porres.* New York: Cambridge University Press, 2014.

Graziano, Frank. *Wounds of Love: The Mystical Marriage of Santa Rosa of Lima.* New York: Oxford University Press, 2004.

Lockhart, James. *Spanish Peru, 1532–1560: A Social History*. Madison: University of
Wisconsin Press, 1994.

Mannarelli, María Emma. *Private Passions and Public Sins: Men and Women in
Seventeenth-Century Lima*. Albuquerque: University of New Mexico Press, 2007.

Osorio, Alejandra. *Inventing Lima: Baroque Modernity in Peru's South Sea Metropolis*.
New York: Palgrave Macmillan, 2008.

Ramos, Gabriela. *Death and Conversion in the Andes: Lima and Cuzco, 1532–1670*. Notre
Dame, IN: University of Notre Dame Press, 2010.

Schaposchnik, Ana. *The Lima Inquisition: The Plight of Crypto-Jews in Seventeenth-Century
Peru*. Madison: University of Wisconsin Press, 2015.

van Deusen, Nancy. *Between the Sacred and the Worldly: The Institutional and Cultural
Practice of Recogimiento in Colonial Lima*. Stanford, CA: Stanford University Press,
2001.

Bourbon Lima

Burkholder, Mark. *Politics of a Colonial Career: José Baquíjano and the Audiencia of Lima*.
Albuquerque: University of New Mexico Press, 1981.

Descola, Jean. *Daily Life in Colonial Peru, 1710–1820*. New York: Macmillan, 1968.

Jouve Martín, José R. *The Black Doctors of Colonial Lima*. Montreal and Kingston:
McGill-Queen's University Press, 2014.

Juan, Don Jorge, and Don Antonio de Ulloa. *Discourse and Political Reflections on the
Kingdoms of Peru*. Edited and with an introduction by John J. TePaske. Norman:
University of Oklahoma Press, 1978.

Premo, Bianca. *Children of the Father King: Youth, Authority, and Legal Minority in Colonial
Lima*. Chapel Hill: University of North Carolina Press, 2005.

Walker, Charles F. *Shaky Colonialism: The 1746 Earthquake-Tsunami in Lima, Peru, and
Its Long Aftermath*. Durham, NC: Duke University Press, 2008.

Warren, Adam. *Medicine and Politics in Colonial Peru: Population Growth and the Bourbon
Reforms*. Pittsburgh: University of Pittsburgh Press, 2010.

From Independence to the War of the Pacific (1821–1883)

Anna, Timothy. *Fall of the Royal Government in Peru*. Lincoln: University of Nebraska
Press, 1979.

Espinoza, G. Antonio. *Education and the State in Modern Peru: Primary Schooling in Lima,
1821–c. 1921*. New York: Palgrave Macmillan, 2013.

García-Bryce, Iñigo. *Crafting the Republic: Lima's Artisans and Nation-Building in Peru,
1821–1879*. Albuquerque: University of New Mexico Press, 2004.

Gootenberg, Paul. *Imagining Development: Economic Ideas in Peru's "Fictitious Prosperity"
of Guano, 1840–1880*. Berkeley: University of California Press, 1993.

Hünefeldt, Christine. *Liberalism in the Bedroom: Quarreling Spouses in Nineteenth-Century
Lima*. University Park: Pennsylvania State University Press, 2000.

————. *Paying the Price of Freedom: Family and Labor among Lima's Slaves, 1800–1854.* Berkeley: University of California Press, 1994.

Markham, Clements R. *Cuzco and Lima: A Journey to the Ancient Capital of Peru, and a Visit to the Capital and Provinces of Modern Peru.* New York: Cambridge University Press, 2014.

McKeown, Adam. *Chinese Migrant Networks and Cultural Change: Peru, Chicago, and Hawaii, 1900–1936.* Chicago: University of Chicago Press, 2001.

Muecke, Ulrich. *Political Culture in Nineteenth-Century Peru: The Rise of the Civilista Party.* Pittsburgh: University of Pittsburgh Press, 2004.

Smith, Archibald. *Peru as It Is: A Residence in Lima, and Other Parts of the Peruvian Republic, Comprising an Account of the Social and Physical Features of That Country.* London: R. Bentley, 1839.

Modernizing Lima (1895–1940)

Aguirre, Carlos. *The Criminals of Lima and Their Worlds: The Prison Experience, 1850–1930.* Durham, NC: Duke University Press, 2005.

Collier, David. *Squatters and Oligarchs: Authoritarian Rule and Policy Change in Peru.* Baltimore: Johns Hopkins University Press, 1976.

Drinot, Paulo. *The Allure of Labor: Workers, Race, and the Making of the Peruvian State.* Durham, NC: Duke University Press, 2011.

González Prada, Manuel. *Free Pages and Hard Times: Anarchist Musings.* New York: Oxford University Press, 2003.

Hiatt, Willie. *The Rarefied Air of the Modern: Airplanes and Technological Modernity in the Andes.* New York: Oxford University Press, 2016.

Mariátegui, José Carlos. *Seven Interpretative Essays on Peruvian Reality.* Austin: University of Texas Press, 1988.

Parker, David. *The Idea of the Middle Class: White-Collar Workers and Peruvian Society, 1900–1950.* University Park: Pennsylvania State University Press, 1998.

Quiroz, Alfonso W. *Corrupt Circles: A History of Unbound Graft in Peru.* Baltimore: Johns Hopkins University Press, 2008.

Stein, Steve. *Populism in Peru: The Emergence of the Masses and the Politics of Social Control.* Madison: University of Wisconsin Press, 1980.

Stein, William. *Dance in the Cemetery: José Carlos Mariátegui and the Lima Scandal of 1917.* Lanham, MD: University Press of America, 1997.

————. *A Peruvian Psychiatric Hospital.* Lanham, MD: University Press of America, 1995.

The Many Limas (1940–)

Acurio, Gastón. *Peru: The Cookbook.* London: Phaidon, 2015.

Alcalde, M. Cristina. *The Woman in the Violence: Gender, Poverty, and Resistance in Peru.* Nashville: Vanderbilt University Press, 2010.

Berg, Ulla. *Mobile Selves: Migration, Race, and Belonging in Peru and the U.S.* New York: New York University Press, 2015.

Degregori, Carlos Iván. *How Difficult It Is to Be God: Shining Path's Politics of War in Peru, 1980–1999.* Madison: University of Wisconsin Press, 2012.

De Soto, Hernando. *The Other Path: The Invisible Revolution in the Third World.* New York: HarperCollins, 1989.

Dietz, Henry. *Urban Poverty, Political Participation, and the State: Lima, 1970–1990.* Pittsburgh: University of Pittsburgh Press, 1998.

Feldman, Heidi. *Black Rhythms of Peru: Reviving African Musical Heritage in the Black Pacific.* Middletown, CT: Wesleyan University Press, 2007.

Gandolfo, Daniella. *The City at Its Limits: Taboo, Transgression, and Urban Renewal in Lima.* Chicago: University of Chicago Press, 2009.

Giampietri, Luis. *41 Seconds to Freedom: An Insider's Account of the Lima Hostage Crisis, 1996–97.* New York: Ballantine Books, 2007.

Greene, Shane. *Punk and Revolution: Seven More Interpretations of Peruvian Reality.* Durham, NC: Duke University Press, 2016.

Lloyd, Peter. *The "Young Towns" of Lima: Aspects of Urbanization in Peru.* New York: Cambridge University Press, 1980.

Lobo, Susan. *A House of My Own: Social Organization in the Squatter Settlements of Lima.* Tucson: University of Arizona Press, 1981.

Majluf, Natalia, et al. *Art in Peru: Works from the Collection of the Museo de Arte de Lima.* Lima: Museo de Arte de Lima, 2001.

Nencel, Lorraine. *Ethnography and Prostitution in Peru.* London: Pluto, 2001.

Pereyra, Omar. *Contemporary Middle Class in Latin America: A Study of San Felipe, 2014.* Lanham, MD: Lexington Books, 2015.

Schönwälder, Gerd. *Linking Civil Society and the State: Urban Popular Movements, the Left, and Local Government in Peru, 1980–1992.* University Park: Penn State University Press, 2004.

Solomon, Juliet. *Yes . . . but It's Different Here*, translated by Daniel Zúñiga-Rivera. Lima: Editorial Arkabas, 2012.

Stokes, Susan C. *Cultures in Conflict: Social Movements and the State in Peru.* Berkeley: University of California Press, 1995.

Taylor Edmisten, Patricia. *The Autobiography of Maria Elena Moyano: The Life and Death of a Peruvian Activist.* Gainesville: University Press of Florida, 2000.

Testino, Mario. *Lima, Peru.* Bologna: Damiani, 2007.

Tucker, Joshua. *Gentleman Troubadours and Andean Pop Stars: Huayno Music, Media Work, and Ethnic Imaginaries in Urban Peru.* Chicago: University of Chicago Press, 2013.

Vargas Llosa, Mario. *A Fish in the Water: A Memoir.* New York: Farrar, Straus and Giroux, 1994.

Cinema

Alias "La Gringa." Dir. Alberto Durant. 1991.

City of M. Dir. Felipe Degregori. 2000.

Days of Santiago. Dir. Josué Méndez. 2004.

Don't Tell Anyone. Dir. Francisco Lombardi. 1998.

Gods. Dir. Josué Méndez. 2008.

The Golden Couch. Dir. Jean Renoir. 1952.

Gregorio. Dir. Grupo Chaski. 1982.

Juliana. Dir. Grupo Chaski. 1989.

La ciudad y los perros. Dir. Francisco Lombardi. 1985.

Maruja in Hell. Dir. Francisco Lombardi. 1983.

The Milk of Sorrow. Dir. Claudia Llosa. 2009.

Red Ink. Dir. Francisco Lombardi. 2000.

Fiction

Alarcón, Daniel. *Lost City Radio.* New York: Harper Perennial, 2008.

———. *War by Candlelight.* New York: Harper Perennial, 2006.

Arana, Marie. *Lima Nights: A Novel.* New York: Dial, 2010.

Charún, Lucía. *Malambo.* Translated by Emmanuel Harris II. Chicago: Swan Isle, 2004.

Faverón Patriau, Gustavo. *The Antiquarian.* Translated by Joseph Mulligan. New York: Grove, 2014.

Gómez Bárcena, Juan. *The Sky over Lima.* Translated by Andrea Rosenberg. New York: Houghton Mifflin, 2016.

Heath, Anna, trans. *Beings: Contemporary Peruvian Short Stories.* London: Berforts Information, 2014.

Melville, Herman. *Benito Cereno.* London: Nonesuch, 1926.

Patchett, Ann. *Bel Canto.* New York: Harper Perennial, 2005.

Ribeyro, Julio Ramón. *Marginal Voices.* Translated by Dianne Douglas. Austin: University of Texas Press, 1993.

Shakespeare, Nicholas. *The Dancer Upstairs.* New York: Vintage, 2010.

Vargas Llosa, Mario. *Aunt Julia and the Scriptwriter.* Translated by Helen R. Lane. New York: Picador, 2007.

———. *Conversation in the Cathedral.* Translated by Gregory Rabassa. New York: Harper Perennial, 2005.

———. *The Cubs and Other Stories.* Translated by Gregory Kolovakos and Ronald Christ. New York: Harper & Row, 1979.

Acknowledgment of Copyrights and Sources

Epigraphs

"Identidad sentimental: Lugar de nacimiento," by Sebastián Salazar Bondy, from *Confidencia en voz alta* (Lima: Ediciones Vida y Palabra, 1960), 59. Courtesy of Ximena Salazar Lostaunau.

"Hermelinda," by Alberto Condemarín Vasquez (1921). Song lyrics.

"Chronicle of Lima," by Antonio Cisneros, from *At Night the Cats,* edited and translated from the Spanish by Maureen Ahern, William Rowe, and David Tipton (New York: Red Dust Books, 1985), 75–77. Used by permission of Donald Breckenridge.

Part I. Pre-Hispanic, Conquest, and Early Colonial Lima

"Pre-Hispanic Lima," by César Pacheco Vélez, from *Memoria y utopia de la vieja Lima* (Lima: Universidad del Pácifico, 1985), 227–30. Courtesy of Rosario Pacheco.

"The Foundation of Lima," by Garcilaso de la Vega el Inca, from *The Royal Commentaries of the Incas and General History of Peru,* translated by Harold V. Livermore (Austin: University of Texas Press, 1966), 114–17.

"The Form and Greatness of Lima," by Bernabé Cobo, from *Historia de la fundación de Lima,* reproduced in Gilbert M. Joseph and Mark D. Szuchman, *I Saw a City Invincible: Urban Portraits of Latin America,* translated by Sharon Kellum (Wilmington, DE: Scholarly Resources, 1996), 61–69. Used by permission of Rowman & Littlefield.

"Lima's Convents," by José de la Riva-Agüero, from *La historia en el Perú* (Lima: Imprenta Nacional de Federico Barrionuevo, 1910), 221–28. Courtesy of Carlos Ramos Núñez, of Instituto Riva Agüero.

"The Spiritual Diary of an Afro-Peruvian Mystic," by Ursula de Jesús, from *The Souls of Purgatory: The Spiritual Diary of a Seventeenth-Century Afro-Peruvian Mystic, Ursula de Jesús,* edited by Nancy van Deusen (Albuquerque: University of New Mexico Press, 2004), 103–6. Used by permission of University of New Mexico Press.

"Auto-da-Fé and Procession," by Josephe and Francisco Mugaburu, from *Chronicle of Colonial Lima: The Diary of Josephe and Francisco Mugaburu, 1640–1697,* edited and translated by Robert Ryal Miller (Norman: University of Oklahoma Press, 1975), 112–14; permission conveyed through Copyright Clearance Center, Inc.

Part II. Bourbon Lima

Part III. From Independence to the War of the Pacific (1821–1883)

"The Saddest City," by Herman Melville, from *Moby-Dick; or, the Whale* (New York: Harper & Brothers, 1851), 214.

"Lima's Carnival and Its Glories," by Manuel Atanasio Fuentes, from *Aletazos del Murciélago*, vol. 2, 2nd ed. (Paris: Imprenta de Ad. Laine y J. Havard, 1866), 290–95.

"The Amancaes Parade," by Ismael Portal, from *Del pasado limeño* (Lima: Librería e Imprenta Gil, 1932), 108–12.

"Chinese Are Not Welcome," by Mariano Castro Zaldívar, from *El Peruano*, February 16, 1884, 175.

"The National Library and the Chilean Occupation," by E. W. Middendorf, from *Peru, Beobachtungen und Studien über das Land und seine Bewohner während eines 25 jähringen Aufenthalts*, vol. 1 (Berlin: Robert Oppenheim, 1893), 454–58.

Part IV. Modernizing Lima (1895–1940)

"The Transformation of Lima after 1895," by José Gálvez, from *Una Lima que se va* (Lima: Evfurion, 1921), 253–62. Courtesy of José Gálvez Dañino.

"A Middle-Class House in 1900," by Luis Alberto Sánchez, from *Testimonio personal: Memorias de un peruano del siglo XX*, vol. 1 (Lima: Ediciones Villasán, 1969), 60–65. Courtesy of Marlene Polo and Joselo Sánchez of Instituto Luis Alberto Sánchez.

"The Growing Popular Taste for Soccer," from *Diario El Comercio*, Peru, June 18, 1908. Courtesy of Sabrina Martin Zamalloa of *El Comercio*.

"The Lord of the Miracles Procession," by José Carlos Mariátegui, from *La Crónica*, April 10, 1917.

"Dance in the Cemetery," from *El Tiempo* (Lima), November 6, 1917. Reproduced from William W. Stein, *Dance in the Cemetery: José Carlos Mariátegui and the Lima Scandal of 1917* (New York: University Press of America, 1997), 99–101. Used by permission of Rowman & Littlefield.

"On the Streetcar," by Martín Adán, translated by Katherine Silver, from *The Cardboard House,* copyright © 2012 by Katherine Silver. Reprinted by permission of New Directions Publishing Corp. Originally published as *La casa de cartón* (Lima, 1928).

"Leguía's Lima," by Guillermo Rodríguez Mariátegui, from "La placa ingrata," in *Lima, 1919–1930* (Lima: E. B. y B. Sucesor, 1935), 263–65.

"The Paperboy," composed by Felipe Pinglo Alva, reproduced in Ernesto Toledo Brückman, *Felipe de los pobres: Vida y obra en tiempos de luchas y cambios sociales* (Lima: Editorial San Marcos, 2007), 169–70.

"Daily Life of a Domestic Servant," by Laura Miller, from "La mujer obrera en Lima, 1900–1930," in *Lima Obrera 1900–1930*, vol. 2, edited by Steve Stein (Lima: Ediciones El Virrey, 1987), 85–90. Courtesy of Laura Miller and Steve Stein.

Part V. Interlude: Nostalgia and Its Discontents

"The True Lima," by Chabuca Granda, reproduced by Raúl Serrano and Eleazar Valverde, in *El libro de oro del vals peruano* (Lima: Tans Perú, 2000), 194. Courtesy of Teresa Fuller Granda, Archivo Chabuca Granda.

"The Mislaid Nostalgia," by Sebastián Salazar Bondy, from *Lima la horrible* (Lima: Populibros, 1964), 11–18. Courtesy of Ximena Salazar Lostaunau.

"One of the Ugliest Cities in the World?" by Alberto Flores Galindo, from "Lima: Crónica de un deterioro," in *Apuntes* (Lima), 17, 1985, 126–31. Courtesy of Cecilia Rivera.

"Understanding *Huachafería*," by Mario Vargas Llosa, from *El Comercio* (Lima), August 28, 1983. Courtesy of Lucía Muñoz-Nájar on behalf of Mario Vargas Llosa.

Part VI. The Many Limas (1940–)

"Malambo, a Black Neighborhood," by Hugo Marquina Ríos, from "Cincuenta casas de vecindad en la avenida Francisco Pizarro," in *Lima y sus suburbios,* edited by Carlos Enrique Paz Soldán (Lima: Universidad Nacional de San Marcos de Lima, 1957), 77–80. Courtesy of Nora Solís, Fondo Editorial San Marcos.

"The Original Mansion," by Alfredo Bryce Echenique, from *A World for Julius.* © 2004 by the Regents of the University of Wisconsin System. Reprinted by permission of the University of Wisconsin Press.

"Diego Ferré and Miraflores," excerpt from *The Time of the Hero* by Mario Vargas Llosa. Copyright © 1962 by Mario Vargas Llosa. Translation copyright © 1966 by Grove Press, Inc. Reprinted by permission of Farrar, Straus and Giroux, LLC, Agencia Literaria Carmen Balcells, SA, and Faber and Faber Ltd.

"The Banquet," from *Marginal Voices: Selected Stories* by Julio Ramón Ribeyro, translated by Dianne Douglas, copyright © 1993. By permission of the University of Texas Press.

"A *Serrano* Family in Lima," by Richard W. Patch, from "La Parada, Lima's Market," in *City and Nation in the Developing World: Selected Case Studies of Social Change in Asia, Africa, and Latin America by Associates of the American Universities Field Staff* (New York: American Universities Field Staff, 1968), 180–86.

"The Great March of Villa El Salvador," by José María Salcedo, from *Quehacer* 33 (1984), 56–64. Courtesy of *Quehacer.*

"Being Young and Radical (Late 1960s and 1970s)," by Maruja Martínez, from "Mil novecientos sesentiocho," in *Entre el amor y la furia: Crónicas y testimonio* (Lima: SUR, 1997), 99–102. Courtesy of Domingo Martínez.

"The Day Lima Erupted," by Enrique Zileri, from "El 'Limazo,'" in *Caretas* (Lima), no. 1604, February 3, 2000. Courtesy of Marco Zileri of *Caretas.*

"A City of Outsiders," by José Matos Mar, from *Desborde popular y crisis del estado,* 2nd ed. (Lima: Fondo Editorial del Congreso de la República, 2004), 69–75. Courtesy of the author.

"The Israelites of the New Universal Covenant," by Peter Masson, from *Consideraciones acerca de un nuevo movimiento religioso: Los Israelitas del Nuevo Pacto Universal,* Ibero-Amerikanisches Archiv 17, no. 4 (1991), 466–68. Courtesy of Cornelia Klinghammer of the Ibero-American Institute–Prussian Cultural Heritage Foundation.

"María Elena Moyano," reprinted from *The Monkey's Paw: New Chronicles from Peru.*

Index